MISSION 'VICTORY INDIA'
A Key to Combat Leadership

MISSION 'VICTORY INDIA'
A Key to Combat Leadership

Author & Editor
Col Vinay B Dalvi

PENTAGON PRESS LLP

MISSION 'VICTORY INDIA': A Key to Combat Leadership
Author & Editor: Col Vinay B Dalvi

First Published in 2019

Copyright © Reserved

ISBN 978-93-86618-77-1

All rights reserved. No part of this publication may be reproduced, stored in a retrieval system, or transmitted, in any form or by any means, electronic, mechanical, photocopying, recording, or otherwise, without first obtaining written permission of the copyright owner.

Disclaimer: The views expressed in various articles are personal. The views in response to some articles and publications are also personal.

Published by
PENTAGON PRESS LLP
206, Peacock Lane, Shahpur Jat
New Delhi-110049
Phones: 011-64706243, 26491568
Telefax: 011-26490600
email: rajan@pentagonpress.in
website: www.pentagonpress.in

Cover Design & Page Layouts
Sudesh Savant, The Design Shop, Mumbai

Printed at Aegean Offset Printers, Greater Noida, U.P.

DEDICATION

Mission Victory India is dedicated to the 'Unknown Soldier' whose deeds of valour and heroism remain buried in the sands of time. He deserves the highest respect and reverence for he has given the highest sacrifice any soldier can make for his country. Although his saga of bravery and grit remains unheard or untold his ultimate sacrifice receives the highest accolades, always and every time!

MESSAGE

Admiral Arun Prakash

"They don't make them like us anymore..." This is the plaintive refrain one frequently hears from military veterans, mostly of ancient vintage, when referring to the younger crop of officers. I must confess that a similar thought crossed my mind, when I returned, after a lapse of 33 years, to my 'alma mater', the National Defence Academy, as Commandant, in 1997.

However, this delusion was shattered within a few weeks of my arrival. Not only did I find the Cadets very highly motivated, but I also saw them coping with the rigours of Academy training much better than we ever did. I found that every single training standard – physical and intellectual – had been enhanced manifold in comparison to what we had to meet. My elation at this discovery was, however, short-lived. From the number of Cadets 'marched-up' to me, and the range of their misdemeanours, it soon became clear, that most of them, had received no inputs about a value system; nor were they provided a moral foundation at home, in school or in the Academy.

This absence of ethical moorings, made it easy for young Cadets to adopt the prescriptions of their 'wiser' (and less scrupulous) seniors, in the form of an 'Academy survival manual', which recommended, lying, cheating, stealing (euphemistically termed; 'managing'), manhandling of juniors and even impersonation. Given the moral vacuum in our social environment, I felt that the Cadet needed a tangible code of conduct, which would spell out, explicitly, what he was expected, and not expected to do.

Intra-Academy consultations on this topic were an eye-opener for me. While the Cadet body was willing to give this idea a try, most officers on staff, were vehemently opposed to it. I recall receiving a sermon from a young Special Forces officer, who told me, sternly, that in a counter-insurgency environment, he would have no use for a subaltern who was not 'smart' enough to 'manage' a few items for himself or his unit; or give and take some physical abuse. Notwithstanding such resistance, a simple Academy Honour Code was instituted, in March 1998 to be managed and implemented by Cadet Appointments under the supervision of the Adjutant. I left the Academy, a year later and am not aware of the subsequent fate of the Honour Code.

We are all aware that India's social and economic transformation has been accompanied by a steep decline in ethical values, as well **in standards of private and public conduct**. The military, which stood tall above civil society, used to be held in respect and admiration, but today we note that they, too, are slipping in the estimation of their countrymen; for good reason. Misdemeanours taking place within our fraternity are spoken about in hushed tones, till they reach the media. They include financial impropriety, misuse of facilities, sexual misconduct, human-rights violations, nepotism and plain bribery. The recent phenomenon of our men indulging acts of open insubordination and even physical assault on officers is a clear sign of leadership failure and a message that we have fallen in the esteem of our men.

Many try to rationalize this, by saying that since the armed forces are a product of Indian society, their conduct is bound to reflect societal decline. We must firmly reject the false comfort of such seductive logic, because it has the potential to destroy the cohesion, morale and self-respect of our armed forces. Instead, we need to focus on the fatal flaw that needs to be addressed; the inability or unwillingness of many in the officer corps to distinguish between moral 'right' and 'wrong' and to draw a personal 'Laxman rekha' that must never be crossed.

My – somewhat simplistic – thesis has been that many of the unethical traits imbibed by 'smart' Cadets in our basic training academies mutate over the years into major character flaws that blight our senior military leadership. The early erosion of a person's moral fibre, if not stemmed, can allow him to rationalize serious misconduct in later life. It was for this reason that the 1998 Academy Order promulgating the Honour Code, contained a paragraph which said, *"It is my hope and expectation that this Honour Code will remain with an NDA Cadet as his creed and guiding light throughout his service career and perhaps the rest of his life."*

It is against this background and context that the reader must view the book that he holds in his hand. This is the fifth volume in a series dubbed 'Victory India'; the brainchild of Col Vinay Dalvi (Retd), through which he has attempted to pinpoint and draw attention to the serious flaws that afflict the whole system of selection, grooming and training the budding leadership of the Indian armed forces. Having enlisted the support of a galaxy of military luminaries, with tremendous experience and interest in training matters, Vinay Dalvi's indefatigable endeavours have turned 'Victory India' into a veritable campaign for introspection and reform. It has delivered, over the past decade, five comprehensive compendiums of essays, focusing on every aspect of selection and training of our young combat leadership.

The thrust of Dalvi's campaign has been that the onus for stemming progressive deterioration of 'quality leadership' in the armed forces rests squarely on the senior hierarchy; the Service Chiefs as well as the Commanders-in-Chief. Only their intervention and directions can bring necessary focus on the military's basic training academies and on introduction of a Military Education Programme that runs in a continuum from subaltern to general.

While my admiration for Col Dalvi's single-minded perseverance and tenacity is boundless, equally deep is my distress at the lack of any response from Service HQs. The plausible reason, that comes to mind, for this status, is the intense preoccupation of HQ staff with multiple routine issues as well as crises requiring immediate action, and the low priority accorded to training issues. But a far more disturbing thought is the likelihood of a belief, at higher levels, that the current emphasis on brawn over brains, that delivers a 'rough-and-ready' brand of leadership, is good enough for counter-insurgency forces.

I sincerely hope that my fears are unfounded, and that the Chiefs of Staff will address this issue in all seriousness, by constituting a high-level committee to study all issues related to selection and training of officers and report to them in a time-bound manner.

Col Dalvi will then, be able to enjoy his well-deserved retirement.

Admiral Arun Prakash (Retd),
25th December, 2018
No. 339 Rangavi Estate Part II,
DABOLIM, GOA - 403801
Mob: 9960584966

FOREWORD

Lt Gen Prakash C Katoch

'Mission Victory India', 5th in the 'Victory India' series of books of the 'Victory India Campaign' (2010-2018), examines the human resource aspects of personnel management, military leadership, training and selection, all of which go a long way in deciding the quality and calibre of a nation's military forces.

This book comes at a time when the spotlight on military affairs has covered the entire gamut of defence matters – from equipment procurement, geopolitical/strategic affairs, military diplomacy to pure tactical level actions, defence business/industry interface; the Make in India conundrum and veterans' issues.

There has been unanimity on the need to modernize the Indian military, primarily in terms of equipment and leadership to tackle our growing threats. How much is achievable with abysmally low defence allocations, manpower cuts with inadequate budget and the fruitless pursuit of rank equivalence; a battle that armed forces cannot win are serious issues in an environment where we are unable to find the correct balance between security and economy.

The 'Victory India Campaign', takes a military insider's view of many of these issues. It provides opportunities to enlighten serving military officers on issues of selection and training of military officers; a primary focus area of the Victory India campaign.

The book critically examines education of serving military officers and the prevailing intellectual bankruptcy fuelled by a lack of reading habits. Suggesting new subjects for dissertation and studies at Tier I institutes like the DSSC, it highlights the scarcity of 'Warrior Scholars' due absence of a reading habit.

Health issues affecting serving officers and their management have also been touched upon. In the context of rising ailments being reported at medical boards, the suggestions made need serious review.

The book also spans core doctrinal and tactical issues like 'Air Cavalry', the Shekatkar Committee Report, effect of CI Ops on Indian military capability, nuances of a two-front war and a radical suggestion of a Sino-Indian alliance.

Analysts blame problems of armed forces on civilian bureaucracy and political executive, but fail to find fault within. Our existing flaws stem from how we select and train our manpower, which can decide the outcome of a battle since it is finally the man behind the machine that matters. The book exposes flaws in our personnel management system – selection, grooming training and promotion. Raised by pioneering, experienced Col Vinay Dalvi, his well enunciated concerns and recommendations have been validated by many veterans.

The primary focus of the Victory India Campaign remains the Cradle of Military leadership namely the NDA (albeit NDA is not the only institution through which officers join armed forces) and selection processes, broadening to allied areas of military management in its subsequent iterations. Adverse effects of ragging at NDA have been discussed in detail albeit whether ragging should be done away completely is debatable. The article about incorporating scientific sports medicine oriented training methodology makes for compelling reading. Structured training to enhance strength and endurance can go a long way in winning battles and reducing health hazards due prolonged service exposure.

The antiquated officer selection system has again been analyzed. The screening test at SSB commencement where almost 70% candidates are discarded without subjecting them to psychological and personality tests denies a fair chance to them to display their full potential. Viewpoints of military and civilian instructors/lecturers reinforce this ill-thought-through waste of potential officer candidates.

The harm caused by appointing ad-hoc civilian instructors have deprived cadets of dedicated teachers due to UPSC laxity in selection is also highlighted.

The book also examines other germane issues, among them the biased functioning of the Defence Institute of Psychological Research (DIPR), a DRDO laboratory with marginal participation by the end user; the Services. There are articles on detailed medical analyses of cadet injuries sustained during training. The book has quality articles on military leadership and leadership traits needed to effectively lead men in war. Overall, the book makes is a compulsive read on critical issues that concern the internal health of the military with suggestions validated by serving and veteran officers.

This is a critical time for the profession of arms. In December 2017, Armed Forces were short of 58,602 personnel including 7,679 officers and 49,932 men (shortage of 15.38%). The Army on an average also has about 10,000 low medical category personnel. This imposes an additional burden on fit (SHAPE-1) officers which needs examination. Has 'grooming' of officers suffered by the killing of the concept of 'senior subaltern' and due to the lack of availability of officers in the units? Of course this is the harsh reality.

The situation is further worsened by the absence of many of the remaining few who are on leave, courses and temporary duty. We once had a Service Chief who could not clear Staff College, but today we see officers not approved for Colonel for not having done Staff College despite winning gallantry awards in operations.

Overall, this work on military reforms in the selection, training and imparting of Professional Military Education (PME) in the main is comprehensive and raises multiple issues. Veterans provide unbiased views – free from pulls and pressures. It is for the military leadership to give serious thought to these issues to stop the drift.

I unreservedly compliment Col Vinay Dalvi for his focus and resolve over almost a decade in persistently flagging these issues and creating a very credible platform for Govt to take urgent action on.

Happy reading!

Lt Gen Prakash C Katoch, *PVSM, UYSM, AVSM, SC*
Special Forces
E mail: prakashkatoch7@gmail.com
10th December, 2018

PREFACE

My journey; obsession really, to write about improvement of selection, training and Professional Military Education (PME) of officers commenced in March 2010 with the publication of my first book: **'Role Model' – A Key to Character Development.** A book on the great Chinese philosopher, **Sun Tzu in 2012; 'Sun Tzu' – The Art of War** followed. His selection, training, mental construct and martial education norms had a great impact on me since childhood and throughout my 37 years in uniform. This book was followed the same year by **'Victory India': A Key to Quality Military Leadership.** In my fourth book published in 2014, I reversed the title of my third book by naming it **'Quality Military Leadership' – A Key to Victory India.** I did so because I was resolute in my focus on selection, training and PME and examined the issue from foundational levels and vice versa. The reader response to these books and the favourable professional reviews drove me to produce two more books in the Victory India Series titled **'A Campaign Called Victory India' in 2016 and 'Beyond the Victory India Campaign' in 2018.**

This book is the fifth in the Victory India series and the seventh overall in the line up of books I have written/edited to improve this most important pillar of the Idea of India – quality military officer leadership from subaltern to apex levels always and every time. Ex Naval Chief, Admiral Arun Prakash, PVSM, VrC, AVSM, NM; a really distinguished sailor-scholar of great depth, guts, grit, conviction and bravery has honoured me in sharing his macro level thoughts about my mission – and they are significant and deep as his professional writing in media has been bench-marked ever since he retired. In addition, I have been fortunate in getting ex DGIS, Lt Gen Prakash C Katoch, PVSM, UYSM, and AVSM, SC to write a Foreword in his inimitable manner. Known to speak out his mind without fear or favour, he has exercised his penchant yet again and in full support of my mission to request those in power and authority at apex levels of Governance and decision making to seriously examine the issues raised by some quality writers and opinion makers on issues that so deeply impact on Victory India.

The articles contained in this seventh book are by the crème de la crème of professional military opinion makers. They have examined the issue of officer induction from the UPSC examination, on to the SSB and its ill-conceived De Novo as well as existing SSB selection system evolved by DIPR; a DRDO laboratory. Handling of cadets at the NDA and equivalent training Academies is examined threadbare in terms of content, physical and mental rigour, medical fitness, ragging and so much more. Also examined are the issues of overall PME, the adhoc as opposed to proper system of education by civil and military instructors and how training and education intrudes into an officer's life from beginning to end. Also added are a few miscellaneous subjects that impact on soldiering in our top quality Armed Forces.

The plea is that the aberrations, lapses, deficiencies noted need correction by taking the user along. I thank all contributors and respondents for sparing their time, effort and content so selflessly.

I also thank my publishers Pentagon Press International and well-wishers, some named, and some unnamed who have helped me selflessly to keep my noble mission alive, pulsating and relevant.

Happy reading!

Col Vinay Dalvi
Pune, 18 November, 2018

MISSION 'VICTORY INDIA'

A Key to Quality Combat Leadership

Author & Editor – **Col Vinay B Dalvi**, *ex 4 Maratha LI & APTC*
Message by – **Admiral Arun Prakash**, *PVSM, AVSM, VrC, VSM, ex CNS*
Foreword by – **Lt Gen Prakash C Katoch**, *PVSM, UYSM, AVSM, SC*

Contributory Authors & Respondents –

1. Lt Gen Harbhajan Singh, *PVSM, 1st Course JSW/NDA, ex Signals Officer in Chief*
2. Lt Gen N S Brar, *PVSM, AVSM, ex DCIDS, HQ IDS*
3. Maj Gen V K Madhok, *AVSM, VSM, ex COS HQ 4 Corps, ADG (TA)*
4. Maj Gen Raj Mehta, *AVSM, VSM, ex GOC 19 Inf Div*
5. Rear Admiral Vineet Bakhshi, *VSM, ex CO INS Shivaji*
6. Maj Gen Anil Sengar, *Ex Offg DGMF & GOC Inf Div*
7. Air Cmde Suryakant N Bal, *ex Flying Instr & Div Offr NDA & ex DS CDM*
8. Brig L C Patnaik, *ex President SSB, Chairman Odisha PSC*
9. Brig I S Gakhal, *ex-Sector Cdr RR & Comdt Sikh Regt Centre*
10. Gp Capt T P Srivastava, *38 NDA, ex Instructor DSSC, CDM, CAW*
11. Gp Capt Johnson Chacko, *ex-Instr AFA, DSSC, CDM, NDA*
12. Col Rajinder Kushwaha, *ex CO 3 Bihar*
13. Col P K 'Royal' Mehrishi, *ex Sikh LI*
14. Cdr Ravindra Waman Pathak, *ex Sqn Cdr NDA*
15. Col C M Chavan, *ex-Air Defence Artillery*
16. Col Pradeep Dalvi, *Mech Inf, ex Instr AWC, DIPR/SSB 'Q' GTO & IO*
17. Lt Col P J Chacko, *AAD*
18. Lt Col Mrinal Kumar Gupta Ray, *ex Inf, 18 Sikh*
19. Cdr Mukund Yeolekar, *ex-Principal, Naval College of Engineering*
20. Col Avinash Wandkar, *ex Signals*

21. Maj Jawahar Thota, *ex Artillery*
22. Prof S P Sharma, *ex HoD, English, NDA*
23. Dr Syed Ehsan Ali, *ex HoD, Foreign Languages, NDA*
24. Dr M K Nagpal, *ex HoD, Physics, NDA*
25. Ghazala Wahab, *Editor, Force Magazine*
26. Shashwat Gupta Ray, *Editor, Gomantak Times, Goa*
27. Nibedita Sen, *Reporter, Gomantak Times, Goa*
28. Parth Satam, *Chief Correspondent, Fauji India Magazine*
29. Nixon Fernando, *ex Lecturer NDA, ex Great Lakes Institute, Chennai*

CONTENTS

Message by Admiral Arun Prakash	*vii*
Foreword by Lt Gen Prakash C Katoch	*xi*
Preface	*xv*
Mission 'Victory India'	*xvii*

SECTION 1
AN EMERGING MISSION

1. Beyond The 'Victory India' Campaign: Articles and Debate by Military Veterans – Book Review   3
   Maj Gen Raj Mehta

2. Subjects for Dissertations, Projects and Studies for Select Officer Training Institutions – NDC, AWC, CDM, DSSC, CME, MCEME, MCTE, AFMC, AIPT & INF, ARTY, Armour Schools of Training   7
   Col Vinay Dalvi

3. Flaws in Basic Military Structure Need Rectification   11
   Col P K 'Royal' Mehrishi

SECTION 2
MILITARY EDUCATION & LEADERSHIP TRAINING OF OFFICERS

4. Read. Reflect. Repeat – "Lack of Reading in the New Generation of Officers is a Serious Malaise"   17
   Ghazala Wahab

5. AFSPA Petition: Army Leadership Needs to Do Soul Searching   24
   Maj Gen Anil Sengar

6. Health of Officers and Stress Management: An Organizational Responsibility   28
   Col Vinay B. Dalvi

7. Catch 22 – Physical Courage or Moral Courage?   33
   Col P K 'Royal' Mehrishi

SECTION 3
THE CURRENT CHALLENGES

8. When Soldiers Ask Questions 37
   Lt Gen N S Brar

9. Debate – Should OROP Agitation Continue or Wind Up?
   A 'Diversity of Opinion' Debate 41
   Col Vinay Dalvi

10. Sanctity, Security & Safety of Military Cantonments: A Debate 49
    Col Vinay B Dalvi

11. National Security: What is it and Who is Responsible? 58
    Col Rajinder Kushwaha

12. Soldiers and Politicians: The Need for Mutual Understanding 61
    Maj Gen V K Madhok

13. Debate: Review of Shekatkar Committee Report and its Selective
    Implementation 67
    Parth Satam

14. Have Prolonged CI Ops Weakened us for Conventional and 21st
    Century Warfare? 74
    Col Vinay Dalvi

15. Into the Mind of the Generals 81
    Col P K 'Royal' Mehrishi

16. Challenges to Value System of the Indian Army 84
    Lt Gen NS Brar

SECTION 4
FORCE OPTIMIZATION FOR STRATEGIC CHALLENGES

17. Debate: Revival of 'Air Cavalry' Concept by Indian Army 91
    Compiled by Col Vinay B Dalvi

18. Paramilitary Forces Need Restructuring, Merger and
    Consolidation 97
    Maj Gen VK Madhok

19. India's Stakes in a Two-Front War – Analysis 102
    Maj Gen V K Madhok

20. Prepare for Three-Front War: India's Security Imperative in 21st
    Century! – Possible Scenario 105
    Col Rajinder Kushwaha

21. Mending Fences – Sino-Indian Détente: A Compelling
    Necessity for Both   112
    Col Rajinder Kushwaha

SECTION 5
SELECTION AND TRAINING AT THE MILITARY ACADEMIES

22. Officer Selection and Training System Needs Re-Appraisal and
    Correlativity – Overhaul Needed   117
    Brig LC Patnaik

23. Lessons to Learn – Intro: Public-Private Partnership can be a Way
    Forward to Military Education and Filling up Officer Shortage 121
    Maj Gen Raj Mehta

24. 'De Novo' SSB from 2019: An Analysis   127
    Debate Compiled by Col Vinay Dalvi

25. National Defence Academy Faces Unprecedented Burnout   135
    Parth Satam

26. Excessive Punishments and Ragging Causing High Morbidity
    and Waste Rates at Premier Military Academies   138
    Col P K 'Royal' Mehrishi

27. Incorporation of Scientific Approaches in Military Training
    Methodology – New-Age Science   146
    Col Vinay Dalvi

28. Selection and Role of NDA Academic Staff: A Debate   150
    Col Vinay B Dalvi

29. Cradle of Leadership Fallen on Hard Times   163
    Brig I S Gakhal

30. 'NDA' The Raging Debate and Way Out   167
    Cdr Mukund Yeolekar

31. Reforming NDA for Leadership Challenges of 21st Century   170
    Nixon Fernando

32. Why the NDA must be Reformed and Reviewed? A Debate   176
    Col Vinay B. Dalvi

SECTION 6
INSPIRATIONAL LEADERSHIP – LIVE EXAMPLES

33. A Tribute to Lt Col J J Fonseca, the Pioneering Army
    Sports Specialist   187
    Col Vinay B Dalvi

34. Sam Bahadur: Leader Par Excellence 191
    Shashwat Gupta Ray

SECTION 7
COMPREHENSIVE MEDIA COVERAGE:
GOMANTAK TIMES, GOA

35. Integration of Tri-Services is Need of the Hour 197
    Shashwat Gupta Ray & Nibedita Sen

36. Media Coverage of 'Victory India Campaign' 201
    Gomantak Times, Panjim Goa – 30 Dec 2018

37. 'Victory India' Campaign Gets Overwhelming Support 206
    Gomantak Times, Panjim Goa – 06 Jan 2019

38. Mission Victory India – Six Part Series 211
    Gomantak Times 3-8 Jan, 2019

SECTION 1
AN EMERGING MISSION

CHAPTER 1

Beyond The 'Victory India' Campaign: Articles and Debate by Military Veterans – Book Review

By Maj Gen Raj Mehta

> *An exhaustive and holistic book review of the one of the most noble and thoughtful campaigns for reforming the selection, recruitment, grooming and training in the Indian military, spearheaded by Veteran instructor, Col Vinay Dalvi.*
>
> *– Maj Gen Raj Mehta*

Observant FORCE readers would have read Executive Editor Ghazala Wahab's 'Read, Reflect, Repeat' column in the Jan 2018 issue with delight and a sense of déjà vu. In her prescient take, she pithily observed not just a decline in the reading and reflecting habits of officers, but, more worryingly, the unexpected, cavalier attitude of a few senior officers towards this decline who disparaged it as an issue of no consequence.

Such deep-rooted concern about this and many other indices of apparent institutional mindset in the selection, training and education of young officers is also the subject for Veteran Army officer Col Vinay Dalvi's 'Beyond the Victory India Campaign: Articles and Debates by Military Veterans', a well-produced effort of Pentagon Press, Delhi and his fourth book in his 'Victory India' series since 2013.

The series focuses on identifying deficiencies in and setting things right in the 'cloaked in secrecy', little understood or openly discussed military selection-training-education domain which is exclusively and inexplicably steered not by the military's HQ Integrated Defence Staff (HQ IDS), but by an inaccessible civilian scientist dominated and led Defence Research and Development Organization (DRDO) laboratory; the Defence Institute of Psychological Research (DIPR). This establishment, much to the chagrin of the military, routinely takes minimal inputs from the military (represented in innocuous junior or medium level positions in its establishment) while conceptualizing the selection/training/education or modifying the domain to meet current and future military challenges.

It has been defending the vintage selection/training norms handed over on Independence and justifying them with obduracy even as the originators, the British, have long since discarded their norms and created new selection norms in line with current realities. Dalvi and his Victory India Team write with frankness, insight and pedigree on what in this opaque DIPR system needs correction and how, backed by substantial research and international benchmarking. If taken up, these suggestions can lead to qualitative military officer improvement to handle current and emerging challenges in the increasingly complex Indian security environment which has mind-boggling external and internal dimensions.

'Beyond the Victory India Campaign: Articles and Debates by Military Veterans' is only superficially a compendium on the vital issues that concern the gamut of Indian military officer quality. It is more pertinently an impassioned plea to move away from legacy methods of selection, training and education of India's military. These methods were hastily and rather thoughtlessly copy-pasted by the British military hierarchy from German selection methods for inducting the vast swathes of 'allied' and British officers it urgently needed on the onset of World War 2. Dalvi makes the point that these methods remain largely unchanged and opaquely institutionalized over the last 75 years but for some pedestrian tinkering such as has recently been initiated to deflect persistent criticism of prevailing systems.

He suggests that this mindset is at odds with emerging realities where officers must learn to 'think-on-their-feet', be multi-skilled, alert, aware in real time, driven by instant 'situational awareness' and decision making skills (almost always at junior levels as occurred recently at Kupwara, when fire had to be opened by the military to save military personnel from mob lynching) besides possessing the timeless qualities of good officer-ship unchanged since the Battle of Megiddo in the 15th century BCE; since the Battle on the Hydaspes (Jhelum) in 326 BCE between Alexander the Great and Porus. Officer like qualities such as heroism, selflessness, inspirational and transformational leadership skills, courage, grit, coolness under adversity victorious under all-weather, all-environment conditions as envisaged by Col Dalvi in his 'Victory India' series.

Not unsurprisingly, these are the very qualities acquired from reading, reflecting and deep study of the past, present and what the unknown future might offer...not mindless application of yesterday by pretending that yesterday offers custom-made solutions for both today and tomorrow. This is the point FORCE Executive Editor Ghazala Wahab makes too and hence the admirable synergy between these two streams of thought: one military; the other an objective appraisal by a civilian lady editor of what the military needs to do as standard, everyday, ingrained practice; not wish away this critical need as irrelevant and superfluous.

The book which has a thoughtful and far reaching foreword by highly decorated ex-AOP Air HQ, Air Marshal Narayan Menon, is laid out in seven sections which cover the entire gamut of officer management in the military from nurturing, selection and training in Section 1 through a truly diverse coverage in the follow up sections.

Col Dalvi in his path-breaking Section 1 article brings out the need for looking at sports medicine as an emerging, 'must-have' discipline in line with world trends. This is needed to ensure preventive injury protection to under-training cadets as also for professional treatment of injury once it occurs. AFMC Pune, a premier military medical college has taken pioneering steps in this direction and Col Dalvi, who has been in touch with sports medicine developments, correctly suggests that our military training academies apply available expertise on priority. This will undoubtedly reduce, for instance, the high incidence of stress fractures which take out a high percentage of cadets across gender in every course from the rigorous training regimen for as much as 8-10 weeks including sick leave. With a crippling existing shortage of around 13,000 officers, surely, we can cut down on such losses by simply taking advantage of available skills and decentralizing them to needed centers of training by placement of AFMC trained Sports Medicine experts.

In the same section, another expert points at the limitations of the much-publicized DIPR-driven 'new' officer selection system by reducing the SSB selection process from the existing five to three days. This will make the job of the GTO, for instance, heavily stressed – if not untenable – and thus make a mockery of the selection system per se. Section 3 carries an article on a general tendency for risk aversion that the writer feels is creeping up in the younger lot of officers. This, he feels, is a serious liability but will happen in an environment where mindsets rule the roost. He quotes Simon Foucher who, in 1673, almost 350 years ago, had written with uncanny truth that, "We are dogma prone from our Mother's wombs". Imagine carrying this attitude forward if we were to carry out a much-needed surgical strike or save a colleague from lynching and certain death simply because the basic selection, training and education parameters treat dogma like a holy cow.

Lt Gen N S Brar in his Section 3 article on cutting military flab to promote muscle makes compelling statements. Vice Admiral Bangara in his article in Section 5 shares pragmatic views on training warriors. He is an erudite ex-Commandant of the NDA who visited the Australian Military Academies during his tenure and picked up important lessons on how to divide the academic-soldiering loads/responsibilities for under-training cadets rationally, pragmatically and brilliantly.

These articles are penned by experienced military Veterans, academics involved with military selection, training and education and by media experts reporting on this portion of military architecture. These bring out what is being done, where deficiencies have occurred, what needs correction and why and how must correction be invoked to bring the regimen of Indian military officer selection-training-education to match the best prevailing systems in the world.

The book covers issues like the contours of future combat leadership; women officers in combat; doctrinal issues (our joint, overarching doctrine does not stand up to close scrutiny both inter or intra-Services besides lacking in battlefield 'jointness'); progressive promotion policies; the choice between ragging and constructive toughening up; need for promoting "soldier-scholars" instead of just soldiers (hence accepting the criticism of inability to read, reflect and repeat as valid)...The book eloquently carries these discussions/debates.

In sum, a well-produced, must-read book for those engaged in military selection, training, education or in decision making positions that oversee these critical military activities including apex political authority and bureaucracy. The Victory India perspective is sufficiently germane and urgent to invite media attention in print, TV and social media platforms and thereby invite much-needed public debate on the Team Victory India to facilitate apex decision making.

Note: This book review was first published in 'Force' magazine, March 2018 issue and 'Fauji India' magazine, April 2018 issue.

CHAPTER 2

Subjects for Dissertations, Projects and Studies for Select Officer Training Institutions – NDC, AWC, CDM, DSSC, CME, MCEME, MCTE, AFMC, AIPT & INF, ARTY, Armour Schools of Training

Col Vinay Dalvi

The u/m twenty (20) subjects and thirty (30) reference books are recommended for dissertations, projects and studies for students and instructional staff at our prestigious officer training institutions. 'Team Victory India' (comprising over 60 military veterans & academicians) consider these subjects to be important and relevant for our present and future generation of officers. The subjects from serial 1 to 12 pertain to our Victory India Campaign books, while serial 13 to 20 pertain to other important issues.

Recommended Subjects (Victory India Campaign)
1. Introduction of mandatory physical tests at SSBs for improving fitness and health of officer trainees and reduction of wastage rates at military academies.
2. Need for coordinated academic and military training of cadets for better academic and intellectual growth?
3. Review and revision of existing SSB selection system and enhanced coordination with military academies for producing qualitatively better military officers?
4. Introduction of Physical Education and Sports Medicine for cadets, recruits and combatants for improving physical efficiency of soldiers and officers.
5. Revival and Prioritisation of Officers Physical Training Course (OPTC) at AIPT to produce more number of effective young PT& Sports officers at unit level and recruit training centres.
6. Increase of Officers Physical Training Courses (OPTC) at AIPT Pune for producing more trained PT & Sports Officers at unit level and transfer of suitable officers into APTC.
7. Blue Ribbon Commission for providing oversight on Defence Forces Entry / Selection / Training / Utilisation.

8. Reformatting the SSB selection system... Need, what ails SSB, what needs doing and attendant time lines.
9. Why should DRDO train the SSB selection staff? Why should DIPR be under / DRDO? Does HQ IDS provide a viable alternative? Examine.
10. Is Ragging acceptable or a violation of military human rights of trainees? Opinions and Recommendations
11. Introduction Basic Physical Education Theory Subjects for Cadets, Recruits and Combatants will make our PT Methodology more scientific as per directions of United Commanders Conference (UCC) decision.
12. Introduction of Basic Sports / Fitness Medicine Theory subjects to cadets and young officers will improve their fitness levels and also reduce wastage rate in context of UCC decision.

Other Subjects
13. Strategies for managing combat stress.
14. Competency building to physical and mental health.
15. Combat stress behaviour and psychiatric disorder.
16. The role of the Armed Forces in national integration.
17. Role of the Armed Forces in creating a caste – less society based solely on competence
18. Leadership challenges in an environment in which followers are more educated than leaders.
19. Is our higher educational training focused on future wars or is we still stuck in the old groove?
20. Does our senior leadership have intellectual competence to deliver in futuristic social and battlefield environment?

Reference Books Recommended
1. On the Psychology of Military Incompetence – by Norman F. Dixon
2. Profligate Governance – Implications for National Security – by Gp Capt T P Srivastava (TVI)
3. The Himalayan Blunder – by Brig J P Dalvi
4. India China War 1962 – By Maxwell
5. Four Decades in Olive Greens – by Maj Gen Anil Sengar (TVI)
6. Battlefields of the early 21st century – by Maj Gen V K Madhok (TVI)
7. Space: Profiles of the Future and Re powering National Security – by Maj Gen VK Madhok (TVI)
8. Restructuring National Security – by Lt Gen Ashok Joshi (TVI)
9. Role Model – a key to character development (2010) – by Col Vinay B Dalvi (TVI)
10. Sun Tzu – The Art of War (pocket book) (2012) – by Col Vinay B Dalvi (TVI)
11. Victory India – a key to quality military leadership (2013) – by Col Vinay B Dalvi & Team Victory India (TVI)
12. Quality Military Leadership – a key to Victory India (2014) – by Col Vinay

B Dalvi &Team Victory India (TVI)
13. A Campaign called Victory India (2016) – by Col Vinay B Dalvi & Team Victory India (TVI)
14. Beyond the Victory India Campaign (2018) – by Col Vinay B Dalvi &Team Victory India (TVI)
15. Demystifying Leadership – by Lt Gen KB Kala
16. Battalion Command, Dare to Lead – by Maj Gen Anil Sengar (TVI)
17. Crises in Command – Mismanagement in the Army – by Richard A. Gabriel and Paul Savage
18. Future Shock – by Alvin Toffler
19. Third Wave – by Alvin Toffler
20. War & Anti War – by Alvin Toffler
21. South Asia Defence and Strategic Perspective 2018 – by Dr Vijay Sakhuja
22. Defence Reforms – by Brig Gurmeet Kanwal
23. Hybrid Warfare – by Vikrant Deshpande
24. India's National Defence – by Gen Gautam Banerjee (TVI)
25. Military Thinking of Ancient India – by Prof Shekhar Adhikari
26. Syrian Jihad – by Charles Lister
27. Baluchistan, the British and the great game – by T A Heathcote
28. Rooks and Knights – by R Chandrasekhar
29. China transition under Xi Jinping
30. Inside Al Qaeda and the Taliban – by Syed Shahzad
31. FAUJI INDIA Magazine Last 25 Monthly Issues From April 2016 to April 2018.

Out of 30 recommended reference books, 13 are authored by members of 'Team Victory India' (TVI) and relate to most of the recommended 20 subjects, especially the first 12 subjects. The help and guidance of these authors would be available if required.

It will be highly appreciated if copy of this letter is sent to Commandants of all concerned 'officer training institutions' of the three services for their information and favorable action as deemed fit.

Kindly find attached a Message from Shri T N Seshan, ex CEC, ex Cabinet & Defence Secretary (from our book A Campaign Called Victory India/2016) – which aptly sums up the vital importance of the subjects recommended and elaborately covered by the 'Victory India Campaign' books and encapsulated in ser 1-12 of the recommended subjects.

With warm regards & best wishes,

Col Vinay B Dalvi
Team Victory India, Pune, 18 April, 2018.

To:

1. Admiral Sunil Lanba, *PVSM, AVSM, ADC – CNS & Chairman COSC*
2. Gen Bipin Rawat, *UYSM, AVSM, YSM, SM, VSM – COAS*
3. Air Chief Marshal Birender Singh Dhanoa, *PVSM, AVSM, YSM, VSM, ADC – Chief of the Air Staff*

Copy to:

1. Lt Gen Satish Dua, *UYSM, SM, VSM, CISC, HQ IDS, New Delhi*
2. Lt Gen Manoj Mukund Naravane, *AVSM, SM, VSM, Army Cdr, HQ ARTRAC, Shimla*
3. Lt Gen P J S Pannu, *AVSM, VSM, DCIDS (DOT), HQ IDS, New Delhi*
4. Lt Gen Ranbir Singh, *AVSM **, YSM, SM, DCOAS (IS&T), New Delhi*
5. Lt Gen Harpal Singh, *DGMT, Army HQ, New Delhi*
6. Lt Gen Amrik Singh, *AVSM, SM – Comdt DSSC, Wellington*
7. Lt Gen Y V Krishna Mohan, *Comdt NDC, New Delhi*
8. Lt Gen Rajeev Tewari, *Comdt AWC Mhow*
9. Maj Gen Sandeep Sharma, *VSM, Comdt CDM, Secunderabad*
10. Air Mshl C K Ranjan, *AVSM, VSM, Comdt AFMC Pune*
11. Lt Gen S S Sengupta, *VSM, Comdt CME, Dapodi, Pune*
12. Lt. Gen Ravindra Singh Panwar, *VSM, Comdt MCTE, Mhow*
13. Lt Gen Paramjit Singh, *VSM, Comdt, MCEME, Secunderabad*

CHAPTER 3

Flaws in Basic Military Structure Need Rectification

Col P K 'Royal' Mehrishi

Every man made structure has an in built life span, no structure created by humans can last eternally, some get created for shorter periods and get obliterated even without registering in general consciousness and some like the pyramids of Giza stand tall over centuries, but sooner or later the law of entropy catches up!

What makes a structure withstand the test of time? Well it has to satisfy the following laws:
- The basic Idea in consonance with objective reality.
- Laws of Physics & Maths related to the structure.
- Team Work & Human endeavour.
- Quality of Material utilized.
- Timely interventions for repair and maintenance if required.

The Indian Army, a product of the British Colonial army, created structured & nourished by the British to further their limited interests has over a span of 70 odd years after Independence developed flaws in its basic structure. I will elaborate:

The Basic Idea
The basic concept of keeping a large standing Army is deterrence (**Chandragupt** had a large, well trained, standing Army of 6 Lakh troops) it also adds gravitas & muscle to following a robust Foreign policy. It is like a living, throbbing with action, mammoth organism with dynamics of its own, based on ethos, recruitment, and training. The topping is prevalent culture. Like in war fighting it is *"Vijay ya Veergati"* (Victory or Death) Army can also deliver in furthering National Objectives & Political aims.

Present Scenario – almost all parameters mentioned above have taken a beating, though we have a large standing Army of 1.3 Million, it is under a lethargic bureaucratic & political control (three RM's in four years). Prevalent culture is materialistic & the political class has scant clue about how to handle the concerns of a well trained professional Army.

Laws of Physics & Maths

Some basic laws of Physics & Maths play a very important role in any structure. Take for example the Pyramids of Giza. The base is wider & stronger to support the edifice & top stones. Interlocking of stones yields a stronger structure; triangle is the strongest geometrical design. **Triangles** are the **strongest shape** because any added force is evenly spread through all three sides. Look closely at any pyramid – it's made of **triangles**! Squares or cubes can be strengthened by adding a diagonal piece across the middle, making it two **triangles** linked together.

Present Scenario – the basics of recruitment, training, ethos, & grooming are all being given a short shrift, with no uniformity & forward thinking in training methods. It is not about numbers alone, that we have in abundance; fact is, the base of the Pyramid is getting weaker. To aggravate the situation, seamless interlocking is missing (integrated training with different arms is an eye wash, with each arm eulogizing & furthering their own concepts of training)

Team Work & Human Endeavour

There is immense sacrifice & human endeavour that is being invested by the Army in terrorist infested J & K, but it is unscientific & not based on sound principles of battling terrorist led insurgencies. Mere human effort will yield diminishing returns. Are the local decisions making politicians, Governor, Army Commanders, NSA, RM & PM always on the same page?

Why in nearly 30 years of terror in J & K we failed to define (an insurgent, militant, terrorist, anti national, terror suspect or misguided youth?) while serving in J & K in anti terror operations, I found multiple agencies working at cross purposes to each other. Till end of 1994 we went into operations without a Bullet Proof (BP) jacket, our vehicles were not BP while the J & K Police moved about in BP Gypsy Jeeps.

Present Scenario – we still lack specific Intelligence to pin point & pick out terrorists. During funerals & *fatehas* of killed terrorists, gun wielding subaltern terrorists throng to the venue openly defying the might of the Army & raise slogans & wave ISIS flags to motivate fresh recruitment. Where are the long range sniper rifles? Does the Army employ professional hackers & data mining experts to read through face book posts & whatsapp messages in J & K? Why are the likes of Mehbooba Mufti allowed to give seditious anti national statements? Even when she is belittling the sacrifices of our brave hearts? Does the Army have a strategic information & public communication structure in place? A full blown insurgency is not only the Army's baby it is National Team Work. Insurgencies which drag on for longer periods (30 years) inure the population against violence & killings by Insurgents or the CI forces.

Quality of Material Utilized

A structure will withstand the test of time only if the quality of material utilized is the best available at that time. Quality is also based on information available about the resource, proximity of the resource, skill or expertise in utilization and abundance of supply for the task at hand.

Present Scenario – The quality of intake has deteriorated over the years is the common refrain. Well what are we doing about it? The quality of Officer intake, Institutions like NDA, moral orientation, grooming, training have all gone down a few notches when we conduct a reality check. In more ways than one it is each one for himself.

Timely Intervention for Repair & Maintenance

Either the structure created is long lasting with no structural flaws or timely interventions for corrections, repair & maintenance need to be activated. The Army as a huge organization has developed vast structural flaws. The concept of war fighting itself has under gone a sea change. War by other Means (WOM) is concepts being put to test by our enemies. The Army basically seams stuck in a colonial mode, training itself has not undergone much change, the basic training academies for Officers have yet not adopted modern concepts of training.

Present Scenario – the entire system is functioning on arms/services concept. Integration, inter-service co ordination is rare. Continued deployment of units in CI grid has taken a toll on Unit training. There is a shortage of Officers in Field areas. To top this all, there is lack of clarity in scientific training methodology, sports medicine, specific syllabus for NDA, IMA etc. and what do we need of a future Military Officer.

Col Vinay Dalvi as the helms man & his team of structural engineers of 60 veterans has come out with path breaking ideas. They have written from experience & expertise with candor in a series of five Volumes, termed as the **Victory India** series. These contributors have the highest goal in mind i.e. strengthening the military might of India. From recruitment to induction, grooming, training, management, leadership indicators, WOM concepts, sports medicine an entire gamut of modern & relevant topics have been debated, vetted, endorsed & verified have been covered in more than 163 articles. The map for restructuring is ready & presented in these volumes. Unit commanders & stake holders at all levels have to rise & start implementing these well researched concepts before it is too late.

SECTION 2

MILITARY EDUCATION & LEADERSHIP TRAINING OF OFFICERS

CHAPTER 4

Read. Reflect. Repeat
"Lack of Reading in the New Generation of Officers is a Serious Malaise"

By Ghazala Wahab

Nearly 12 years ago, when I first heard the refrain from a retired Indian Army lieutenant general that young officers do not read any longer, it was a lament. He ruled the fact that the counter-insurgency operations – the endless and thankless low-level war (now referred to as no-war-no-peace) – leave young officers with no time to read even professional material, let alone literature. As a result, the overall intellect level of the officer class has progressively been on a decline.

But why a professional soldier would need to read literature, if not for mere pleasure, I wondered aloud.

It is true that reading literature is pure pleasure, he argued, but it also trains your intellect to absorb new ideas and concepts. It can also be inspiring, he said, adding that, he is not even expecting young officers who are overworked and hard-pressed for time to read fiction. "But at least they should read professional literature and not take short-cuts by memorising the précis to clear various examinations," he insisted.

Recently, at a public event, I heard a retired army commander talk about the lack of reading habit amongst the young in the uniform. There was no lament in his tone; there was a touch of pride, because he qualified the lack of reading as a new trend of the modern world where social media forums like twitter and Facebook are not mere sources of entertainment but news as well. This is what they read and this is how they express themselves, he said. Today, they have no time to write professional essays, as was required of them. But this does not mean that they are any less intelligent or smart than their predecessors, he claimed. What the older generation said in their essays, the younger lot is saying in tweets, he said in all seriousness.

His final point was that the new crop of officers should not be judged by their poor command of the language, neither by the absence of grammar nor by spelling mistakes. They should be judged by their enthusiasm and initiative.

Safe to say, 12 years have had their impact. The fear of intellectual atrophy that haunted the old timer has come true. His successor, 12 years hence, not only rubbished the habit of reading, he also downplayed the importance of language. Clearly, for him too, the fountainhead of all wisdom was social media, where independent thinking, clarity of ideas, dispassionate assessment, language and spellings are slaughtered every minute at the twin altars of propaganda and herd mentality.

The 17th Century Irish writer, playwright and subsequently politician, Richard Steele is known to have written once that, 'Reading is to the mind what exercise is to the body.' To this, I would add that language is the tool which facilitates reading and writing; and grammar a mechanism by which you express your ideas. All of these are the most basic necessities of civilised living.

If you don't have words at your command how are you going to say what you want to say? Complex ideas do not need complex words, but they certainly need a vocabulary without which the receiver of your ideas would be left struggling in the maze of incomprehensible sentences. And you would be left making excuses about being misunderstood!

Another great writer, this time a German and one of the earliest critics of Nazism, Heinrich Miller had said, 'A house without books is like a room without windows.' Without the windows, how would you know what is happening outside? Whether there are friends or enemies outside, or whether your friends have been canoodling with your enemies. When you can't see for yourself, you will have no choice but to believe what you are told.

The importance of reading, thereafter reflecting and finally, writing, especially for the military officers can never be overemphasised. More than any time in the past, today there is a need for military officers to be well read, so that they are able to understand better, assess fairly, advice sensibly and are able to take far-reaching judgement calls. Reading is a habit that grows on you gradually, one book at a time. If you don't read when you are a junior officer, you will not understand when you become a senior officer. And you will continue to repeat what you learnt from your superiors without questioning its efficacy. You will remain stuck in theories of the past, as your intellect will neither be able to absorb nor process new ideas.

It is not about literature alone. Once the mind is made supple by continuous and varied reading, it is able to connect what it has read with the events around. Prescience is not a supernatural trait. It is the ability to take a broad overview of the past to put your present in a context, so that you can understand how events are likely to unfold in the future. Isn't this ability essential for all military leaders? Where will this ability come from if not cultivated early on?

Military power is one of the prongs of national power. By celebrating the age of illiteracy amongst military leaders we are ensuring that as a nation we continue to hobble on borrowed wisdom.

Letters

Executive editor Ghazala Wahab's column (January 2018) 'Read. Reflect. Repeat' has drawn a lot of response from the readers with many of them offering their own suggestions. We reproduce a selection.

Reintroduce Officer's Week

Ghazala Wahab, in the January 2018 issue, has written on an important matter felt by the veterans – lack of reading habit in the new generation of defence officers (*Read. Reflect. Repeat*). The article reflects the predicament faced by the defence force but what is intriguing is the fact that some of the senior officers take it in their stride. They feel that spelling mistakes, vocabulary and lack of expression are well compensated by their enthusiasm and initiative!

There is no denying the fact that due to the commitment of the officers; especially those in the field areas have no time and energy left to read. Over indulgence in WhatsApp and Twitter probably is another reason for deterioration, as the expressions on these platforms is abbreviated and in short forms. Then there is the issue of intake of the officers who are from all walks of life and lack the environment wherein they can form the habit of reading. Thus, the result is there to see. Therefore, an officer has to somehow find at least half an hour in a day to devote to reading.

Medium of instruction in India is largely English hence, to grasp any subject one must know the language well which also helps in reproducing the same whenever so required. Grasping allows one to express the same in different ways and one doesn't have to bank on mugging.

I remember that till the late Eighties Officer's Week were planned as a part of annual training schedule at Brigade levels. During this week all officers were required to present a book review and speak for half an hour on any subject other than their profession. In units, the Commanding Officer used to encourage officers to speak on general topic during tea breaks. This is how the officers were encouraged to form a habit of reading which was a very good trend.

Knowing the language well helps to project oneself and stand out in any gathering. Grasping any matter helps in the growth of an individual as he can participate in any discussion and debate on it logically. Thus, the advantages of mastering the English language are far too many, and moreover it is the official language in the Forces. There is no denying the fact that reading alone helps in improving one's language and learn different nuances of expressions. The reading can be on any topic of general interest of an individual like fictions, autobiographies, thrillers, military history etc. As one forms the habit of reading one can start selecting choicest authors, who have distinct methods of expression.

Those cadets in academies, who have some mastery over the English language, generally fare better than the other cadets. It does not take them time to understand a topic and reproduce the same as when required. It is, therefore, essential that right from the academy days the cadets should be encouraged to read. The instructors should tweak the minds of the cadets and make them understand the advantages of knowing a language well. This trend should start at the school level as well; wherein teachers should make the students write essays on innovative topics as an impromptu competition. Most importantly, the hierarchy in the Forces should take it on to themselves, as an improvement agenda of officers under their command. As command over the English language is an important tool for the growth of an officer.

It is, therefore, the bounden duty of teaching staff at academies to endeavour to develop the habit of reading amongst cadets earnestly. It could also be made a part of assessment as a part of syllabus. At unit level, the Commanding Officers should inculcate the habit of reading amongst officers, irrespective of seniority as a part of training programme for every quarter, wherein an officer should read a book and speak on it before all the officers for half an hour and questions should be asked by the audience at the end. The Officer's Week can be reintroduced at Brigade levels of Command and time permitting; the Divisional Commander should make a surprise visit as per the training programme.

Col C M Chavan

Need for Intellectual Development

Kindly refer to your piece in 'First Person' column on page 79 of FORCE magazine January 2018 issue.

You have touched upon a very critical issue, that of the imperative need of 'intellectual development' of our military officers. I have been leading a campaign called 'Victory India' for past six years relating to issues for improving the quality of our military leadership at all levels.

Your piece has highlighted the need for intellectual development through reading, reflecting, repeating and reproducing/writing. This glaring shortcoming has not only adversely affected the military but also the vast civil world from where our intake is inducted.

Your noble intention has been well comprehended not only by me but many other senior veterans with whom I been regularly interacting. The piece has already been circulated by me for a serious debate amongst military veterans and academicians in the civil world. Views and Counterviews are being obtained to reach a consensus and conclusion to enable the drafting of a practical vision/ way forward to address this serious shortcoming that has already negatively impacted the intellectual level of our military leadership even in the apex/ higher levels, especially in the Army.

Col Vinay Dalvi

Reading Distinguishes Leaders

The author is bang on! On one side it is an established fact that reading distinguishes leaders. Research shows that one fact that distinguishes the best men/women who rise up as leaders is that they spare time amounting to a few hours of reading every week.

On the other hand, there is this vision about making military men and junior leaders in the academy where there is no relief from running around just to 'survive'. 'Blind obedience', 'if they start thinking they will not obey', 'don't think, and leave the thinking to us' and such other notions rule the roost at the academy.

The cadets pledge themselves to a life of obedience in a military context when they sign on and they are aware of it. You don't have to rub it in needlessly. Rather the aim should be to make them rise intellectually so that they can be military leaders with vision, erudite, and capable of holding their own in a forum of intellectuals. They must have the depth to understand their men, the context they come from, their aspirations and a whole lot of other things. This is an absolute necessity to be able to lead anybody for that matter.

NDA does not provide that opportunity, meaningfully at least, in the present context. 'Cradle of military leadership' or 'Cradle of military heading', what is the vision that is presently driving the NDA?

Nixon Fernando

Immediately Implement Reading

Ancient India, the cradle of civilisation and learning, nurtured the concept of saint-soldier. For a soldier/commander/king, virtues of mental balance and equanimity would emerge from values being impacted by a saint. Never hitting a man when he was down, never coveting somebody's wife/land were some of the basic values passed on to generations. Some of the *rishis* were equally adept in the art of warfare. However, one thing was common and that was erudition. Lord Rama is an iconic example of a learned saint-soldier, his gurus (Vashist and Vishwamitra) not only taught him all the *Vedas/shastras/ganit*, but also taught him the deployment and use of *Brahamastra*, which was the ultimate deterrent. Late 18th century again witnessed this concept playing out in the battles fought by Guru Govind Singh and his band of legendary fighters.

Without reading how can the intellect are developed? Reading opens up the mind to different ideas, concepts and alternate ways of doing things. Had it not been for the reading of military history and some well-known classics we would be constantly staring at failure in battles as some basic concepts of warfare are perennial gems to be learnt and implemented:

- Never reinforce failure (choose a different route)
- Surprise is a force multiplier
- Moral courage to Physical Force is 3:1

- Know the enemy
- Look after your men better than their mothers do

These are a few nuggets taken from classics like War and Peace (Leo Tolstoy), Sun Tzu, Napoleon Bonaparte, Gen. Douglas McArthur and George S. Patton Jr.

Reading, reflecting, discussing, debating, writing and doing basic arithmetic puzzles develops abstract/creative thinking. Most of the complex solutions in battlefield are going to emerge from 'out of the box implementation of ideas'. Following the tried and tested beaten path will yield diminishing returns as the enemy would also have studied our standard reaction patterns in a set piece of given situation.

I whole-heartedly endorse the concerns raised in the article 'Read. Reflect. Repeat' by Ghazala Wahab regarding lack of reading habit among the new generation of officers. Her contention that 'reading is to mind what exercise is to body' deserves immediate attention and implementation among the officer class.

Col P K 'Royal' Mehrishi

Read, Write and Grow

When I was seven years old my uncle told me to not only read but write as well. Writing could be anything from letters to poetry to stories et all. He further added that 'Son as you grow you will see/hear lots of things that in your opinion ought to be changed.' But he cautioned me that before opening your mouth (and putting your foot) you must consider writing your proposal. Sleep over it and read the next day. He elaborated further and said that 'in most cases you will find that your proposal, which was delivered verbally, was a proposal put forward by an ass'. So, write before you open your mouth was the dictum.

Gp Capt T P Srivastava

Additional Response

Anyone who feels that WhatsApp can replace reading is a moron, for one, studies establish that 70 to 80 percent of information on WhatsApp is fake. The problem, you do not know which 20 percent is not fake. If a General said this, clearly, he has gone way beyond his level of incompetence. And that is one of the issues with our promotion system. There is no audit of your 'phronesis', a Greek word which means practical wisdom which is a product of intelligence, experience and common sense. An average officer can reach the highest rank in our army if he has mastered the art of keeping his boss happy. And ACRs being the only criteria of promotion and not spoken reputation based on a 360 degree input, you will have officers who believe that grammar and spelling mistakes are fine if you have enthusiasm. That is fine for a JCO but not even a young officer, for soon he will be a senior officer and clear unambiguous communication skill is essential to passing clear orders that are in any case prone to misinterpretation and expressing yourself with clarity and confidence.

Reading leads to learning, and learning is an indispensable part of effective leadership. They go together. While ignorance is bad enough, some senior army officers have illusions of knowledge based on ranks. That is more dangerous.

As for time, the person who understands the benefit of reading will find it in a fox hole. The current CO 5 Guards, Col AP Singh, an ever smiling and a relaxed commanding officer has read more than 200 books in his 27 months of command and practiced ideas picked up from reading to make the battalion effective in every way. Now, when does he read? He rises at 3.30/4 am in the morning. Before PT parade, he has already read for a few hours. The battalion, its officers and men have benefited from his reading, professionally and personally in a big way. The battalion under him in his formation is a case study.

I hope the WhatsApp General will read this piece.

Maj Gen Anil Sengar

CHAPTER 5

AFSPA Petition: Army Leadership Needs to Do Soul Searching

By Maj Gen Anil Sengar

"If the troops stop bringing their problems to the commanders, they have either lost confidence in their ability to solve their problems or have concluded that they do not care."

Although the Armed Forces Special Powers Act (AFSPA) has been a bone of contention for many since its inception, an on-going tussle over dilution of the said act has now even forced Army men to take their stand. In a first, on August 14, an unprecedented writ petition filed "collectively" by 356 Army officers of Eastern Command in the Supreme Court against alleged dilution of the AFSPA in disturbed areas such as Manipur and Jammu and Kashmir has raised many eyebrows. This move was later supported by few hundred more, taking their number to over seven hundred.

Days after Army Chief General Bipin Rawat, speaking to officers of the Army Headquarter in Delhi, questioned the need for serving Army officers and soldiers to approach the Supreme Court in personal capacity against the above-mentioned issue, a serving Major General, currently posted as Chief of Staff of a Corps in the Eastern Command, has filed an application that he be made party to the petition filed by 739 Army personnel.

What does the Army Chief think of him? In my perspective, he is a rare breed of Generals who possibly answered the call of his conscience and set an example. Better, he should have got the military leadership to act when the dust storms were gathering. This is not a solitary case. In September 2017, more than hundred officers of Army Service Corps had gone en masse to the court against a perceived discriminatory promotion policy.

Why should that Happen Time and Again?

A large number of people including law experts, such as Dushyant Dave, and General Panag, the former army commander, joined to condemn these officers outright, referring to the action as mutiny and an act of gross indiscipline. Dushyant Dave was particularly severe on this and, given his legal background, gave many reasons to justify the Supreme Court's action and how this act had the potential to lead to all-out confrontation between the Judiciary and the Army.

Well, it is a fashion to condemn army actions that do not fit the frame of reference of either armchair human rights experts or legal experts or the self-proclaimed righteous within the military. Lt Gen Prakash Menon, former military advisor of National Security Council, in a very well-articulated article, The Indian Soldier Feels Let Down by the Army Brass, Supreme Court and Politicians, brought out the larger dangers of the judiciary wading into the combat space.

Debate is the strength of democracy, and it must be encouraged. My observation is that more often than not, these experts tend to look at the issues from their narrow respective fields of expertise, without comprehending the dynamics and complexities of the military situations that have a character of their own, which cannot be put into a narrow frame of reference of one field.

I wish to contribute my bit to put across why fixed templates of experts, such as those of Dushyant Dave or General Panag, can create serious misunderstandings in public and intelligentsia and create an unwarranted alarm.

No one in the Army sees the institution above the law. In fact, nowhere else in the country is law enforced and disciplinary action taken more expeditiously and severely than in the Army.

Why actions of the Army in counter-insurgency environment will not fit in to the straitjacketed frame of the law or the Army act?

Counter-insurgency operations pose multiple challenges. Insignificant incident can be blown out of proportion in this age of (morphed/doctored) social media with no accountability. Conflicts can arise out of constraints and caution imposed by military hierarchy. It creates an environment where plethora of agencies – human rights organizations, political parties and media – are always looking for breaking news and sensationalizing military errors.

The situation in disturbed areas is really complex and seeks utmost attention and skills so as to minimize any chance of mistake. However, owing to different nature of enemy while fighting with either soldiers of enemy nations or civilians of our own country, it is very difficult for a soldier to counter those of our own nation, such as stone-pelters in Jammu and Kashmir.

In war, the whole nation rallies behind an Army man, whereas in Jammu and Kashmir, a group of own countrymen, the political establishment, as has happened now, and even the judiciary could be against him. As it happened in the case of Major Aditya, 10 Garhwal Rifles, against whom an FIR was lodged, reportedly in consultation with the then Jammu and Kashmir CM Mehbooba Mufti and the Defence Minister Nirmala Sitharaman.

Where do the cases like the one of Major Aditya fall. Those who have operated in active counter-insurgency areas will only understand that those are very dangerous situations to handle for the young officers. The decision is impulsive, for there is no time to seek counsel or anyone's advice. Choice is to take action or make a mockery of the security forces and get your men killed. Such actions which result in deaths of stone-pelters or those aiding terrorists to escape or hinder the operations are very necessary in situations like these. By no stretch of imagination should such actions be investigated, for no investigation can fathom the situation or the mental state of the men whose lives and honour were in danger. The political leaders were wrong to initiate an FIR in the case of Major Aditya.

Military Leadership must Look Inwards
The chief was quick to express his disappointment at the officers going to the Supreme Court. Frankly, he could have done nothing else, unless he was a man of different breed. What does he think of Major General Rajeeva Kumar, who reportedly joined the petitioners?

One obvious question no senior army commander or the chief posed is why did these officers and men go to the court, if, as he says, they were already pursuing the AFSPA case with the government. The possible reasons might be as follows:

- Lack of clear information on how the leadership is working to safeguard Army's right.
- Lack of confidence in the ability of the senior military leadership to deliver.
- Fear among average officers and soldiers to fall prey to the recent demands to dilute the act.

All these issues have left an impression that the military leadership is either incompetent or does not care. Well, what does the chief expect the men to do? Clearly, these officers and men lacked the confidence in their leadership to deliver.

When an incident had happened in 2015 in the Valley where the Kashmiri youth racing in a car refused to stop at a check post and then crashed, resulting in his death, Lt. Gen. Hooda, Northern Army Commander, was quick to fault the troops even before the court of inquiry had concluded. Following this occurred the Uri incident where about 18 soldiers including an officer died. I see a direct connection between these two incidents. The army commander had psychologically disarmed his men, rendering them incapable of acting against a threat, for fear of their own commanders. This action to go to the Supreme Court is a reflection of that lack of confidence in their leadership.

Heed the Dangers that Lie Ahead
The champions of human rights may question the Sri Lankan Military for war crime and human rights violations. In reality, common people there are grateful to their Army for getting them rid of the LTTE menace and bring peace to the country.

Indian Army has restored normalcy in the valley many a times. What has the government done to leverage that stability and achieve lasting peace? Even today, the government has no clear long-term strategy for resolving the Kashmir issue. This delay is really making the situation even worse.

It is my assurance to Dushyant Dave that the Army will not get into a confrontation with the Judiciary. It is not part of Army's DNA. But, there is a bigger danger, as Lt Gen Menon points out in his article The Army Feels Let Down by the Army Brass and the Government. They will continue to serve the country, but not the way they have been.

The real danger comes in the form of loss of morale, passion, commitment and trust in the leadership. All of these are capable of destroying the core pillar of our army that is unity.

AFSPA

The decision whether to revoke or dilute the AFSPA will solely be taken after analysing the present and future complications that will crop up after its removal. It is also important for the Centre to not dilute the Army's power in today's environment when our neighbouring nations are always on a lookout for a chance to disturb our integrity.

The Way Ahead

Asymmetric warfare is not about rules; it is about fighting without rules. It is about neutralizing the advantage of the stronger adversary by any means. And that is exactly happening in Kashmir.

At the same time, the Army is not above the law or the Constitution. There is a serious need to understand the difference between actions done in good faith and those done with bad intent.

Thus, for our forces to remain effective, the Judiciary should keep out of the combat space and leave it to the government to address the balance.

Note: This article was first published on 02 Nov18 by NPM Team

CHAPTER 6

Health of Officers and Stress Management: An Organizational Responsibility

Compiled by Col Vinay B. Dalvi

Most common cause of stress these days is dealing with self-centered and/or corrupt seniors who misuse their command for personal gains. Professional superiors with high ethical and moral values can be hard task masters who do not cause unreasonable stress and keep their command contented, healthy and happy. Stress is one of the top causes of heart attacks and working with difficult or unreasonable people is one of the deadliest forms of stress. This research finding is very much relevant to the disciplined military environment particularly when your immediate superior officers or seniors in the chain of command fall in the above category or description.

"There are two types of officers in the Armed forces; a good officer and a successful officer. A good officer is competent, steady, loves his men, merges his identity with the unit and is a source of strength to his subordinates, colleagues and superiors. On the other end of the scale is a successful officer. He is keen, intelligent, industrious, ambitious, competent but self-centered and a self-promotee. To him, his men and unit are tools for his professional progress. If in the bargain his men and unit benefit, it is incidental." – *Lt Gen Sardesh Pandey*

Most common cause of stress these days is dealing with self-centered and/or corrupt seniors who misuse their command for personal gains. Professional superiors with high ethical and moral values can be hard task masters who do not cause unreasonable stress and keep their command contented, healthy and happy. Stress is one of the top causes of heart attacks and working with difficult or unreasonable people is one of the deadliest forms of stress. This research finding is very much relevant to the disciplined military environment particularly when your immediate superior officers or seniors in the chain of command fall in the above category or description.

Military officers are used to unquestioningly obeying orders and instructions from their superiors. Hence, very few have the moral courage to oppose or challenge wrong, illegal or stupid orders. This invariably leads to frustration or disgruntlement causing severe stress to the concerned officers who prefer to remain silent and cope with their adverse/stressful situation due to their own career interest and survival in the organization.

Background

The recent spate of deaths and serious medical ailments in officers is not only shocking but alarming. Each such unfortunate incident has been most disturbing and demoralizing for not only the serving fraternity, but the Veterans too. Whenever such unfortunate deaths have taken place, other than paying rich tribute to the departed soul and offering moral support to the bereaved family nothing serious seems to have been done to analyze the actual/true causes for these unfortunate deaths with a holistic approach to all intricate issues related to officers' health, diet, routine, lifestyle, fitness regime including physical and recreational training activities.

Health of officers and stress management are command and organizational responsibilities that cannot be wished away or palmed off to individual officers by commanders at all levels. There is now an imperative need to get to the root causes of the malady that have plagued the system. The tendency of some senior officers in the establishment to blame the entire officer community by calling them 'unfit' and thereby passing the buck on to the officers themselves is not at all a mature and pragmatic approach.

Commanders at all level cannot absolve themselves of their primary responsibility towards all officers under their command by merely issuing/ circulating advisory letters related to 'stress management', 'fitness', 'health' and 'welfare' and obtaining their signatures. There is a need to identify and resolve the issues/impediments confronting the officers that prevent them from leading a healthy, happy and stress-free life.

There is a need to realize the harm being caused by unnecessary/ unproductive late hours in office which prevents him from taking timely meals, rest and participation in regular physical, recreational and social activities. The physical fitness tests for officers in the form of BPET and PPT schedule is laid down keeping in mind the age profile of the officers. Before conducting these tests, the concerned officers must be given adequate time, opportunity and facilities to prepare.

Great care must be taken particularly for the endurance runs of 5km and 2.4 km tests, more so for higher age group officers when they have been leading sedentary lifestyles due to nature of job/appointment. Every individual case must be considered/weighed differently, and medical advice followed religiously where required. Unnecessary pride and ego of the officer or his superior must not become a cause for anybody to lose his life. Three great principles of PT must always be remembered – 1) Harmonious Development 2) Systematic Progression & 3) Continuity.

Most deaths are taking place due to overlooking or ignoring the third great principle of 'Continuity' or due to negligence or overlooking medical ailment or illness due to need/pressure of being medically fit for the next promotion. There is a serious lack of awareness and knowledge of the principles of physical training/education and sports medicine and sports sciences and faulty physical training methodology imparted to the officers in military academies. The recent joint decision of the United Commanders Conference (UCC) to "...incorporate sports medicine in physical training methodology of cadets, recruits and combatants" will surely make our PT methodology more scientific and ensure better health and fitness of all ranks, provided it is taken seriously and followed in letter and spirit. Hence, the senior military officer hierarchy/cadre must accord top priority for implementation of this recent UCC joint decision.

RESPONSES

Lt Gen Harbhajan Singh

Stress is for those who do not know their job and profession are lazy, reactive, lack self-confidence and courage of conviction, whose priorities are topsy turvy and may be doing wrong things. A real professional will not be under undue stress.

Air Cmde Suryakant Bal

Stress is here to stay. Stress does not kill – the individual's dysfunctional response does. Sometimes a mild degree of stress can actually act like a catalyst. It is foolish to transfer the responsibility entirely to the organization. That is an act of cowardice and easy escape from responsibility – howsoever 'intellectual' it may appear in the populist media to people who do not wish to think – or are actually incapable of thinking. The individual alone is ultimately responsible. Of course, the organization can play a positive supporting role by creating an environment of equity and justice, effective policies and procedures, thereby removing stressors that it can, but the individual is ultimately responsible. To allege that the organization does nothing at all is not a statement of reality but simply a populist slogan. If the organization is to do all, it would reduce the individual to the status of a puppet. Of course, much more can be done. We all did that during service. This is my conviction based on own experience and that of others.

A Serving Officer, *Infantry, Commando & OPTC Qualified*

Very true Sir! It is the organization's responsibility. Measures have to be taken to cut down unnecessary work drastically. Senior commanders have to realize that filling the calendar with events one after another, just for their entertainment is only making life hectic for people under them. This tendency has to stop!

A Serving Officer, *Medical Officer & Sports Medicine Qualified*
This is true! There is no letter or guidelines on 'how to reduce stress'. Physical exercises/games are the only option available to officers for reducing stress. Morning time/periods should/must be religiously utilized for collective physical activity, either with troops or partner for exercises. PT must be made an enjoyable training activity and not viewed as a burden. Being 'fit' in Annual Medical Examination (AME) or Promotion Medical Examination (PME) does not mean you are fit. Even in AME or PME, one should have sports/fitness medicine evaluation for an officer to know his actual physical fitness. Only medical fitness does not guarantee a healthy life. Physical fitness (related to the nature of your job/trade) must also complement it.

Col C M Chavan
As a hypothesis; if an individual is NOT put under any stress and kept under ideal condition and exercise regimen, what would be his life span? No one can answer for sure. Hence body is composed of complex organs which can function differently in different bodies and genetics probably play an important function. A good officer and a successful officer act as per their own conscious and are fully aware of what they are doing; when they stretch their limits hence no one should be blamed for it.

Self-centered or corrupt senior officers, who misuse their position, are the very officers who have been selected by a system and nurtured by the organization. Most of the senior officers, aim for perfection in all the activities, endured day in and day out which co-relates to something called as 'zero error syndrome'. It is this very trend which needs to be kept under check. Senior officers should get used to results which are near about perfection which do not spell doom always. This definitely will not apply to operational requirement where; the need will be that of precision and perfection.

An officer therefore should keep himself fit by participating in the daily activities with the men and play regular games and should sleep well. One should avoid smoking and should not drink heavy and not indulge in over eating. He should heed to the body signals and take proper medical treatment as and when required and should not avoid the same, because of promotional prospective. The commanders at all levels should ensure the same by keeping the routine under control and check.

Cdr Mukund Yeolekar, *ex-Principal, Naval College of Engineering*
Physical and mental fitness of every individual contribute directly to the overall organization's efficiency as well as the career progress of the individual. The organization's priority and goals will always take precedence over the individual. The organization being made up of several individuals has to harness the synergy of all members for improved performance. It is a matter of pride and the duty of every individual to keep him/herself in fit condition in order to perform to

the very best of capabilities and achieve the goals and objectives of the organisation.

The organisation is responsible to create/provide an environment such as sports/gym facilities, balanced time schedule, social harmony and developing an ethos for maintaining high physical and mental fitness. Scientific methodology has to be adopted to train every individual so that benefits of latest developments are accrued. The organisation has to ensure a high morale, team spirit and professional competence among its members so that it is able to accomplish its goals. This is also achieved by exemplary leadership.

Considering unforeseen circumstances, limited resources and certain inevitable situations, the organisation is bound to stretch the physical and mental limits of its cadres so as to achieve the set targets – come what may. Therefore, 'burning the midnight oil' sometimes cannot be avoided. Battles have been won by transcending limits of human endurance. This can be achieved not only by a strong body but also on the body being complemented by a stronger mind. In sum, the individual and the organisation have to complement each other in keeping with physical and mental fitness.

Conclusion

The unfortunate loss of our officers is one of the symptoms of a bigger and deeper malady that has engulfed the entire system. The 'Victory India Campaign' books, which aim to improve the quality of our military leadership at all levels have done complete research on all possible aspects, issues and subjects of selection, training and grooming of officers with a holistic approach. A lot of focus has been on physical and recreational training, sports and games and health and fitness of military officers. Sports and fitness medicine has also been elaborately covered. All the causes for 'what ails our system' have been identified and solutions presented and well-documented on a platter. One needs to only peruse, comprehend and follow it in 'letter and spirit'.

The Air Force and Navy have already acknowledged and endorsed the books. It is the Army that is taking time. The earlier these subjects are taken seriously, the better it will be for the military officer cadre and the Armed Forces. The UCC joint decision to incorporate sports medicine in the PT methodology of cadets, recruits and combatants is a positive development which must be transformed positively on ground at all levels with a vision and an action plan.

CHAPTER 7

Catch 22 – Physical Courage or Moral Courage?

By Col P K 'Royal' Mehrishi

An unprecedented event occurred on the eve of Independence Day this year. 356 serving Army personnel filed a writ petition in the Supreme Court asking for legal protection against prosecution by CBI & the Courts for doing their duty in areas where AFSPA is in force. 14 August 2018 will go down in national history as a day when we as a nation failed to safeguard our Forces from judicial harassment & 'hauling over the coals' by a select few who have a personal agenda to belittle the good work done by the Military.

Army works in a tight hierarchy wherein disobedience of Command /Orders can incur the wrath of the superior Officer & unleash immediate reprisals ranging from an explanation to a Court martial depending on the gravity of offence & circumstances preceding it. Under this shadow of Army Act (passed by an act of Parliament) the entire lot of subordinates work to defend the territorial Integrity & sovereignty of India.

The law itself is binding but a vast majority keep this factor in the background & perform diligently to uphold intangibles like regimental honour, camaraderie, *naam–namak–nishan, izzat* & so on. Officers when they join are fresh faced, idealistic, without malice, have tremendous drive & do or die spirit. It is overvaulting ambition in later service that does them in!!

Since no action/operation can take place without it being cleared by senior HQ's, what is all the more intriguing in the writ petition is absence of the names of Brig's/Maj-Gen's/Lt-Gen's who control insurgency & anti –terror operations in Manipur & J&K.

Questions that arise are:
- Did these 356 Officers (Col's/ Maj's/Capt's) act of their own voilition?
- Did they disobey orders at any juncture?
- Who was monitoring these operations?
- Were no written reports generated after the conduct of operations for perusal by higher HQ's?
- Were the orders to conduct operations given verbally or in writing?

- Who all are the beneficiaries of the successful conduct of operations (by way of citations/awards/promotions)?
- When things failed or did not go as per plan who was left holding the CAN & who covered his tracks?
- The lowest hanging fruit in any hierarchy is the junior officer; did he by default or by design get picked for the fiasco when "s...hit the fan"?

Answers to these questions will never be available, but what scares us in the face is an unfolding tragedy of massive proportions. Is Physical Courage enough to get selected, face operational conditions, rise in one's career & act like "to each his own" or are we missing out on the strongest pillar of a Military man's Leadership trait & character, his adherence to moral courage in times of crisis & distress.

Field Marshal Manekshaw had this to say about Moral courage "You have got to have the moral courage to stand up and tell them the facts. Again, as I told you before, a 'yes man' is a despicable man". In many cases of Life & Death situations it is understood that written orders may not be given, yet the subordinates have to act & complete the mission. It's a win-win situation if everything goes well according to plan. A senior's moral compass is put to test when he has to face his superiors (even politicians) & give the unpleasant news or fall out of an operation gone awry. Many Generals of the day have been found wanting of this noble quality of Military profession to stand up for their juniors when the times get rough. It is all good when accolades/awards & rewards come their way for an operation well done & executed by subordinates. According to the law of averages for some missions that don't go as per plan & get the desired result there is always a Moral escape route, Feign Ignorance!!

We need to urgently train our future Leaders to face moral courage dilemmas with sagacity & choose the harder right (resignation/demotion/inquiry) than the easier wrong (fudging reports/ yes sir syndrome/staying aloof) In fact Physical courage may be tested as a one off situation in an Officer's career but it is Moral courage which will he will continue to draw on till he serves in Uniform.

SECTION 3
THE CURRENT CHALLENGES

CHAPTER 8

When Soldiers Ask Questions

Lt Gen N S Brar

The country is at war, make no mistakes about it. Many eyebrows will be raised asking 'Where is the war?' Von Clausewitz had many aphorisms, of which the most famous is "War is the continuation of politics by other means." And today the 'other means' has graduated from direct conventional conflict to pursuing national objectives through low cost terror, proxy surrogate insurgents, disinformation or misinformation, propaganda, undermining instruments and institutions of state and in fact any means aimed at imposing your will on the adversary. We are witnessing all this in J&K. That is where today's war is being fought. When all instruments of state fail to contain the situation, the Army is employed, albeit for a role it is primarily not trained, structured and legally and constitutionally mandated. For any conflict which has a military dimension, the triad of Government, People and the Military must complement each other. The Government must set clear policies and objectives, the people must support the objectives and the military must thereafter prosecute the military objectives from the sub conventional and in the ultimate to all out war. A clearly defined politico-military objective is the base on which national policies are formulated, military capabilities created and action directed.

National security is ultimately a question of evaluating security threats and national interests and deciding on capabilities to meet or secure them. Capabilities in turn mean expenditure. The first must take the shape of a 'Strategic Defence Review' and define our responses in terms of military capabilities to be created and maintained. In our context we are unique in never having formally articulated our security concerns and how we intend to address them. We are insecure in stating our security concerns. Universally, countries spend in proportion to their economic development or in direct response to immediate security threats. We seem to be guided by neither. Defence spending as a percentage of GDP is the lowest since 1962. We have a dysfunctional civil-military equation and no formalised and structured forum for collective analysis and policy formulation at the highest level. Views and concerns of the military are more often ignored and sidelined and all is assumed to be well. If and when a crisis situation does develop, the response is naturally ad hoc. In other words there is no formally articulated policy and approach for handling our security concerns.

The lack of adequate funding over a long period has resulted in 'hollowness' in our capability to sustain a conventional conflict. Resultantly, we do not have the wherewithal to move up the escalatory ladder in response to sustained Pak sponsored proxy terrorism. We have an Army which has never been adequately equipped with even the basics like boots, helmet, rifle and bullet proof jackets. Not much has changed since the Army Chief's Kargil declaration to 'fight with whatever we have'. The option of conventional response has been foreclosed.

As Churchill said the Armed Forces are not like a limited liability company to be reconstructed from time to time as the money fluctuates. It is a living thing. If it is bullied, it sulks, if it is unhappy it pines, if it is harried it gets feverish, if it is sufficiently disturbed it will wither and dwindle and almost die, and when it comes to this last serious condition, it is only revived by lots of time and lots of money.

What then is our perceived policy towards the proxy war in J&K? Indian policy appears to be on one hand to eliminate as many 'terrorists' as possible to force a political solution and at the same time accept security forces casualties as acceptable. What has not been factored is the intangible and intrinsic aspects of terrorist staying power of fresh recruitment, home-grown or externally sponsored, and the attitude of the local population. The Americans in Vietnam hoped to achieve a 'tipping point' forcing the North Vietnamese to negotiate due to the aerial bombing of the North and killing Vietcong in the South. It never came. Unremitting Pak sponsorship of the proxy war would and should result in moving up the escalatory ladder to the full conventional level to deter and punish. That response is precluded due to lack of capability or 'hollowness'. Handling insurgencies has followed a pattern of 'military pacification' followed by 'political purchase'. Military pacification has been brought about in J&K on more than one occasion; however, the political purchase has eluded the political leadership. J&K is essentially and ultimately a political problem.

Pakistan may not have achieved cutting away Kashmir from the Indian Union but the three decade employment of the Army in its sponsored Proxy War has resulted in the Army being permanently employed on an armed constabulary role while the 1.4 million strong Central Armed Police Forces and Para Military has practically relinquished their primary internal security mandate. The nomination of the Army Chief by stepping over others for his experience in 'counter insurgency' has put an official stamp on this role. The next chief in all probability will also be selected by supersession citing similar experience. This was further reinforced by the Pay Commission equating, and in some areas, lowering the armed forces in relation to these forces. Three decades of armed constabulary work has resulted in the Army imbibing the ethos, culture, attitude and approach to the civil population of these forces. It may not be too far off when the Army too thinks acts and performs as such with the attendant duplicity, political game play and un-soldierly conduct.

The Army cannot be deployed on internal security duties in 'aid to civil power' or 'disturbed areas' without the mandated legal sanction and protection. The Armed Forces Special Power Act was enacted for this purpose. Politics and judicial intervention has practically left the soldier devoid of this cover with resultant prosecution and confusion.

In the past the military shrugged off the politician and politics as not concerning them. The politician's disinterest in matters military was a consequence of total ignorance of such matters. While the ignorance remains, the new found interest of the political class is driven by political mileage and not the interest of the military or national security.

Perception of successive pay commissions handing out an unfair deal, ignoring the anomalies, disrupting rank equation and issues like non functional upgrade rankle both the serving and veteran community.

Under these conditions a soldier perceives himself as being expendable, inadequately equipped, equated with a policeman, failed by his senior leadership, used by the politician and unfairly compensated. The country has failed the Army by not providing the clarity of objectives, legal framework, capability and ethical backing. The senior military leadership has failed the rank and file by not taking the inbuilt correctives within the military justice system and discipline to deal with any actions outside the laid down parameters, if there was any transgression, and not standing by the rank and file if there was none and they were being hounded on false grounds. The rank and file perceives the senior leadership to have failed or been unable to safeguard institutional and collective interests of the personnel.

The middle rung of the Army leadership, most affected by their employment and informed through social media, is the most disenchanted unlike the lower ranks that are relatively indifferent in their ignorance and bound by discipline and the higher echelons cocooned in their self centered careerist pursuit. This is manifest in the recent Supreme Court petition by nearly 800 officers and men. This portends far reaching effect on the ethos and cohesion of the Army. Any qualms about going to the courts by servicemen, once considered un-soldierly, were laid to rest when a serving chief sought redressal from the Supreme Court. Not many supported his claim and the relief sought, but many supported him for taking on the government perceived to be insensitive to the soldiers concerns.

The Army has been, and has consciously con-sidered itself, the neutral instrument of state policy. When ordered it does not ask "Why?" or "What for?" If the military is to be used for political ends and their concerns ignored, can it continue to be the innocent automaton? That soldier fights best who has the least questions and doubts about why he is fighting. Under the prevailing circumstances the soldier asks 'Why am I risking my life and limb?' That question is being asked in the Supreme Court. When he does not perceive or receive a convincing answer his response and attitude turns to indifference if not avoidance of the task for which he is deployed. When this attitude becomes all pervasive the consequences are that the last resort for the country is also gone. Let the soldier's questions be answered before we reach a stage like the Americans in Vietnam where the soldier saw himself as the unwilling, led by the unqualified, to kill the unfortunate and die for the ungrateful, with ignominious consequences.

CHAPTER 9

Debate – Should OROP Agitation Continue or Wind Up? A 'Diversity of Opinion' Debate

Compiled by Col Vinay Dalvi

Backdrop

In the backdrop of a letter written by Gp Capt T P Srivastava to IESM Chairman Maj Gen Satbir Singh, proposing the movement to be called off for it having lost its apolitical character, this debate was initiated. Gp Capt Srivastava cited several reasons in his letter, relevant extracts of which are reproduced below to enable the reader to grasp the main crux issues of OROP that led him to justify why the OROP agitation should be wound up unconditionally.

Based on the contents of the letter several Veterans of the three services were requested to send their honest and forthright views if the OROP agitation should continue or wind up as advocated by Gp Capt Srivastava. The debate is in the form of an article, where views for and against the proposition have been obtained and attributed to the concerned Veteran respondents. The reason behind carrying such an article is to foster a healthy debate on such matters of military management, and gleaning workable solutions for the benefit of the armed forces and the nation at large. It is hoped that this exercise produces a remedy that settles this intractable dispute, which seems to be turning into an impasse.

Trigger

Relevant Extracts of Gp Capt TP Srivastava's letter to Gen Satbir Singh
"I believe that OROP issue is no longer an issue involving military; it is slowly but surely taking shape of a political movement. If and when it happens, it would be a national disaster. Military must remain apolitical and loyal to the government in power not on the basis of pre-poll promises made by political parties...Unfortunately this cardinal principle was broken by both major political parties, BJP and Congress...Indian politicians have no love for the military because institution of military cannot serve and support their nefarious activities.

"...Numerous articles, chats, views of all and sundry are openly talking about not voting for BJP/NDA in the forthcoming elections in 2019 primarily because current government failed to implement OROP in Toto. Current government led by Shri Narendra Modi started implementation of OROP with few modifications to the original concept...unacceptable to Military. There has been a quantum and many fold rise in the pension of military personnel during the past decade, primarily due to implementation of VIth and VIth pay commission recommendations. Most of these increments have been during post 2015 period.

"The OROP agitation commenced to force the government to implement OROP as contained in Koshiyari committee report. Nearly three years have gone by and the issue remains on the boil... neither in national interest nor in the interest of Military. Out of the ten Agenda points for proposed rally on 13th May, 2018 in Maj Gen Satbir's letter nine points do not concern OROP. Indeed all points merit a look into but not by retired military personnel. It is the job of Serving Chiefs to look into each issue and take it up with the government."

"We are making a mess of the OROP issue by mixing it up other issues... attempting to create a parallel organization. Let the Service HQs do their job. Highest court of the country is already seized of the issue. Satbir, you have accomplished what many failed to accomplish... carry this as a reward from the almighty, who gave you the courage and wisdom to lead from front."

"A word for PM, FM and RM. Onus lies squarely on all three of you, individually and collectively, to resolve the issue amicably...so that the undesirable agitation does not affect national power...Military personnel are...requesting/demanding what is due to them. FM's intransigence is evident as he refuses to accept annual revision as against five yearly revisions."

VETERANS' RESPONSES (FOR)

Maj Gen V K Madhok

I was commissioned in the Indian Army after 4 years training at JSW and IMA Dehradun in the early 1950s. The salary at the end of 40 years of service was pittance compared to what has been paid since 01 Jan 06 with implementation of 6CPC. 7CPC further enhanced the pay of military personnel from 01 Jan 16. Since the pension paid to veterans is only 50% of last pay drawn depending on the operative CPC of that time, there was a vast difference of pensions between military pensioners who retired in the same rank with same length of service. Hence this led to an unfair deal by the consecutive governments to create a vast disparity in pension scales of Veterans of same rank and service.

Despite representations for more pension to match the prevailing cost of living, the governments failed to meet their minimum expectations leading to further frustration amongst the entire pre-1996 lot. The present BJP government in their pre-election campaign promised the Veterans to grant them OROP to remove the wide gulf in pension scales between pre and post-2016 pensioners of same rank and service.

However this promise was not destined to be fulfilled. However due to the exemplary leadership of Maj Gen Satbir Singh and his dedicated group of ex-servicemen, the OROP agitation compelled the government to relent and half-heartedly grant OROP. In this country, politicians and bureaucrats are hand in glove and have no love lost for the soldiers. Hence, the soldier can only get their justified demands met only through peaceful agitation.

I for one and many more like me would not have got increased pension had it not been for the OROP agitation. The agitation must continue and take up more justified demands for the pensioners and the serving fraternity too. Advice to call off the agitation and cancel the planned 13 May 2018 rally must not be paid heed to. The BJP government must not be trusted to meet any further demands of ex-servicemen. A united organisation led by Gen Satbir Singh must be strongly supported.

Wg Cdr SP Singh

I fully support the views expressed by Maj Gen VK Madhok and one should not object any individual's effort just for the sake of objecting. Must support with fact and figures! By giving OROP has the government become any poorer? On the contrary, lakhs of ESM have been benefitted. If we are hell bent on objecting, then we should object to government policies where people run away to other countries after taking thousands of crores of rupees as loans, waiving off crores of bad loans of PSUs.

Brig S K Kakar, *ex-EME*

Immediately after 1971, the pension for soldiers, which was 75% and 33% for civilians, was brought at par to 50% for all government employees without going into the divergent terms of conditions and younger retirement age bracket of 35-45 years for majority of soldiers, in comparison to 60 years for all civilians. This is the genesis of the issue that triggered the prolonged tussle. This issue has also adversely affected war widows, disabled soldiers and dependents of martyrs.

Some Veterans feel that after one OROP pension hike, two earlier hikes and implementation of 7 CPC, the pensions have increased substantially. Hence, do not feel or advocate the need to continue the OROP agitation. In simple words OROP means, 3-5 % increase every year. Presently there is a big disparity of Rs. 4000 in the pension of soldiers who retired in 2003 and in 2017. For a soldier, his widow and dependents, this amount is quite large. A Jawan with 17 years of service is losing Rs. 4296 every month. A widow is losing Rs. 2548 every month. The pension has been fixed as Average of Maximum and Minimum of rank and service and number of years served as basis for a pensioner. The increments earned by the serving person are 'not' taken into account, thus affecting the correct fixation of Pension.

The majority of officers, especially those who retired after 01Jan 06, have by and large benefitted from the increase in their pensions and hence feel satisfied. These officers need to comprehend the plight of over 80% majority of the pensioners, the OR fraternity, including NCOs, who still haven't received OROP as per its true definition. The strength of officers is approx 3-4 %. The strength of JCOs is about 13-14%. Balance strength of NCOs and OR is about 80%. Hence, the imperative need to continue the OROP agitation.

The Reddy Commission on the 7 CPC anomalies has given its recommendations to the government over a year back but not being made public. The OROP team has clarified that they have only used the platform of political parties because they were denied audience by RM, MoD and PMO. The Veterans have not yet accepted back the medals that they handed over.

Col Avinash Wandkar

There were several shortcomings in the sanctioned OROP scales, especially for the majority Other Ranks (OR) category (from Sepoy to Havaldar rank). The implementation of the 7CPC further complicated the OROP and led to adding more demands and representations for a better deal for the military fraternity vis-a-vis their civil counterparts, as per OROP definition of the Koshiary Committee. This strong majority of OR fraternity feel betrayed.

An objective comparison of their pay scales, allowances and terms of service and retirement age with the Civil Services and even Para military forces will amply reveal that they have always received a raw deal. The OROP agitation apparently represents not only the ex-servicemen but the serving fraternity too, as all serving personnel will sooner or later also be ex-servicemen. Hence, what is granted to the pensioners will positively or negatively impact the serving personnel too. Hence, the OROP agitation under Maj Gen Satbir Singh must continue till they achieve their set aim and objective.

VETERANS' RESPONSES (AGAINST)

Maj Jawahar Thota

I agree with the letter written by Gp Capt TP Srivastava. The services start off by guarding the borders, the coastline and the airspace, which is their primary task, and then take on flood relief, helping out during natural disasters, contain and battle terrorism on a daily basis and in return we ask for nothing. It is just OROP and respect for the uniformed. The money spent on OROP is a negligible fraction of the GDP, in comparison to the trillions that people stash away underground and run away with.

A government, if it honors and respects it's soldiers, will not humiliate us in this way, by denying what we deserve. It will be gratifying to see if the government hands in the balance without the planned OROP on 20 May, 2018. It is time the country separated politics from the patriotism and sacrifice by those who fight for the security of the country and keep the national flag fluttering even in nil wind conditions. Veterans should not be humiliated and forced to do what they are doing at Jantar Mantar. Instead the nation's voice should reverberate with: "Thank you for your service. Welcome home. Be at peace."

Col Rajinder Kushwaha, *ex-CO 3 Bihar*

I am of the opinion that one must distinguish between just demand and ambitious project. OROP is no more an issue to lose your sleep for. Fact remains that 80% objective has been achieved and rest 20% can be achieved through other forums available. As far as NFU and other details of OROP/7CPC are concerned, they are being tackled in the courts, in which Gen Satbir has no role.

Finally, to say PM Modi had backed out of his promise is unjustified. And to think he gave it out of pressure that had been exerted by Gen Satbir and the agitation is a gross misrepresentation of facts. When PM Modi promised OROP at Rewari in Sept 2013, he did not understand the full financial implications of OROP, until he took over. He became cautious, yet he gave us 80% of what we wanted. I think we should adopt different approach to get 20% and stop falling prey to political parties who wants to misuse us. For 40 years Congress did not do anything and now it wants to become champion if our cause through Gen Satbir and company. It is best avoidable.

Gp Capt Johnson Chacko

There is a Grade known as Higher Administrative Grade Plus or HAG+ where the pension is based on 'Revised Pay' and not on 'Last Drawn Pay'. I believe that all the C-in-Cs and equivalent and Chiefs fall into this category. It means that whenever the pay is 'revised', they get an increment in pension as of the person retiring that day. If it is so, then the top most hierarchy may never fight for OROP as this is actually OROP. Doesn't matter what the Koshiyari Committee says.

Hence, the top most hierarchy cannot be motivated to look after this aspect of those placed below them. It undermines the principles of leadership. Cost of living is supposed to be compensated by Dearness Relief for pensioners. It does not neutralize it fully. That is proven by the fact that when a new Pay Commission is implemented the pension for similar service and rank is higher. This difference is what needs to be bridged. If the rule is changed to base pension on Revised Pay, OROP issue will be resolved. The money involved will be nowhere near the NPAs of banks that we are grappling with. A small price to pay for a stronger India!

Col Pradeep Dalvi

I thank Maj Gen Satbir Singh and his team for their untiring efforts. Without their efforts, the pre-1996 pensioners would not have got their increase in pension. The agitation has met most of its goals and the balance should be achieved through other means and pursuit by serving fraternity. The saddest part of the OROP agitation was the manhandling of Veterans by the police. Lack of response from the serving hierarchy enabled the political masters to lower the image of armed forces in the society. This must never happen again. The remaining issues of OROP can be resolved through 7CPC and recommendations of the Reddy Committee.

Many Veterans have now become more aware to obtain their justified demands and even dragging the government to courts. Ironically, the same Veterans, especially the senior lot, who served during 1975-2000 period, failed to take up these legitimate issues, while serving with the then Congress government.

With 2019 elections now being round the corner, the Veterans must remain apolitical, maintain military dignity, and not be permitted to use the OROP platform for their personal agenda or political ambition. The May 2018 meeting agenda contains issues that are not related to OROP and hence should be taken up with the government by the Service Chiefs. Finally, the OROP agitation must be wound up before it turns counter-productive.

Col C M Chavan
There are two schools of thought emerging at this point of time. First, should pressure be put on the present government to fulfill the balance of OROP issues, which we deserve rightfully, especially in view of the forthcoming elections? Second, since the present government has at least given 80% of OROP which no government could do and be content with a hope that the issues will get settled in due course of time, as the matter is already seized by the highest court.

Putting pressure by coming on the roads with our issues at this opportune time would indicate the political swing of the Veterans, even if that is not the intent. It also shows us in the poor light when the entire world is in awe of the PM. At the same time, it also goes to the credit of Maj Gen Satbir that we got the major chunk of OROP. Having said that, however, most of the points in present agenda of agitation are not related to OROP! As brought out by Gp Capt TP Srivastav, all these points fall under the care of Chiefs.

Going ahead intelligently would be better to gather in large number on 13 May and declare that the Veterans would like to entrust the present government to resolve balance of the OROP issues in amicable time bound manner and return home. This will display solidarity and appeal to the government to consider the matter sincerely and possibly turn out to be a win-win situation for both.

Col P K 'Royal' Mehrishi
OROP is akin to a dead issue now with only the carcass remaining for the opportunistic vultures to feed. Strong cognitive imagery but the lesson

underlying it is clear. No doubt Gen Satbir Singh led from the front and became a rallying point for many but some of our own with deep rooted political ambitions axed the initiative by pushing their own agenda & hijacking the forum to build a parallel narrative to suit their political masters.

The purity of the movement was lost when one witnessed retired Generals squabbling in public and trying to outdo each other for that extra sound byte. Such movements lose steam after sometime when the "way ahead" has not been thought through in detail (so much for planning by ex-military stalwarts). Nadir was, when the Delhi Police (DP) forcibly evicted aging Veterans from Jantar Mantar before the RD parade.

The irony of this could not be missed, on the Rajpath some of these Veterans in their younger days may have led Contingents/Military Equipment/ Squadrons with badges on their chests with pride, and here was a situation where a force like DP, perceived to be corrupt and inefficient was seen roughing up old Veterans, the image that went viral amongst serving and retired fraternity was of an old NCO with his torn kurta and medals hanging precariously for want of a modicum of deserved dignity and respect. Why wasn't this scenario thought through? Many aging Veterans and their better halves were seen pleading with constables of DP to behave and accord respect, which of course was not provided. The then Defence Minister Arun Jaitley chose to keep silent, and our serving tigers and lions (nice sounding aggressive titles for appointments) like over-obedient circus animals did not even roar at any ring master.

The foremost nationalist institution, the military, has over the years been eroded of its status by a self-serving political class (ever heard of a self-proclaimed 100% increase in pay and allowances) and a servile bureaucracy. The issues regarding the military can only get resolved when the serving top "honchos" once in a while rattle the sabre in its sheath. Since the military is not a vote bank or a political lobby, (rightly so) the only way forward is a dynamic vision by the persons selected to sit on the high table at the Commanders Conferences in Delhi.

Cdr Ravindra Waman Pathak
The IESM led a successful agitation to force the government to announce OROP. What was announced was not the OROP as per definition given by Koshiyari Committee and accepted by government. The agitation continued even after announcement of OROP and the government agreed to look into the balance of grievances by appointing the One Man Judicial Committee (OMJC). Frankly the agitation should have ended then.

Once the OMJC was announced all parties made their presentation before it and the report is now in cold storage with the government for over a year now. The IESM also decided to take the matter of OROP to court and filed a case. Hereafter any agitation is meaningless for seeking full OROP. The agitation has lost its meaning moment the OMJC was appointed and further lost its meaning when IESM went to court. We are at a deadlock at this stage as IESM has annoyed the government and closed all doors to any talks. He has further complicated the matter by his political games of hopping with parties. Even if this party hopping is seen as building pressure it is not going to work as it did in 2014. The ground realities are different.

The very fact that Veterans are losing as a result of not having got the full OROP is reason enough to call of the agitation specially, since it affects a large number of JCO and below Veterans and start a dialogue with the government. The agitation is simply compounding the loss month on month. The denial of talk was a result of adamant attitude of the IESM in continuing agitation mode. Incidentally, the Veterans must also understand what they have gained by whatever OROP orders that have been issued so far.

The way ahead would be to call off whatever the current form of agitation is going on at JM, even after some internal doubts within the IESM governing body to continue with the same. Then approach the government for talks on the subject and press for action on OMJC. The situation now is same as in pre-2014 era and despite the bravado, the BJP will need Veterans support as in 2014. It would be in the interest of all if IESM calls of the remnant of the agitation which is only an irritant value now and engage the BJP and government on actual issues.

CONCLUSION

The Veterans are almost equally divided in their views on the continuation of the OROP agitation. One section feels it should be called off and the other feels that it should continue till the 20% balance of OROP is granted as per the definition of Koshiyari Committee. However, one common point of agreement is seen, that 80% OROP was granted to the military pensioners largely due to sustained efforts and perseverance of the OROP agitation spearheaded by Maj Gen Satbir Singh. The scheduled OROP rally at Jantar Mantar now postponed to 20 May 2018 and subsequent events would surely indicate which course of action was a better proposition.

CHAPTER 10

Sanctity, Security & Safety of Military Cantonments: A Debate

By Col Vinay B Dalvi

Background

The recent directive of the Defence Minister/MOD to the military authorities for opening of all roads passing through 62 Military Cantonments for all civil vehicular traffic has undoubtedly stirred a hornets' nest.

The directive was apparently issued by the Defence Minister at the behest of the recommendations of the elected Vice Chairmans of the 62 Cantonment Boards and the political pressures of the MPs of concerned area/region with the focus being primarily on gaining votes from the civil fraternity for the crucial 2019 Lok Sabha elections. The immediate and long term implications of this recent controversial decision have led to a lot of confusion and chaos in the minds of the civilian population who are the prime focus for garnering votes through such popularistic actions without realizing the negative and long term negative implications to the Sanctity, Security and Safety of these 62 military cantonments.

Hence, there is an imperative need to spread the right awareness of all these 62 military cantonments including the history behind their creation, the justification for their continuation for 71 years post independence and the dire need to protect and preserve them from rampant and unplanned development of adjacent cities or towns by the civil authorities at the behest of the local vote seeking politicians.

It is time that the serving military hierarchy spoke up and took tough stands on such critical military issues. The veterans must project their true voices through their individual articles and responses debates. The collective efforts will enable the projection of a holistic picture not only about these 62 military Cantonments and the need to preserve them but also protect the character of the military institution, their personnel and families who reside in these Cantonments.

Need For Responses

This debate will become objective and meaningful only if both sides of the issue/problem are projected to give a holistic vision to the issue, enabling analysis leading to logical conclusions on the issue/s and facilitating recommendations on the 'way forward' and possibly meet the needs and expectations of the concerned civilians besides ensuring the safety of military personnel, their families and the overall security and sanctity of the military cantonments. It is pertinent to mention the imperative need for well prepared and effective Quick Response Teams (QRTs) of the military units, institutions and formation/command HQs to face any threat or contingency arising out of this development. The local police also need to gear up to meet the likely threat perceptions to protect the citizens and institutions in their civil area of responsibility or jurisdiction. Both the military authorities and civil agencies including local police must get their act together to meet any possible threat perception in the larger interest of the state and its citizens.

With a view to compile varied views on this subject of debate your individual responses are sought.

RESPONSES

Col P K 'Royal' Mehrishi, Jaipur

Military Cantonments (Cantt's) are by their very nature of upkeep and maintenance, islands of beauty and perfection amidst squalor, dirt and grime of the City which it is a part of. Has someone asked this question as to why and how be these spaces so neat and well maintained? Not a bit of litter, no doggy pooh next to the roads, grass neat & trimmed, roads well swept and clean. The answer is a bit complex and requires detailed explanation.

The Military firmly believes in the three fold manifestation of human energy i.e. Body, Mind and Soul. All Military persons are taught the virtue that a healthy mind resides in a healthy body; hence the PT and early morning exercise routine. To further this, are academic and training classes for all to shape the mind and encourage learning. To top this there is a noble concept that cleanliness and order is next to Godliness. It is for this reason in Military Cantt's all over the country vector diseases, dengue, malaria etc., are negligible.

Next is the administration of Cantt's which is efficient and not corrupt like the municipal bodies in the cities. There is no politics over clearing filth and garbage. The persons who inhabit the Cantt's come from the same villages and tier two or three cities of India but adapt to the prevalent ethos and culture of decent living. Not one keeps a cow or a goat or creates a mess over hygiene as it concerns community living.

Most important are the routine inspections by senior officers who have a penchant for looking at every nook and cranny and checking defaulters to pull them up for not measuring up to the high standards which are now bench marks.

Are our citizens and the RM jealous of the efforts put in by each and every resident of the Cantt's? Is there a pressing need to compromise the safety and security of families who are separated from their husbands deployed operationally? Is there a larger agenda of belittling whatever is left of the Military's pride stemming from Institutions they love, respect and nurture? If citizens need more roads build them around our Cantt's, not through them!

We are getting angrier by the day because of repeated flawed decisions of the Govt, beware the fury of a fully angered Military, the last bastion of our Nation's strength!!

Brig S K Kakar, Delhi

The political angle is the trigger for the opening of the roads in only 62 Cantonments (Cantt's).

Why representatives (reps) of only 62 Cantt boards were called from over 400 Cantt's in the country? Why nobody was called from Cantt's like Chandigarh, Jallandhar, Amritsar, Siliguri and Kolkata? Reason is not far to see as they are from different political streams with different views, perceptions and interests. Cantt roads episode started from Secunderabad. It is reliably learnt that there is a school in Cantt and owned by relative of an influential person wanting access through the Cantt.

Also, Telangana Govt wants to build new Secretariate in Secunderabad Cantt Area. Location is Army Polo Ground and Play grounds of Army Centre. For this CM has asked PM to tell Army to give land to Telangana Govt.

Govt has already been eyeing Neelayam Niwas (of President of India) in Secunderabad.

It seems that In order to meet all these requirements the reps of 62 Cantt's came together for their vested interests after nudge by ruling political authorities.

Hence, it is obvious that the decision of opening of Cantt roads was taken hurriedly to meet vested political interests, without realising the strong reaction would draw from families of serving persons and security of installations that will be compromised.

Thus, subsequent backtracking and seeking support of Army Chief Gen Bipin Rawat was only a face saving exercise!

Nixon Fernando, Chennai

As a person who has seen several such cantonments, I loved the green patch amidst the concrete jungle and the old world charm that comes through as heritage.

I am not too well versed to comment on the security aspects, but on the face of it I am sure it is challenging as the inhabitants can become soft targets of terrorists and other enemies of the state. I am also aware that for the soldier at the border the motivation level has been dropped by one more level because of this, as his family back at the cantonment is a little less safe. And given that families are getting increasingly nuclear, this is really a big issue. I hope the authors of such a drastic step have thought through enough counter measures before taking such a big leap.

In any case, I would request the citizens of the concerned cities to ask for the preservation of the green patches in their pristine beauty as it matters to their and their children's health. Today passage is granted, tomorrow something else, and creeping up it may ultimately be the seed planted to destroy this green wealth for the city. Let it not start at all.

Gp Capt T P Srivastava, Delhi
Most pertinent issue is whether Raksha Mantri consulted Gen Bipin Rawat (COAS) before taking the decision? As a soldier views of CoAS are the only thing that matters to me on this issue.

Rest of the issues doing rounds are merely historical in nature.

Bipin Rawat's pregnant silence is indicative of his tacit approval to the proposal of opening cantt roads. I sincerely hope I am wrong in my assumption.

Lt Col P J Chacko, Pune
Security has been the guiding imperative for locating troops at any station in the country. That being the factor, a closer look at the various cantonments established since the British days reveals that they were located far from existing civil areas, eg. Nasirabad, Jullundar, Agra, Poona, Khadki, Dehu-Road. Post independence especially after industrialisation civilian areas expanded exponentially unplanned and unchecked often succumbing to greed. Civilian authorities responsible need to have ensured connectivity to the civil areas without impinging the security and safety of the military cantonments. Apportioning the blame now on the military authorities for denying access to the civilians through the cantonments, finds little justification. Arguments put across to relocate the cantonments to tide over the encumbrances to the civil traffic is not a reasonable suggestion.

Col C M Chavan, Pune
I am sure that RM must have consulted the Army Chief before taking the decision of opening the roads passing through 62 cantonments. It is learnt that the Army Chief has since directed the Army to be extra vigilant to ensure the security of the cantonments. This has obviously increased the burden on Commanders at all levels and consequently deprived units coming from field areas of much needed time for rest and recuperation during their peace tenures before preparing for their next field tenure. The repercussions of this decision will be detrimental to the morale of families and soldiers residing in these military cantonments. The little peace and brief reunion that the soldiers were getting with their families

will be adversely affected as they will be required to be more vigilant and alert than hitherto fore to safeguard their own safety and meet the additional security burden in their 'so called' peace stations.

Acceptance of diktat from politicians on the Army way of life revolving around security by the top brass should be firmly repudiated. Army alone should not be expected to make concessions always. Examples from other countries should also be looked into.

Mr T N Seshan, Chennai, ex Defence Secy, Cabinet Secy and CEC of India

As explained to Nixon Fernando

In Mr Seshan's view, the decision to open the cantonment areas to civilian traffic is an old question and it had been discussed for ages. Even when he was a sub collector in the 1950s it was being discussed. As the pressure of population and the pressure of traffic increases over the available roads the administration attempts to open the roads in the cantonments for non-military traffic. The military looks upon that with grave worry, and both points of view are understandable. The administrator faces the question of what he can do when there is excessive traffic. He must take it on the available road. The military can have only as much road as the civil public can afford. An administrator will not consider it apt to reserve roads for the military in the cantonment while traffic comes to a grinding halt in the rest of the cities. Mr Seshan says, 'for me it is a non-issue; nothing to do with Civil Military relationship. It is just a population issue'.

Lt Col M K Guptaray, Pune

The direction of the Defense Minister Nirmala Sitharaman on recent opening of closed roads in 62 Cantonments across the country has created hornet's nest among the army circles especially among veterans and ladies fearing opening of cantonments will affect their security, safety and moral of the army. It is also commented that such decision has political and financial connotation.

With increase of population from 22–25 crores when the cantonments were established to 130 crores today, space has shrunk. The cantonments have now been surrounded from all sides by the sprawling cities and towns. Civil populations, from toddlers of nursery classes to super senior citizens, perforce, need to use these roads in these 62 cantonments to commute from one place to the other. In fact they had been using these roads since time immemorial, specially where the army and civil population co-exists, to carry out daily activities till the recent closure a decade ago consequent to recent spurt in terrorist activities. Closure of these forces them to take long detour which is expensive in terms money, when the petrol price has reached Rs. 85/- per liter, and time in tremendously increases traffic on the few roads those are available. All need to share this poverty of space.

Such arbitrary closure of active roads by the LMAs, mostly without following necessary procedures, has created bad feelings in the mind of the local civil population and has also thwarted civil military interaction which is essential for harmony. We must remember that, unlike British period, we are part of them and not an isolated body. Some of our parents, brothers, sisters may be facing same problems like other civilians, somewhere, for such drastic acts. We can no longer live in colonial style.

Army populations who are staying in the cantonments are of migratory nature, stay for a tenure of 2 to 3 years and leave the station. They are practically not aware of the tribulations of the local civilians. I am sure many of the propagators of closure might be staying far away from the cantonments and not aware of the problems. But we must understand that proper attention must be given to the need of the civilians who will live in or around the cantonments for generation after generation.

There has been a misconception that Defence Minister Mrs. Nirmala Sitharaman has taken arbitrary decisions to take political mileage out of it. This is far from the truth. RM had taken numbers of meeting with all concerned. There have been constant interactions between Army HQ, LMAs, DG of Defense Estate, CEOs and vice presidents of 62cantoments and concerned MPs of all parties. Last meeting was taken on 9th May after the return of the Chief of Army Staff Gen Bipin Rawat from Shrilanka visit, before final decision was taken. There are 862 roads in 62 two cantonments which were closed. Many of them were arbitrarily without following proper procedure. She insisted that even if decision is taken after one month to close certain roads after evaluating their security aspects, proper procedure must be followed and decision must be taken with proper justification. She has also mentioned that roads are being opened in those areas of the cantonments where there are only living and administrative accommodations and not in the places where sensitive things like depots etc lay.

However, all of us are equally concerned for the safety of the soldiers and their families. Every unit or family station must be well guarded. If required degree of protection can further be enhanced by augmenting number of guards, carrying out patrolling, constructing high boundary wall, having well equipped Quick response team, introducing CC TV and other gadgets etc. But please do not change all cantoments, most of them located far away from the border, into war zones. Let's show some boldness. Civil population looks up to the army with awe and admiration and feel secured living among them. In contrary army is projecting a feeling of fear and detachment and showing lack of concern and compassion to their civilian brethren.

Before any conclusive direction, a tripartite meeting between LMA, PCB representatives and local user representatives must be held to arrive at an unanimous decision.

The gravity of the situation can be gauged by the fact that all MPs and CEOs of 62 Cantonments unanimously represented for opening of the roads. This has been unprecedented.

Army or Defense Ministry is merely a custodian.

Cdr Ravindra Pathak, Pune

The order of MOD at the behest of the Raksha Mantri (RM) to open all cantonment roads is seen as a populist move since the decision was apparently taken at a meeting where there were no representatives of the Local Military Authorities (LMA) concerned or the Army HQ with just the 62 Vice Presidents (Elected members of public) of the Cantonment boards in attendance. May be her own house in Secunderabad is affected and that could have played on her mind. Never know how a political mind works.

Further what was horrifying was the kind of celebrations that some political activists indulged in as if they had won a war against the enemy.

It is no one's case that the LMA has not erred in some cases but that may well be an isolated case.

The military environment has rightly been vocal on the subject and as such there has been some back tracking on the issue by stating that order is subject to review after a month and RM being forced to give out details which none do believe.

In this entire din the silence of the Army Chief is thundering. Wish he had stalled the issue for a better understanding by the RM than to play along and expect his juniors to take action like blocking roads to allow soldiers to exercise on them. Child like really – as if his troops had no other area other than a road to exercise on?

Let us understand the issue.

The Military lands are covered by many acts and the cantonment board areas have Restricted, Prohibited and Protected areas besides the civil areas that form part of the cantonments.

The duties of the cantonment board are stated at Para 62 of Cantonment Board Act 2006 and I see no role of the board in the process of closing or opening the roads.

The issue is how to permit movement of those from civil areas from one side of the cantonment to the other civil side of the cantonment. This is where the cantonment areas have been divided into Restricted, Protected and Prohibited areas. It is very clear that only restricted areas could possibly be opened to civil vehicular traffic. In many instances transit facilities have been approved through such areas in the interest of the public like the Metro line in Delhi.

The Vice Presidents (and it seems the lead was taken by Secunderabad) have largely complained that LMA have not followed Rule 258 of the Cantonment Act. This is a subject beyond their charter of duties as laid down.

I see most of the cause of concern by veterans and serving officers wives is the security of the families and about the exclusiveness of the Defence areas being lost. To the best of my knowledge security of families have been threatened more in units that were located in disturbed areas prone to attacks by anti nationals, terrorists and insurgents rather than peace areas.

It is nobody's case that all road closures are not without fault but surely there are cases wherein the closure is justified as far as the LMA/ Station Commander is concerned and that I feel is the final authority in the absence of any regulatory requirement to go beyond him.

CONCLUDING REMARKS

Gp Capt Johnson Chacko, Pune

A few years after independence, there were civil disturbances in Lahore, Pakistan. The Army was called out and they resolved the issues. The disturbances subsided. The Army was told to return to barracks. They asked for a week more before returning to barracks. In that week they cleaned up the city and brought in some order to the chaotic lifestyle of the civil population. The civil population was very satisfied and they enjoyed it. They set standards for the civil administration to emulate and they haven't been able to do so thereafter. After that whenever Martial Law was declared the population welcomed it as 'Masha Allah' and not 'MartialLaw'. A small price to pay for better living, I guess. Why can't better living be extended to the City from the Cantonment rather than ruining the Cantonments?

Cantonment roads are designed for the load that it is expected to carry. Funds to maintain them are allocated from the Defence Services estimates and maintenance is done by the Military Engineering Services. The funds are barely sufficient to meet the needs of repairs and maintenance. With heavy vehicles and quantum of vehicles expected to shoot up the roads are expected to give way. Can the respective Cities fund the maintenance of these roads?

Now that the Cities have grown around the Cantonments, there is a need for the population to reduce travelling time and hence traffic through the Cantonments needs to be allowed, which in many cases is already allowed except for heavy vehicles that ruin the roads. Restrictions are few and there is no need for a civilian to go to those places. Allowing civil traffic through Cantonments reduces expenditure of fuel and probably it may cause an invisible dent in the foreign exchange we pay to import crude, though the users of these roads will benefit. Assuming that there are procedures for civilians who live within the Cantonment, the problem is for the civilians who want to cross the area. What is the solution?

Build flyovers, so that civilians who want to go to the other side can fly through without hindering the Cantonments. Have broad enough roads for a detour. Probability is very low as the area around is heavily populated in an unplanned manner.

If the roads are open to all with no security checks, then security threat to the families of Armed Forces personnel living in the Cantonment is high. The Police are not capable of providing the required intelligence or security to prevent a terrorist attack in the soft underbelly as has been witnessed earlier. It will have a tremendous adverse impact on the morale of soldiers who are deployed to protect our borders. High quality all weather cameras that give a warning of undesirable deviation of traffic from the permitted routes and effective interception by tactically positioned Quick Reaction Teams manned by Army and Police would be cheaper than a Flyover. This will not tie down Army personnel to unnecessary guard and patrolling duties.

The apparent practical solution is that Cities should contribute to maintenance of roads that are opened for civil use and for use of high quality all weather cameras to monitor and intercept deviation. The cost of these needs to be met by the city concerned before traffic is thrown open through the Cantonment.

Note: This debate was published in Fauji India magazine, Aug 2018 issue

CHAPTER 11

National Security: What is it and Who is Responsible?

Col Rajinder Kushwaha

Plain Speak

Then, there is a lot of confusion between national security and law and order problems. Not only this, national security has been further sliced into internal and external security and being assigned to different organs of the Central Government. NSA to MHA; MoD to State governments, have, thus, all become executive authorities to conduct national security operations. National security cannot be segmented into compartments and thus distributed as sweets to different proponents. It must have a single executive authority, whether it was internal threat or external threat.

In recent years, issue of national security has become a Ping-Pong ball and everyone was kicking it. From the media to social organisations like RSS; National Security Advisor (NSA) to state Chief Ministers; politicians to bureaucracy and government organs such as MHA, MoD and MEA. All of them have been behaving as if security of the nation was their sole responsibility. There is an utter confusion.

Do any one of these people/organisations know what comprises national security? Chief of a social organisation thinks that in three days he can create a private army who can handle security more effectively than current bunch of security forces. A state Chief Minister thinks that she was the boss and AFSPA-1958 (Armed Forces Special Power Act) is all bunkum. She ordered lodging of a FIR against an army officer who acted in self defence when some miscreants pelted stone on his party. Sometime back, the highest court of the land had passed an order to say that FIR would be lodged in all cases of encounters.

Then, there is a lot of confusion between national security and Law and order problems. Not only this, national security has been further sliced into internal and external security and being assigned to different organs of the Central Government. NSA to MHA; MoD to State governments, have, thus, all become executive authorities to conduct national security operations. When there are so many bosses, confusion has to take place as it did during terrorist attack on Pathankot Air Force base on 01 January 2016 and more recently during terrorist attack on Sunjuwan Military Garrison on 11 February 2018.

There are number of such incidents. Why does everyone want to get into the arena? Simple answer is that terrorism and counter terrorism have become a glamour bazar for everyone whether one, who perpetrated terror and the other who counters it. Lack of clear cut definition and areas of responsibilities make everyone rush into it to get their pound of flesh.

National security cannot be segmented into compartments and thus distributed as sweets to different proponents. It must have a single executive authority, whether it was internal threat or external threat. Unfortunately, India has divided this role between Home Ministry and Defence Ministry. On top of that, there is the confusion about law and order problem, which is a state subject. Herein lies the glitch. It needs to be sorted out by defining national security and law and order.

National security is the assessment of intended, demonstrable and executed threats to national integrity and unity by external and internal foes. It is one big whole and it cannot be segmented. Internal foes are separatists and terrorists. They need to be treated as "enemies" and not as "our misguided boys." Unfortunately, "our misguided boys" concept leads to ineffective and half-cocked measures to deal with internal threats. We, courts and legal system included, fail to note that whoever picks up arms against India, is her enemy. This is the position of the Constitution of India. This brooks a no-nonsense approach, when AFSPA was imposed in a region or a state. Security forces must have a free hand. Appeasement and softness are the biggest enemy of internal security measures.

Armed forces of a nation are organised and equipped to deal with these threat to national security. Therefore, the responsibility of national security must devolve upon armed forces, whether it has a Chief of Defence Staff (CDS) or not. Defence Minister can take on this role till government decides to appoint a CDS. But with the fast spreading insurgency and militancy across the nation, the need for a CDS is becoming utmost. The NSA cannot take on this role because he must focus on strategic affairs and regional environments. NSA can only advise the Ministry of Defence but he cannot be the executive authority.

The Ministry of Home Affairs (MHA) must focus on law and order for which it has the Central Reserve Police (CRPF) and state police forces. Time has come when threat to a nation needs to be defined in broad terms. Some of the issues clubbed with law and order need to be delinked. Mass agitations, communal violence, organised crime under mafia, such as drug/narcotics trafficking, smuggling, militancy and terrorism must fall into the ambit of national security. Therefore, all such forces dealing with them are assigned to MoD. This would include BSF, ITBP, CISF, SB, and Assam Rifles and so on.

Law and order should focus on individual crimes such as murder, extortion, kidnapping, criminal harassment, crime against women and children and corruption. CRPF should be an added force with the centre to beef up state police. Conduct of elections can be grouped under Law and order. In order to ensure proper coordination of national security; one has to get at the most potent threat endangering a nation. To do so, we might have to fall back on the sayings of Chanakya or Kautilya. According to him, there were four kinds of threat to a nation. One, which emanates from outside but aided and abetted from outside. Two, which emanates from the inside but also aided and abetted from insides. Three, which emanates from the outside but is aided and abetted from the inside. The last one, more dangerous is the one emanated from inside and aided and abetted from outside.

It is the last one which India needs to focus – whether it was North East, MP, Chhattisgarh, Jharkhand, West Bengal, Andhra Pradesh, Punjab or J&K. It is therefore utmost important that overall responsibility must lay with MoD, who should work out an internal security grid and allocate forces accordingly. This job must not be left to state governments.

Having done this, we ought to look at AFSPA-1958. It was designed to deal with the Naga Insurgency in 1958 to provide immunity to soldiers. However, over the years, the insurgency has taken a more diabolical shape with political and legal complications. It needs to be replaced by a COZA-2018 (Combat Zone Act), which would ensure once a state has been placed under COZA, state governments would not interfere with the national security apparatus, as has been happening in NE and J&K. The declaration power be given to combined houses of the parliament and not with central government. Once COZA is imposed in a state/region then, only High Courts and Supreme Court be allowed to intervene in so-called alleged atrocities by soldiers. Time has come to act tough.

CHAPTER 12

Soldiers and Politicians: The Need for Mutual Understanding

Maj Gen V K Madhok

Good Sense

In peace, the chances of friction between the soldier and the politician are enhanced. While the latter is trying to find ways of saving money, the former is constantly demanding increased allocation. No doubt, as mentioned earlier, the habit of obedience prevents the soldier from pressing his case too far. But the politician, skilled in the manipulation of men, is an adept when it comes to overcoming the resistance of professionals. But when war breaks out, at the first clash of steel, the pattern of values is turned topsy-turvy. The soldier is invested with tremendous powers. The lives of others are in his hands and the future of the country hangs on his decisions. The whole nation looks upto him and the politician sees with amazement this over-riding power suddenly springing up from the ground and bringing the soldier on to a level of equality with him.

It is a historical fact that in all countries soldiers find it difficult to give unquestioning obedience to the civil authority. There are sufficient examples around us in Pakistan, Bangladesh and Myanmar, where the soldier took the extreme step of dislodging the Politician. Reverse was the case during the Korean War, when US President (Truman) sacked the soldier (MacArthur). And where this has not happened it is not because the soldier finds happiness in a sense of subordination but because the sense of discipline has become so ingrained in him that there is seldom any refusal to obey orders. His loyalty goes to the minister's office rather than the man who happens to fill it. This tussle is unavoidable, and it would continue because the politician and the soldier bring to the common cause of serving their country, entirely different approaches, fears and methods which are bound to lead to friction. But before that, two incidents of misunderstanding which took place owing to a lack of communication between soldiers and politicians.

There was uproar in the Lok Sabha over some remarks reportedly made by General SF Rodrigues, ex-COAS, on March 16, 1992 concerning "the need for good governance of the country and to fight siege within". His dismissal was demanded by some MPs. Subsequent efforts were made by the then Defence Minister, Sharad Pawar, to defuse the situation. He issued instructions to completely cut out interviews between the Chiefs and the media. Certain interesting observations were made during the debate: One, military commanders are dismissed for defeats, moral turpitude and cowardice in battle, but certainly not for the types of remarks reportedly made by the then Chief. Two, public censure of a serving Chief who also happened to be the Chief of Defence Staff, would become a topic of discussion, not only in army barracks, but by troops at the front, military institutions, by officers and their families, in messes, by soldiers travelling in trains and at the sentry posts on the border, and this was the worst type of a situation for any army when the merits and demerits of its Chief become a topic of open discussion by his troops and common citizens. And last, are not "good governance" and "to fight siege within" the concern of the armed forces? After reflection, one cannot but come to the conclusion that both as citizens and defenders, it is.

The second incident took place on May 23, 1995. Some MPs in the Rajya Sabha questioned the Army Chief's authority when he made a statement regarding Pakistan backing different insurgent groups and the need for a dialogue with the militants. Also, that there was an undeclared war on between India and Pakistan in Kashmir. Now these are matters on which a great deal has been written and spoken in the last seven years. Even a school child will support what the then COAS, Gen Roy Chowdhury, had said. "Besides, a Proxy War, all said and done, is an undeclared war." What the MPs had failed to analyse and appreciate was the reason why Service Chiefs were going around making such statements. More serious statements have been made by the Service Chiefs in the recent past based on facts and nearly all politicians have remained silent instead of rectifying the situation.

To list a few instances: on taking over in November 1994, the then Army Chief made a statement of far-reaching consequence to the scribes, "Indigenize or perish." Again, besides officers, armies need tanks, all-weather surveillance equipment, attack helicopters, missiles, medium guns and a hundred other things. If 75 to 80 percent of this has to be imported from abroad at exorbitant cost, then the Army is truly handicapped. Foreign countries can curtail or stop this supply or increase the cost. Imagine the impact of this situation on the troops when they realize that they are held hostage to foreign countries so far as their defence equipment is concerned.

In addition, the Naval Chief made statements towards the end of 1996 about the ageing naval fleet and non-availability of replacements. The Air Chiefs have voiced their concern on more than a dozen occasions about the shortage and non-availability of spares for combat aircraft and the AJTs on which a decision has been pending for the last 19 years.

Now these are matters which should have made our chosen representatives sit up. They should have grilled the government and taken the MoD or those who are responsible, to task. But nothing of the kind has happened and serious issues concerning the nation's security have been glossed over. Therefore, when Service Chiefs are asked questions over security, either they have to give facts or keep quiet, nothing in between! Obviously, the accountability factor plays heavy on their minds, as they head the instruments of security. Besides, they are in an unenviable position wherein they have no say in the making of the defence policy.

In such circumstances, to pick up an excerpt from an interview or a briefing to the press and make the man who made the statement, the butt of censure in the Parliament is not only unfair but uncalled for. Instead, our chosen representatives in the Parliament need to do some solid homework on defence and rectify some of the more important shortcomings. If we do not do that, as a result of this ticking off, the Service Chiefs may keep quiet, but others may speak up. How are we going to control them?

Therefore, it is true and most desirable that the Service Chiefs do not advise their government from public platforms, as this shows a clear communication gap between them and their political masters. Nor should they speak openly about the shortcomings of their respective services because such statements are not only demoralizing for the services but for the nation as well. The right place to sort out these crucial issues is the Defence Minister's office, where solutions to various problems have to be found. In fact, a good Defence Minister should not only be fully seized of such problems but tell the MPs in Parliament as to what measures his Ministry is taking to obviate current as well as future deficiencies.

As regards the differing approaches of these two servants of the state: the politician reaches his goal by roundabout ways, the soldier by direct approach. The one is long-sighted, sees realities as complex and sets himself to master these by diplomacy and negotiations. The soldier sees what there is to be seen in front of his nose, thinks it is simple and capable of being controlled with determination. In dealing with immediate problems, the politician's first concern is what people will say of him, while the soldier looks for guidance from his principles. The disparities contribute towards misinterpretation and the soldier regards the politician as unreliable, inconstant and greedy.

Broken in as he is to a life of hard duties, self-effacement and respect shown for services rendered, he is astonished by the number of pretences a politician has to make, his dominant concern with the effect to be produced, and the judging of others not in terms of their merit, but their influence.

Accordingly, the politician plays the chief role in peace time. The masses greet him with applause or boos, but their eyes and ears are all for him. When suddenly war starts, the soldier appears on the stage. With the limelight on him! The politician is pushed aside – the country is now all for a Manekshaw with an Indira Gandhi on the flank. However, both are interdependent.

The politician aims at dominating public opinion since it is from this that he draws his authority. His skills in pleasing and making promises are far more effective than his abilities and arguments. As a result, he concentrates all his efforts in captivating people's minds – he must pose as the people's servant to become their master. He knows when to dissemble and when to be frank. Outbidding his rivals with a thousand intrigues and long agenda, even when he finds himself in full power, he can never afford to be open in his dealings. His authority always remains precarious, as he must continue to please, gratify popular passions, sooth the anxieties of business interests, convince the Parliament and keep an eye on public opinion – that inconstant mistress. Being ungrateful like all mistresses it downgrades the efforts put in by him and is only too ready to listen to his opponents. If the politician makes a mistake, the pack is at his heels.

An intrigue or a shift of opinion in the Parliament can snatch the empire from him. Fallen from his pedestal, he finds nothing but injustice awaiting him. He swings between power and powerlessness, between prestige and public ingratitude. A politician's life and the sum total of his work are marked by instability, turbulence and public ingratitude.

But the soldier's world is different. From the moment he enters his profession, he becomes a slave to a body of regulations and remains so throughout his life. The army is like a jealous but generous wife. She guides his steps, develops his gifts and supports him in his moments of weakness. But it always keeps a tight hold on him – holding his over-enthusiasm in check. Its demands force him to give up personal liberty, renounce the chances of making money and sometimes even sacrifice his life. But at this high cost, it opens the door for him to armed might, and though he often grumbles about his slavery, he clings to it and loves and glories in the price he pays for it. Bound by discipline and tradition, under the shield of regulations, he marches straight ahead. The soldier's predilection for system, self-assurance and rigidity inbred as a result of prolonged restraint, seems tiresome and unattractive to the politician. In his eyes, the soldier is narrow-minded, arrogant and difficult to handle. As the politician is committed to a career in which public speaking and general ideas play so vital a part, he can scarcely fail to feel uncomfortable when confronted with the display of brute force.

But these contrasts are really not disadvantages. They are necessary to balance the opposing tendencies in the governance of a State. As such, one ought to be grateful and satisfied that those who govern the country and those who direct its armed forces are, to some extent, estranged from each other. Good politicians do not meddle with the army, particularly in its selection system which must be solely based on military merit and not public opinion.

So long as a country is not immediately threatened, public opinion will remain opposed to increasing the burden of armaments and additional manpower. Only too often, money spent on an army not engaged in actual combat is considered a sheer waste. But the politician has to produce a budget in which the defence estimates make an ugly hole. Naturally enough, military problems are anathema to the bureaucracy and the men in authority. But soldiers are unaffected by such considerations. For them, armed power is sacred. The ideal for their profession is self-sacrifice and they find it difficult to digest the idea of a compromise. As the soldier is in a constant state of preparation, he is too ready to believe that war may break out any moment. Because, war after all, is the first and the last purpose of his life! It is high opportunity where he can give off his best. It is rightly said that a soldier who prefers a life of peace, needs to be put on the retired list.

Therefore in peace, the chances of friction between the soldier and the politician are enhanced. While the latter is trying to find ways of saving money, the former is constantly demanding increased allocation. No doubt, as mentioned earlier, the habit of obedience prevents the soldier from pressing his case too far. But the politician, skilled in the manipulation of men, is an adept when it comes to overcoming the resistance of professionals. But when war breaks out, at the first clash of steel, the pattern of values is turned topsy-turvy. The soldier is invested with tremendous powers. The lives of others are in his hands and the future of the country hangs on his decisions. The whole nation looks upto him and the politician sees with amazement this over-riding power suddenly springing up from the ground and bringing the soldier on to a level of equality with him.

At first, carried away by a concern to set an example to the country, both reach complete agreement without the slightest difficulty. Each finds in the other a thousand good qualities which until then one had scarcely suspected. But then the war progresses with mounting casualties and the demand for the resources of the nation to flow to the battlefield under the control of the soldier who will not tolerate intruders or interference. This is the time when the politician is left with no alternative, but to entrust the fate of the people as well as the government to the soldier and go through a period of anxiety and irritability.

But the best servants of the state, whether soldiers or politicians, are seldom the most pliable of men. True enough, while the conduct of war is the business of the politician, its fighting is that of the soldier. But where does one cease and the other begin? Are we to assume then that soldiers and politicians must rely on chance inspiration at the moment of crisis? As things go now, soldiers and politicians rarely find themselves working for a common end in peace. The life of a soldier with its discipline and aloofness scarcely ever brings him into close contact with civil affairs. While the politician's life is filled with such a press of complicated obligations that he neither has the time nor the wish to think about his own immediate problems. All the same, a vague sort of attraction does exist between them. Their wishes, anxieties and their activities are so different in kind that they seldom make contact. Of course, the soldier is called in as an expert and takes part in exclusively technical discussions, then duly seated in order of seniority on ceremonial occasions, he listens to the politician's speeches.

An enlightened state would therefore not hesitate to find ways and means to reduce, if not cut out, this communication gap, and bring in the soldier for consultation and advice even on matters other than military (of which a long list can be drawn), instead of leaving him out with a feeling that he, like the doctor and God, would be required only in times of crisis.

Tailpiece

The recent outburst against the Navy at a public function on Jan 11, 2018 at Mumbai, in the presence of a union Minister Nitin Gadkari, civilians and naval personnel and Vice Admiral Luthra, C-in-C Western Naval Command and Chief Minister Devendra Fadnavis has left us Veterans wondering as to whether the armed force will now be chastised by politicians in public?

His remarks that he won't give an inch of land to the Navy or that, Navy's job is to go and defend the border against Pakistan and that, it had created obstacles, in development of Mumbai, Were uncalled for, insulting and defamatory. What will the rank and file of Navy think about Vice Admiral Luthra? Loyalty and a sense of discipline do not permit soldiers to answer or counter charges levelled by superiors in public. This will lead to indiscipline. I therefore very strongly urge the Prime Minister to reflect and that the proper place to discuss such issues is in the government offices, and not in public.

CHAPTER 13

Debate: Review of Shekatkar Committee Report and its Selective Implementation

Compiled by Parth Satam

Background

The Shekatkar Committee (headed by Lt Gen DB Shekatkar) was constituted by former defence minister Manohar Parrikar to 'recommend measures for enhancing combat capability and re-balancing defence expenditure of the armed forces with an aim to increase 'teeth to tail ratio'. The committee submitted its report to the Defence Minster (MoD) on December 21, 2016. Out of the 188 recommendations made, the MoD has accepted 99 and issued implementation orders for 65 (in phase one, to be completed by end 2019) mainly pertaining to the army, involving redeploying some 57,000 personnel.

The highlights of the approved reforms include optimization of Signals establishments, restructuring of repair echelons in army, redeployment of ordnance echelons, better utilization of Supply and Transport echelons and Animal Transport units, closure of Military Farms and army postal establishments in peace locations, enhancement in standards for recruitment of clerical staff and drivers in army, improving the efficiency of the NCC, plus retired Officers and Jawans to replace serving personnel for running NCC, performance audit of non-combat organizations under MoD, plus Defence Estates, Defence Accounts, DGQA, Ordnance Factory Board (OFB), DRDO be accountable, establish joint services war college for training middle-level Officers, 'roll on' plan for fresh acquisitions be introduced to overcome 'surrendering' funds at the end of every financial year and financial powers of all three Chiefs and Vice Chiefs be enhanced further to quicken the pace of acquisitions.

Reacting to the development as reported by 'Gomantak Times' Panaji, Goa on 31 Aug 2017, Lt Gen Shekatkar said, "It is a welcome step but the government must implement all 188 recommendations made by the committee and not only 99, otherwise the purpose of this entire exercise would be lost." According to Lt Gen Shekatkar, "What has come out in the media is just the tip of the iceberg and there were more issues taken up by them like DRDO, Ordnance Factory Board and streamlining the arms lobby." He further said, "If you produce weapons in India in large quantities and export them, the cost of production will come down."

He recommended, "Anybody and everybody paid from defence budget should be looked at, examined and held accountable irrespective of their nature of responsibility." He said, "The aim of the report was not to send people home but to reorganise their services in such a way that there is optimum utilisation of manpower and other resources for better combat readiness." He also said, "The committee took into account the changing nature of war, both independent and twin threat from Pakistan and China besides prevailing internal situation."

Lt Gen P C Katoch in his article said, "These reforms, termed Phase 1, are to be completed by 31 Dec 2019. Significantly, the Committee had stated that if all 188 recommendations are effected within five years, it would result in saving Rs. 25,000 crore that could be utilized for modernizing the Armed Forces. Interestingly, MoD sent only 99 of the 188 recommendations to the Armed Forces for making the implementation plan, of which 65 sent to the Army have been approved, while balance 34 are to be taken up in Phase 2. It is unclear how many, if not all, of the 89 recommendations not sent to the Armed Forces are being shelved.

"Significantly, of the 57,000 personnel being redeployed, 31,000 are civilian-defence officials. Was there scope of phasing out the latter after attaining normal retirement? Where are they being redeployed? And what functional problems will aggravate with the Army already facing this with civilian-defence officials paid more than their military counterparts based on which they claim superiority over same ranks?

"The creation of new posts in AFHQ Civil Service is catalyst to the problem. When we are calling for nationalistic rock concerts in universities, how about 'combatizing' the AFHQ Civil Service? The bit about performance audit of non-combat organizations under MoD like Defence Estates, Defence Accounts, DGQA, Ordnance Factory Board (OFB), and DRDO accountable is inherent responsibility of MoD, which has been utterly lacking. Mentioning these as part of 'Army reforms' is meant for impressing the public.

"Similarly, the 'Roll On' plan for fresh acquisitions to overcome 'surrendering' funds at the end of every Financial Year is a misnomer, as it still leaves loopholes. Why not simply say that the unutilized defence budget will be carried forward to the next Financial Year, as was recommended by a defence minister during NDA I, and also in various reports by the Parliamentary Standing Committee on Defence?"

RESPONSES

Lt Gen Harbhajan Singh

One has seen a number of such studies not only in defence but police and other departments also. Only cosmetic changes which suit the bureaucracy (IAS) are undertaken when the topic is hot and then the reports languish in cupboards. Shekatkar Committee Report is not going to be an exception!

The quick reaction/announcement by the government is to counter Doklam Crisis. In depth examination and discussions could not have been done by Shekatkar Committee. It is amateurish for the government to say that so many recommendations out of so many have been accepted. This is crude propaganda. The main issue is higher defence management and not saving of a few thousand men and or a few thousand crores. The government announcement is quiet on bigger issues. The bureaucracy would not allow any meaningful reforms to take place in the working of MoD, defence R&D and so on, which affects their standing/power and perks.

No doubt we need to reduce our tail as Indian forces are primarily to fight within/close to our borders. We should therefore use civil resources to the maximum, as long as these are close to the borders. Some of the measures suggested by the Shekatkar Committee regarding Military Farms, Ordnance, ASC, and EME seem to be on the right lines. However, let us be forewarned that Indian industry's performance lacks quality and timeliness. They can resort to legal system to fight any damages levied on them for unsatisfactory performance. There is ample proof of this in civil works executed through contractors by the MES. Some laws may have to be enacted to ensure that as far as defence is concerned, civil contractors and companies will have to deliver works of quality and on time, otherwise face penalties.

There is a problem in the East of India which is vulnerable to Chinese offensive/attack and hardly any civil industry exists in the area. Logistics and maintenance support for troops around Siliguri and east of it requires special consideration.

As regards changes in Corps of Signals, some reorganization is overdue. The role of Corps of Signals in Electronic Warfare, Signal Intelligence and Cyber Warfare, which are force multipliers, needs greater emphasis. India must not overlook large capabilities built by China in these areas. Provision of signal communications no doubt remains the core task. It is hoped that the top military and MoD brass would realize this and readjust Signals resources.

Lt Col M K Gupta Ray
Before we carry out any study about defence forces, we must remember that there is a vast change of scenario between peace time and war time situation. What looks cost effective in peace time may become very expensive in war in terms of battle effectiveness.

In the army there are peace and war equipment table. The equipments or services which look redundant during peace time may be well needed during war. While with the development of resources, it is imperative to take periodical stock of tooth to tail ratio but once war starts it is equally important to ensure that tooth has the capacity to bite. War is a field of destruction. It is better to save the destruction by having a powerful army than being involved in war. Too much endeavour to save manpower and money should not become counterproductive. Such studies must have following considerations.

- Optimising existing resources
- Modernising forces in keeping with the overall development
- Employment of troops
- Futuristic operation: limited or all out, within the neighborhood or at continental/ intercontinental level. Limited war may land up in greater escalation
- Foreign policy

Since our country is having different terrains and degree of development level, the same structural changes may not work specially in northern and eastern border. We may have to make tailor made organizational changes. The overall study report seems to be a welcome measure. But where government seems to be keeping quiet is in the higher defence management. We must be able to get maximum effect by deploying and employing our resources at the maximum level. It is only possible when all the three services fight in a cohesive manner.

Maj Gen Anil Sengar
In principle, reforms are much needed and most of these can be done to improve the teeth to tail ratio. What one needs to remember is that many of these organisations may look redundant in peacetime, but they may have a role in war. Any restructuring that sounds good in peace, should not affect operational functioning. Any outsourcing should be doable and functional in war.

The other thing is, all units especially combat units, are required to perform many ad-hoc tasks, for which no manpower is authorized as such it is better that combat arms have ten percent more than one percent less. Then there are categories with restrictions in employment etc. In short, each recommendation must now be studied with a tooth comb before a blanket restructuring is initiated.

Col C M Chavan
Lt Gen N S Brar, former Deputy Chief Integrated Defence Staff, in his article has very rightly brought out the futility of the government in trying to save money of the exchequer by cutting down the so called flab of the army which actually is the support system of the armed forces. It is envisaged that 57,000 personnel are likely to be released. However, as very well brought out, a large area of prime land will be available to the government by dissolving military farms. Next in line will be the golf grounds. If we come to see, almost 40% of the defence pension accrued is due to defence civilians which should not be actually accounted to defence budget.

As the General has very rightly brought out, our approach to security has been political rather than military. We are shy of demanding what is essentially needed on ground with firmness. Our Chiefs should at some stage put their foot down rather than accepting the unilateral cut down in acquisition of Rafale fighters and putting on hold the raising of a Mountain Strike Corps. Recent example is that of Gen Pierre de Villiers who said in his statement that he could no longer "guarantee the durability of the army model" (due to cut in defence spending) that he considered necessary to ensure France's protection and resigned.

In actual fact there was a requirement of drastic changes in the MoD. This is substantiated by an article in Times of India dated 01 July 2017, in a news item given by Newton Sequeria where he quotes previous RM Manohar Parrikar, when he took over in November 2014, "When I was the Defense Minister, and I can tell you this, when I took over, the Defense Ministry was in pure shambles...There was total chaos."We need drastic changes in the functioning of the government.

Brig L C Patnaik

Optimal employment and deployment of complex weapon systems, requires a high level of quality military leadership. There is an urgent need to enhance our intake quality and improve our training methodology.

Given the compulsion of containing the fiscal deficit and eliminating the revenue deficit under the Fiscal Responsibility and Budget Management (FRBM) Act, it is unlikely that the allocation for defence would ever exceed more than 2% (far below the Committee's recommendation of 3%) of GDP in next ten years. Assuming the current share of revenue and capital spending of 55:45 to be maintained over next ten years, the capital expenditure is expected to be a staggering US $200 billion on an incremental basis.

As nearly 85% of this allocation goes towards modernization and imports leaving very little for capital works, lands and married accommodation etc. Hence there is an urgent need to rebalance the capital expenditure by upgrading our indigenous defence manufacturing capability, rationalization of offset investment inflows, public-private partnership/outsourcing and reinforcing 'Make In India' through technology infusion and incentive of a captive market.

The Army's Army Design Bureau (ADB) must be supported through adequate budget allocations for prototype production in conjunction with leading technological institutes. The Committee should have actually suggested measures to reduce the share of revenue and capital spending substantially in next 10-15 years. This should have been the basis of major recommendations rather than recommending restructuring of Signal Corps, military farms etc.

Reduction of man power and consequent attenuated saving to the defence exchequer has achieved limited success in the past. The Army's previous suo-motto in-house initiatives of manpower reductions in EME, AOC and AEC were restricted by the courts and civil unions. Notwithstanding the above, the recommendation of reduction in OFBs/DPSUs are noteworthy as it would help in reduction of defence pension budget (40% of annual pension budget goes to defence civilians).

The defence budget currently allocated to DRDO is around 6%, while the capital acquisition, maintenance and upkeep of the imported equipment and credit servicing is around 70%. To balance this, allocation to DRDO should be adequately enhanced with provision for collaborative research with leading national and international research institutes, exchange of scientists and joint prototype production. The additional allocation could be given from defence off-sets.

The DRDO be allowed to create technical capabilities in the private sector by concurrent transfer of technology during the design and development stage and gain adequate share in 'build to specifications' in foreign R&D collaborations. The defence offsets in next ten years are expected to be in the range US $ 50-60 billion, considering the minimum mandatory level of 30% obligation. It is essential that the Service HQs, DRDO, Defence PSUs, OFBs constitute a Joint Technical Planning Board(JTPB) to lay down their priorities and prepare a focused roadmap to augment the defence industrial base.

Establish joint ventures to reduce the life cycle operation costs, maintenance of imported weapon systems and creation of state of the art overhaul facilities. Substantial manpower can be saved by modernization of Base Workshops and amalgamation of inter-service repair and maintenance depots. Defence resources management should form part of the joint strategic logistic staff team under the IDS and the proposed JTPB. Representations of DPSUs, OFBs and DRDO should be incorporated on a need basis for optimal resource management, both during war and peace.

An integrated IT system to provide information on a real-time basis would enhance timely expenditure of allocated budgets. Five-year review audit on tenets of zero-based budgeting will ensure smooth expenditure and minimize surrender of funds. There is need to drastically cut down the scales of stocks at the PSUs/OFBs and Ordnance Depots to avoid dead stocks and reduce maintenance costs. This alone could bring down the defence budget substantially.

CONCLUDING OVERVIEW

by Gp Capt T P Srivastava

The bane of the Indian military is poorly equipped soldiers and not poor or wasteful utilization of manpower. The committee in recommending withdrawal of 57,000 men from so called non-combat duties and arriving at savings of Rs. 25,000 crore is hogwash. 'Teeth to Tail' ratio improves when our soldiers are equipped with better personal weapon than INSAS rifle against an adversary equipped with predator class UAVs, M4 assault rifle, Glock model 19 pistols, ceramic plated body armour, satellite telephones, GPS trackers and so on.

In fact on the basis of the report, which essentially has delved on regrouping, the service HQs would be burdened with sending monthly/quarterly feed back to the ministry regarding implementation of recommendations. Shekatkar Committee has deliberately undermined the status of Service Chiefs by recommending the appointment of a Four Star General to act as a coordinator amongst the three Service Chiefs, directly implying that the Service Chiefs are not capable of resolving their differences in the interest of national security. To sum it up; Shekatkar Committee report is an 'Auditor's Report' submitted to the 'Super Auditor' of the nation, and has 'nil' to 'negative' operational value.

CHAPTER 14

Have Prolonged CI Ops Weakened us for Conventional and 21st Century Warfare?

Compiled by Col Vinay Dalvi

Background & Trigger

In a recent article by Manoj Joshi published in TOI on August 18, the author suggests the Indian Army to should show greater 'self-restraint' and consequently suffer greater casualties than the militants like the British did in fighting insurgency in Northern Ireland and which the Israel Army has failed to achieve against the Palestinians.

In context with the joint petition filed by 356 serving army officers in the Supreme Court, the author opines the move to be disturbing and trade union like act. Joshi perceives that Armed Forces Special Powers Act (AFSPA) does not give the Army absolute protection against the law of the land.

Combating insurgency for decades in J&K and North East is taking its toll in India with the Army paying for it dearly not only by losing its honour, morale and reputation but more importantly its overall fighting capability and efficiency for a futuristic two front conventional war. Further, the military is not being adequately equipped and reformed.

There is now an imperative need to change this narrative and not keep the Army bogged down only with fighting insurgency as it can prove to be disastrous in the times to come. Both the political and military leadership are to blame for this sorry state of affairs. Solution has to be found with improved Civil-Military Relations and better military and political leadership at all levels.

RESPONSES FROM TRI-SERVICE VETERANS

Lt Gen Harbhajan Singh

I have read Manoj Joshi's article and do not find much wrong with it. However, he has covered only a small part of the problem to pick holes with the Army top brass and even Veterans. He should have taken a holistic view instead. Some of the points that he should have discussed before finding fault with the Army hierarchy are mentioned.

The Indian Army has been misused in counter insurgency for over 70 years since Independence to tackle unrest among Indian population due to political, bureaucratic and police ineptness, selfish interests and even corruption. No other Army in the world has had to be deployed against its own citizens so many times and for such long periods. In spite of this, the record of the Indian Army as far as self-restraint, human rights and self-disciplining are concerned cannot be matched. Look at Pakistan, they even used gunships against own tribals!

The Army has taken disciplinary action against a number of officers and soldiers who have violated engagement rules. Manoj Joshi is quoting wrong example in this regard. Time and again situation in Nagaland, Manipur, J&K, etc., has been brought under control by the Army but the opportunities were squandered away by the politicians and bureaucrats.

As far as nearly 300 officers and men going to the Supreme Court is concerned, what would anyone do if even after years of retirement from the army, you get summons from a court in some remote corner of the country for actions taken by you at the cost of your life to safeguard the integrity of the nation? Perhaps, the likes of Manoj Joshi do not realize as to how and why some politicians and even the judiciary has been extra active to fix soldiers who have obeyed the orders of their superiors/GOI?

It is failure of top Army Hierarchy and above all MoD where nothing moves, and Army's view point is given least consideration. Look at the way the Raksha Mantri held scores of meetings in two months or so to take decision on opening of roads (one fails to understand why there was such urgency to deal with these matters), but issues like dealing with stone throwers and those bearing weapons against security forces gather dust! Those responsible for law and order find it rather convenient to call in the Army to do the dirty work after they have made a mess due to their lethargy/dereliction of duty.

Earlier, the civil authorities had to render a certificate that they have used all resources to maintain law and order. Now this provision has been done away with quietly. They are the same people who later sit on judgment and process complaints against officers and men for human rights violation/use of excessive force etc., who have discharged their duty in bringing normalcy. Prolonged deployment in counter insurgency/terrorist activities adversely affect the operational thinking of affected officers and men and take it away from his primary role. Though in their own country land, soldiers have to operate in hostile environment as in the affected areas the population is invariably sympathetic if not supporting the insurgents/terrorists.

Even feelings of local civil government functionaries are likely to be with those who have taken up arms. This alienates the local population from the Army, whereas the Army is meant to be protecting the same people and needs their support in times of war to safeguard their bases and lines of communications.

Constant operations against alienated citizens where it is often difficult to distinguish between friend a foe, where a woman or a child may throw a grenade or set off an IED, ensuring least collateral damage and keeping in mind highest standards of human right violations makes the task of the Army soldiers full of tension and takes its toll on the soldiers' psyche. The soldiers are trained and taught how to eliminate the enemy and not get killed. Let him be embedded with a RR company for a month and then write a similar article!

Air Cdr S N Bal

Manoj Joshi has given grounds for deep introspection by all – the Armed Forces, government and society in general, as also the media. While it is indeed true that the AFSPA (like any other law) does not grant absolute protection, it is necessary to examine several aspects connected to it. Why is the Army always called in by State Governments invoking the AFSPA – is this not tantamount to continuous (and demonstrated) failure by the civil administration in maintaining law and order? Why is the state government not held to account for such repeated failures?

While the AFSPA does provide protection to the Army in the discharge of legitimate duty as demanded by the State, it does not (and should not) accord blanket protection in cases of blatant violation of all norms and acts that are clearly established as illegal (if not actually criminal). If this were allowed, it would make the Indian Army like the Nazi SS – above all laws. A classic case in point is the action by General Dyer in 1919 – there was no valid case for what he deliberately did in Jallianwala; and the consequences were cataclysmic.

My service experience suggests that commanders are reluctant to prosecute violators – more out of a misplaced feeling of camaraderie, and for requiring to be seen as 'a good boy', and sweeping wrongdoings under the carpet. It must not be forgotten that a criminal act is a criminal act – even if done by Faujis (or anyone else for that matter). During service I had four individuals arraigned before courts martial: and secured four convictions – my stand was that an offence was unacceptable, and that the accused must be punished. A cleanup job begins at home. That earned me a lot of flak both from juniors and contemporaries as also from higher formations.

In stating that many serving and retired personnel have developed a sense of victimhood, feel that the country is not giving them their due and seek to be placed on a pedestal above the citizenry, the author has indeed stated an unpalatable degree of truth. If the military feels that it deserves to be placed on a pedestal, then that cannot be demanded, but must be established by strict adherence to the law of the land. A Fauji must never demand respect – but command it by demonstrated conduct that is unimpeachable – both in and out of uniform. Of course, in a fluid situation and in the heat of battle, excesses could well be (and sometimes are) committed. In such cases there could be valid mitigating factors, but total absolution under the AFSPA is not a valid demand. Military Law is quite capable in addressing such situations: but must be invoked.

In all countries and at all times, Civil-Military Relations are (at the very best) rather troublesome. Civil society (and government) expects the military to do a job where the government has failed (repeatedly) but are quick to pontificate from the comfort of air-conditioned offices. The bitter truth is that a Fauji is no more than a citizen who is expected to obey the law. The AFSPA accords protection in the discharge of legitimate duty – but is not a blanket cover for deliberate transgressions (without sufficient cause). Where such things happen, military law must come down with a heavy hand.

Cdr Ravindra W Pathak
It's wrong for the author to call it a trade union like activity. It is a call for justice and direction from the Supreme Court so that they do not have to face action years after retirement for doing a job they were mandated to do. The personnel have not asked for any special protection. Consider a situation where in a group of army men surrounded is by stone pelters and their life is in danger or there is threat to their limbs. Now what they wish to know is should they wait for clearance from the court to take action or take action to save their lives and face the court later.

Lt Col Mrinal Kumar Gupta Ray
It is most unfortunate in India that all kinds of comments on specialist issues on matters of defence are made more by generalists and less by defence officers, who have gone through this situation for decades and in numerable times throughout their professional lives. AFSPA situation is not a one-day new phenomenon. Armed forces are living with it from the very next day the country was born. India was born with only one problem that was Kashmir. Thereafter came Nagaland and Assam in 50s, Bengal, Bihar, Madhya Pradesh, in 70s, Punjab in 80s, Maharashtra, Chhattisgarh in 90s and continued one after another.

Who created these problems and why were these created? Not by army I am sure! Those who were responsible to provide good governance had miserably failed to provide that and sent army to wash their dirty linen. Is the army as demonic as projected by the judiciary and so-called intellectuals and human rights propagators? How many human right cases have been reported and convicted in the last over seventy years? Can there be a better example of the restrained manner in which the army operates?

I, myself, took my Battalion to Sri Lanka where the Indian army had spent about three years under most trying conditions. Casualties to Indian Army were almost 1400. One of my company officers was killed very next day. I know of an incident where a 10-year-old girl had shot an officer when the officer turned his back after seeing a huddle of women and thinking them to be harmless. But there was no retaliation. Under such gruelling situation when the LTTE was operating mixed and covered by the inseparable civilians, how many human right violation cases had been reported? Not even one. Just imagine the extent of self-restraint.

I as a human being knew the pressure one withstood in remaining within the perimeter of humanity when the provocations were plenty. On the contrary, their own government carried out genocide to get rid of LTTE. The UN and the world remained a mute spectator. World military history has unanimously hailed the Indian forces as most disciplined and professional one. It is in our own country where from leaders and so-called intellectuals – the only so-called country lovers – are making unabashed allegations against their only savior i.e. army. If the same army ever lowers their guard even for one day these people will be nowhere. Adversaries will cut them to pieces as the Mohd Ghazni or Khiljis or Mughals or British people had done. I do not say that in the army of 1.3 million all is well, but that is negligible to the proportion. Pakistan army raped and killed more than a million of their own countrymen in 9 months in their own country, East Pakistan. Indian Army went in, fought and liberated them. Not a single case of rape and murder reported.

In AFSPA, Army Act works as inbuilt corrective system. Army Act and Army Rules caters for all the situations and so worked well so far. I do not know how local police, CBI or judiciaries are coming into it? What our top brass is doing? Is there degeneration in military leadership? There is only one Chief in the million-strong army. There is no second such authoritative post. In fact, instead of 365 army personnel going to the court army top brass should have felt the pulse and taken corrective measures.

In short it appears that Mr. Joshi has found all wrong in the army. Before attributing trade unionism to the soldiers didn't stop for a while to think as to what level the frustrations and fear have permeated in the minds of these army personnel which have prompted to break all the ethos and traditions and knock the door of the highest court of the country. This has been unprecedented with far reaching consequences.

The writer even finds it objectionable as to why none of the 50 (I do not know where he got this exact figure) solders were punished! He pronounced verdict of guilty even before hearing!

Col Rajinder Kushwaha
There is a raging debate amongst military circles, whether army should be employed in Insurgency environments or it should be left free to prepare for a future conventional war? Such a question smacks of the hollowness of the understanding of emerging form of a future military conflict. Manpower heavy armies with dud weapons and ammunition, serviced by unintelligent soldiers, are the sitting ducks for the 'Designer and Customised wars 'of the future. Weapons of mass destructions (WMD) and Revolutions in Military Warfare (RMA) have changed the very concept of war in a 'Nuclear Zone'.

In the South Asia context, Hybrid war, as a major component of 'Designer War', is the only war India is going to fight in the next half a century or so. Hybrid war is what you might call insurgency/terrorism/proxy war or fifth generation warfare. It is felt, what was being done in the army was to prepare for a future military conflict in a 'nuclearized' environment. Pakistan's Full Spectrum Deterrence (FSD) is being countered by India's Cold Start Doctrine (CSD). In other words, to counter the threat of the Tactical Nuclear Weapons (TNWs) of Pakistan, as is being propounded in her FSD doctrine, India needs highly light-weight but mobile and self-sustaining mission-oriented Task Forces to bounce off the border in a short notice. This is why Indian Army has been locating her forces in the military Cantonments near the border.

The Indian Army is readying herself for a 'Designer War' of the future, which has three components: Information, Hybrid Warfare or Fifth Generation Warfare and finally Surgical Operations to further the gains of Hybrid and Information Warfare. Therefore, what is being visualised is an assessment that land battles would remain confined to border skirmishes, such as Kargil-99 or DokaLa-2017. In the same breath, The purpose of the 'designer' and 'customised', on one hand, is to soften and weaken the enemy from inside through Hybrid operations, such as militancy, terrorism and insurgency and then, on the other hand, carry out Surgical Strike through 'space and seas' to bring about the final collapse of your adversary.

Hybrid war seeks to exploit internal vulnerability of a nation through 'Irregular Soldiers', call them militants, insurgents, non-state actors, terrorists, fifth columnists and so on. 'Triggers' and 'sparks' are used in the form of support to separatist movements. This is preceded by Information Warfare to create favourable international public opinion. Therefore, it is a considered opinion that proposed changes in the army is a first step towards gearing up for a future military role which would need light weight forces to implement CSD in a FSD scenario.

In the long run, it would save the army from a 'Future Shock' which can lead to a military disaster like the manpower heavy army of Saddam Hussein of erstwhile president of Iraq. Remember, in a modern military conflict, what matters is quality and not quantity. Finally, we must also realise that we have been in a state of war since Pakistan – sponsored Azadi Movement in J&K and Khalistan Movement of Punjab.

Let us stop calling it insurgency or terrorism and then dismiss it as a law and order problem. Call it the modern conventional war, which India would have to fight. Dread the day terrorist or the separatist organisations lay their hands on TNWs. Therefore let army reorient herself.

CONCLUSION

The recent article by Manoj Joshi is most disgusting and demoralizing to the Indian soldier both serving and retired. However, the bigger question which begs an answer is, what is the price that the Army has paid for their heavy and unbroken deployment in counter insurgency warfare particularly in North East and J&K involving one third of their strength? The biggest loss is that they have become unfit for conventional warfare and not geared up to meet the complex challenges of 21st warfare like hybrid and designer wars. The time has come for the Army to stop fighting internal disturbances and counter insurgency wars created and fuelled by the enemy within the country. These must be dealt with by the PMFs under the MHA which has an equally large and capable armed force (parallel army).

The Army rest, recuperate, reorganize, reform and refocus on their basics of conventional warfare and prepare for the multifarious challenges of the 21st century. If the primary threat perception is a two/three front adversary, with one third of our force already deployed in CI Ops, how is the army/military possibly going to meet these multiple threats? The perceived threat is not to be dealt only by the Army but must be tackled as a cohesive national effort involving the three services (under RM), the PMF (under HM) and all the State Police forces. A united and integrated national effort is the imperative and inevitable need of the times. The time to make this happen is in fact the need of the hour!

Way Ahead

Conventional war is now being considered to be redundant in the Indian subcontinent. The last one was fought during the 1971 War for the liberation of Bangla Desh. Hybrid War, a part of Designer Wars (also termed as Insurgency or Proxy war or Fifth generation warfare) is the only war our Army is going to fight in the next half a century. At best, Land wars will remain confined to border skirmishes, be it against China or Pakistan.

The conventional war which Indian army was/is waiting to fight was disintegrated through Hybrid war machinations of our enemies within and without. The INTERNAL ENEMY is now more dangerous than the external enemy. Indian army must fight it with all its might.

The great Indian thinker and strategist, Chanakya and Kautilya had stated that a nation has four kinds of dangers to its existence. They are:
- One that emanates from outside and abetted by an outside;
- Two, one that emanates from outside but abetted from inside;
- Three, one that emanates from inside and abetted from inside;
- Four, and most dangerous threat is, the one that emanates from inside and abetted from outside.

According to Chanakya it is the Fourth Threat that disintegrates a nation. India is facing this 4th type of challenge, not only in J& K but in North East. The internal Maoists/Naxalite movements in Chhattisgarh, Jharkhand, MP, Bihar, Andhra and Bengal, with the active support of China, are part of this 4th and most dangerous threat!

Note: The debate was published in Fauji India Magazine, Sep2018 issue

CHAPTER 15

Into the Mind of the Generals

Col P K 'Royal' Mehrishi

1. The Nation is going through a crisis of epic proportions. At the political level, opportunistic alliances to defeat the incumbent party are a matter of unending soap opera.
   The venomous, vicious 'tukde tukde' brigade is losing no opportunity to attack the government & the security agencies particularly the Army after prompting by foreign handlers who have a stake in slowing down the strides & growth the Indian economical Juggernaut is now taking. The professionalism displayed by the Army is a cause for worry for Pakistan as nowhere in the world does an Army under constant attack by terrorists use the same small arms to hunt them down as against Pakistan, Syria, Russia who roll out the big guns including Armoured Personal Carriers (APC's) & Air power to eliminate terrorists. Indian Army does this to avoid collateral damage & wishes to avoid mass alienation of the local population. In the present scenario whom does the Nation look up to in providing a coherent vision & some semblance of order in these chaotic times? To make matters worse the valley is again on a boil due to ill advised short sighted view of mandarins in North Block.
2. Expecting politicians to understand grand strategy, relentless operations to keep the initiative, not allowing terrorists to regroup is like propping a three legged stool on two legs a sure contraption for disaster. Politicians especially in Government have an over inflated ego, like to believe they know everything but are insecure of order, meticulousness, boldness & clarity of vision. Most have grown through chaos, babble, shouting & lack of long term vision. This is where the professional General steps in. Gentle persuasion, disarming style of functioning, steely resolve & a sense of humour can bring a dyed in the wool career politician to the Operations Room asking for more. General Sunderji & FM Manekshaw excelled at this with glorious results.
3. The question being asked in the Military fraternity is, are our Generals up to it? Let us put one thing in perspective before moving to the nuts & bolts of the practically flawed selection system for higher ranks. The Indian Army

has the most copy book perfect system for selection to higher ranks. Most of the top ranking Generals have risen because of near perfect appraisals (9 on 9), ability to keep their professional views to themselves or best become verbose when there is an audience of subordinates & maintain a deathly silence in front of seniors who matter! At times one can notice robotic precision in their climbing abilities, 'A' grade on all courses, 9 points throughout in the ACR, the right courses like Senior/ Higher Command/ LDMC / NDC & Courses in Foreign Countries, phew !!. A common denominator is to always blindly follow instructions given from the top with little or no application of mind as it may tantamount to insubordination or breach of discipline thus creating a atmosphere of breeding " yes men" & gradually becoming another "yes man" oneself.

4. Grant it to the guy who has risen through thousands of course-mates, slogging on courses, managing pinks (DS Solution) for Grades, pleasing his superiors, never expressing a professionally differing opinion, a perfect clone to many like him before & after. A person of such magnificent abilities is fit to be lead into the parting of the earth if it so happens, but redemption will only come when the core constituency of a General the Junior Officers & men who execute orders on ground are in perfect sync with his thinking. When his subordinates praise him behind his back. Nearly all the Generals are fond of Military History often quoting from campaigns & lessons learnt but alas very few adapt the good qualities of speaking up to be counted when necessary to save the nation & its polity. For example General Douglas Mc Arthur the renowned American General of WW II, who could stand up to a powerful President like Harry Truman. His speech delivered in the US Congress after the war is a benchmark for clarity & die hard nationalism by a brilliant professional soldier.

5. The issue of quality (best man for the job) can easily be set right as mentioned by Maj Gen Anil Sengar in his book (Four Decades in Olive Greens – Pentagon Press New Delhi)
   - Set right the promotion policy, the root is the flawed ACR System.
   - Introduce 360 degree appraisal (the author of this article has a format developed by his efforts)
   - COAS to be accountable for promotion of Major Generals (no arbitrariness)
   - Remove the Infantry only bias in posting of Important Appointments like. MS, AG, DG MP etc
   - Army Commanders should display moral courage during promotion boards (in differing) when required.
   - Remove Pro-Rata Policy for promotions (only merit based)

6. In addition to the points already covered by the General, I have my own take on the promotion policy:-
   - Subservience displayed by any Officer any time should be "nipped in the bud".

- Honest reporting & non fudging of reports should be encouraged & recognized.
- Wide, peer group admiration & respect is a good barometer of contemporary character.
- Harp on moral courage for higher ranks, as this is one trait most required.
- Encourage plain speak, precision & execution of plans rather than long winded verbose briefs with thick documents plagiarized from old files.
- Reward innovative & creative thinking (it is always at a premium)

7. The Army & the Country is looking at our top leadership to deliver, not just to read & analyze the Army list on a daily basis to see who has fallen in the sweepstakes to make it to the next rank. Good for persons who make it because of good qualities of head & heart with a dash of soul; we need them now more than ever. We live in an imperfect Universe with flawed personalities around us. We need real leaders (A Man to Respect) as these are testing times for practical, hardnosed, tough as nails, clear headed Generals alas not for the copy book seemingly perfect ones!

Note: This article was first published by Gomantak Times, Panaji Goa on 21 Jun18 and Fauji India magazine, Jul 18 issue.

CHAPTER 16

Challenges to Value System of the Indian Army

Lt Gen NS Brar

The purpose of the profession of arms has been and will remain the management of organised violence and is inextricably linked with the ultimate question of life and death. The shared uniqueness of the profession moulds its members into the 'Brotherhood of Arms' with shared values, beliefs, standards and codes of conduct; be it the Spartans, Zulus or Samurai. Fundamental to this profession are the behavioural standards defining one's conduct which relate to a set of principles, morals, values and ideals subscribed to by the brotherhood. Values are an unwritten commitment of conduct rather than commandments for conduct. Values are an enduring belief that a way of conduct is personally or socially preferable. It drives attitudes and actions. It is taught and learnt in absolutes of 'All' or 'None' – in other words seen in black and white with little or no place for grey. The encompassing collection of such values and beliefs creates the value system which cements the covenant between the organisation – the Army – and its components – the men. In turn it creates, promotes and upholds the ethos of the Army; the spirit and inspiration contributing to the fighting power of the Army.

In essence it's the intrinsic moral component as distinct from the material or physical. The core values of the Indian Army may be summarised as

Honour – *Izzat*.
The committed word – *Vachan or Vada*.
Honesty and Integrity – *Imandari*.
Loyalty – *Wafadari* – *Namak*.
Courage – Physical and Moral.
Discipline.

The immediate question arising in relation to these values and the prevailing environment is 'Do values change with the environment?' The answer would be an emphatic 'No' with a qualifier that the changed environment may demand increased emphasis on some values but not substitute or discard any of these values. On the other hand, the manner, method and nature of war and conflict may change, the fundamental purpose of the military to manage violence in this changed conflict environment remains. Undoubtedly, conflicts and security challenges of today, increasingly driven by political and ideological ends, are more likely to produce moral strains unlike the conventional conflicts of the past.

What are the challenges to our value system? At the outset it needs to be understood that the values necessary to defend society or those fundamental to the intrinsic capability of the military have historically been and will remain at odds, if not at conflict, with the values of society itself. In our context and at the very basic level, the emphasis of society at large to reduced deference, if not indifference, to authority and discipline and enhanced awareness of individual rights with lack of corresponding obligation towards duty are at odds with what the military emphasises. The military must concentrate on the hard values and requirements of the battlefield as against the prevailing values of a liberal society like ours.

Ours is a society in deep transitional turmoil. Like the rest of society, India's military too is in the turbulent and unsettling throes of transition. The established feudal, class, cast and privilege based societal order is in the process of being transformed into an egalitarian, equitable and competition-based system. We are perhaps at the tipping point of this transition. Globalisation and economic liberalisation has thrown open opportunities and choices not only in matters of goods and services but equally in matters of jobs, vocations or professions. In a free market driven environment does one opt for the military for reasons of patriotism, a traditional calling, an entry into a way of life or simply as an economic choice relative to one's economic aspirations, capability and qualifications which may preclude other options? If this is true, and the prevailing shortage of officers suggests so, then in such an environment an individual opting for the military, both soldier and officer, would in its extreme interpretation be a mercenary. The challenge then would be to mould this 'mercenary' into one who treats the profession as a calling and willingly forms part of the brotherhood. That is where the role and the associated challenge of the relevance and reinforcement of the value system would come in. Also, under strain, and needing to be addressed, would be the cherished separateness of the military from the civilian society.

The Indian Army today is a common man's army. The elite, the privileged and the upper professional classes no longer seek a career in the military. Military rank and advancement are a means and an acknowledgement of relative social advancement. Securing a commission or even being enrolled is a step towards such advancement. Further progression adds to this advancement. This generates intense competition and a desire to excel but, and more importantly, also creates an environment of protecting self-interest, placing self before service, diluting camaraderie and perhaps indulging in what was earlier said to be 'not done' – seeking political and bureaucratic patronage for career enhancement. The average individual opting for military service from such a background also brings to the service extremes of either a rigid and stubborn resistance to injustice and graft – of this there are very few – or an attitude of accommodative acceptance of impropriety – the larger and predominant majority. All this undermines the core strength of the military which demands ethical actions which are fundamentally built on moral courage – the question of choice between right and wrong - the ability to talk straight, take a principled stand on what is right and take the path of 'harder right than the easier wrong', as such an approach is perceived to undermine the prospects of advancement. Dealing with such attitudes and behaviour needs a conscious and harsh approach. This also demands that discipline to cultivate integrity and moral courage must be emphasised at the training academies and in service. Moral courage must promote the highest values of the service – not a particular agenda, individual pride, interest or parochialism. Without courage all other attributes and capabilities are of little value as they cannot be used.

In the transitional turmoil of our society, perhaps the biggest concern is that of corruption. Our society at large is no longer resigned to its fatalistic acceptance or even accepting it as being a part of our national culture. The media being the catalyst for this awareness and resistance! In an all-pervasive environment of petty graft, seen and experienced before entering the service and when back in the environment on leave, how does a military man reconcile to the core value of 'Imandari' the profession demands? What may be a minor or non-issue on Civvy Street amounts to serious misdemeanour in the service with the consequential harsh dispensation of military justice. When viewed and weighed up against the prevailing societal standards, those dispensing military justice also tend to dilute the dispensation. Impropriety condoned or overlooked always comes home to roost. The need to uphold the values of Honesty and Integrity may need a streak of ruthlessness and may be perceived to be harsh, but when dispensed without fear or favour the purpose of the larger good and the higher objective will prevail.

Political expediency, regional aspirations, reservations and assertion of local identity has created political competition based on cast, creed and such like considerations. This is compounded by our social inheritance of the culture of patronage. This undermines the fundamental character of secularism of our constitution and fair play in our dealings. This cannot but impact our military culture of apolitical secularism and honest fair play. Within the military, parochial considerations, regional affiliations and above all misplaced regimental loyalties threaten the 'professional secularism' of the army. Regimental spirit and regimental loyalty are great strengths of our army, if misplaced they can also be a grave danger. Loyalty as a value needs to be emphasised as a higher loyalty to the Service, Constitution and the Nation and not loyalty to the immediate objective or superior authority.

Modernity militates against tradition. Tradition is an important facet of pride, self-esteem and identification with any social or organisational grouping and more so for the military or the brotherhood of arms. Tinkering with tradition in matters of uniform, drill, ceremonials, social conduct etc undermines the contribution of tradition and loosens the bonding of the brotherhood. The need to resist this tinkering is imperative.

An unspoken social contract exists between the Indian Army and the people of India. At one end of the bargain exists a deep sense of admiration, respect and intrinsic affection for the soldier. At the other end the people expect the Army to deliver when required, no matter what the demand or cost. The people believe it to be the one institution that has not been affected by the all-pervasive moral decline of Indian society. This social contract is vital for the future of the Army given the indifference or ignorance of matters military by the politico – bureaucratic combine. This contract will endure as long as the Army lives by its values of Honour, Honesty and Integrity, Loyalty and Discipline. The soldier owes it to the future of this country to abide by and honour this social contract.

In a free democratic society, unlike despot regimes backed and propped by the military, soldiering has been and will remain an occupation in honourable poverty. Any comparison with the corporate or business world in terms of lucre and the consequent lament will not alter this reality. Central to this reality will be the bedrock of honour, the poverty component being constant. Accepting this reality and reinforcing the honour component would be the way forward and will become increasingly challenging.

In the prevailing societal changes, conditioned by market driven economic considerations, what is the place for values and ethics. Contrary to popular perception the corporate and business world too lays emphasis on its values and ethics. Fundamental to any corporate culture are the values embedded within the organisation, both extrinsic and intrinsic. There is increasing talk of 'business ethics and values'. The Tatas are a very pertinent example of corporate success based on very high standards of business ethics and refusal to indulge in graft. Values remain relevant in any environment.

What then is the approach to the challenges posed by the emerging environment and how will military values be defined to cope with this environment? Experiences of other militaries in somewhat similar circumstances are relevant. The British Empire, perhaps the greatest the world has ever seen, was made possible by the Royal Navy which ruled the waves worldwide enabling the British to project power around the world and secure its connections. The sailor who manned this navy was forcibly press ganged from the slums of the industrial towns and ports of England and then whipped into shape to man the empire winning navy. Churchill called it 'Rum, Buggery and the Lash'. The British Army which gained and held this empire similarly found its manpower from the lowest rungs of society. The Duke of Wellington called them the scum of the earth. Yet the Royal Navy and the Army created that winning ethos in their service which created and held the Empire.

At the end of the Vietnam War the US military had fallen to its lowest in terms of self-esteem, public acceptance and ethical standards. American society itself was in turmoil on issues of civil rights, segregation, anti-war pacification, women's lib etc. The officer corps collectively conscious of the need to self-correct, set into motion self-regulating measures to cleanse the system. By the time of the Gulf War it had reinvented itself. The transition came from within.

These two examples are cited to emphasise the fact that the prevalent challenges have to be met from within.

The most critical challenge to our value system today comes from the erosion of Discipline - in all its facets, and declining standards of Honesty and Integrity – probity in service life. The redeeming feature is the inbuilt ethos of the Army to discipline itself and the legal framework of the service to enforce discipline. It similarly provides for ensuring probity. What is required is the will at all levels of leadership to meet these concerns.

Very seldom does a democracy give preference and primacy to the military. The prevailing environment hits at the roots and remains at conflict with the military's value system. In our context, our institutional identity appears to be unable to cope with the changing environment. Where then do we stand as an organisation and as individuals and how do we meet the challenge. Organisationally, relevance can be gained and maintained by acquiring the moral high ground created by professional and ethical conduct driven by adherence to our core values. Such moral high ground once secured will need to be defended and the interest of the service promoted, if need be by staking one's career. The onus on this count lies on the senior leadership. At the individual plane the need is for the practice of value-based leadership to face the challenges of today. Gentlemanly behaviour and soldierly conduct. After all, we invented phrases such as "officer-like conduct" and "an officer and a gentleman". The British have coined the terminology 'Officership'. Simply put it is leadership by example. Colonel Nicholson (Sir Alec Guinness) in the movie *Bridge on the River Kwai* instantly comes to mind. As individuals, the correct ethical choices may often be against the grain of the attitudes and approach of the larger component. Individual strength of character would then be the compass to steer the right course. In this context two quotes come to mind. The first from Robert Frost

Two roads diverged in a wood, and I .... I took the road less travelled by, and that has made all the difference.

And Mahatma Gandhi's favourite

Jodi Tor DakShune Keu Na Ase Tobe Ekla Cholo Re, Ekla Chalo Re...

If no one responds to your call, then go your own way alone, walk alone, walk alone. (Rabindranath Tagore)

SECTION 4

FORCE OPTIMIZATION FOR STRATEGIC CHALLENGES

CHAPTER 17

Debate: Revival of 'Air Cavalry' Concept by Indian Army

Compiled by Col Vinay B Dalvi

The Indian Army has tested in the desert terrain of Rajasthan the military concept of 'Air Cavalry' that was used by the US Army to locate and assault enemy ground forces during the Vietnam War. This being with an eye on the future, which is focusing on strengthening its combative air assets by procuring attack helicopters. Under the 'Air Cavalry' concept, attack helicopters are fully integrated with tanks and mechanized ground forces.

Background & Trigger

PTI release of 13 May18 about Indian Army's testing 'Air Cavalry' Concept revived a four decade-old philosophy of employment of Air Cavalry in close/intimate operations between armed helicopters and troops on the ground (tanks, APCs, infantry). In fact, the case for Army Aviation Corps in 1975-76 was justified on this basis through a convincing video from foreign sources showing close cooperation and fire support by helicopters to troops on the ground, to emphasis the need for Army Aviation to the defence ministry.

It is ironic, that after 40 long years the recent trial has made headlines for this subject of critical importance and underlines our priorities in military decision making. Decades seem to have been wasted in 'in-fighting' between Army and IAF, as to who should own armed helicopters!

Highlights & Characteristics of Air Cavalry

This concept is being tried and executed by the Indian Army, with an eye on the future, which is focusing on strengthening its combative air assets by procuring attack helicopters. Under the 'Air Cavalry' concept, attack helicopters are fully integrated with tanks and mechanized ground forces. To enhance its defence capabilities, the Army tested the concept under which weaponised helicopters carry out combined action against the enemy in coordination with tanks and mechanized ground forces.

This is a new concept for the Indian Army and it is aimed at reshaping land battle by defeating the enemy by offensive punch from the air in coordination with tanks on the ground. The concept was implemented after a detailed deliberation, sand-model discussions and war gaming. In normal battle scenario, attack helicopters are called in on requirement basis by forces moving on the ground to launch an attack where the ground forces are not able to neutralize the target due to many reasons, including difficult terrain. Under the 'Air Cavalry' concept, attack helicopters are fully integrated with tanks and mechanized ground forces. A fleet of armed helicopters simultaneously flies in air and performs a number of tasks, including troop insertion in forward areas, on the spot aerial recce, launching attacks and it proves more powerful and a good speed in the action is achieved.

An Army chopper during the 'Vijay Prahar' military exercise at the Mahajan Field Firing Range near Bikaner in Rajasthan (PTI Photo)

This requires a very high degree of precision, coordination and continuous up gradation. It saves time and energy. The forces achieve more flexibility and fluidity in an operation and multitasking can be performed more quickly, swiftly and effectively and the ground commanders can act decisively, boldly and offensively.

Under this kind of arrangement, attack helicopters can engage targets in the shortest possible time and the mission can be accomplished in a very flexible and effective manner. This concept can be executed in different kind of terrains depending upon the feasibility. While the US used this concept in the jungles of Vietnam during the war from 1954-75, India tested it in scorching heat in desert terrain to sharpen its teeth. The Army is gradually inducting helicopters equipped with ultra-modern sensors and high-precision weapons and therefore a need was felt to use the "Air Cavalry" concept for increasing capabilities in monitoring and protecting both eastern and western borders of the country.

RESPONSES FROM VETERANS

Lt Gen Harbhajan Singh

Air Cavalry Assault could be possible in an asymmetrical situation. Against a better or equally equipped enemy, a surprise operation like the surgical strikes or attacking a bridge / communication center could be possible. Great deliberation needs to be exercised trying such an assault against a well-trained and equipped adversary. Lessons of Battle of Arnhem in WWII (Movie: A BRIDGE TOO FAR) should be kept in mind while planning any such venture.

As part of a large offensive:
- Complete air superiority is a pre requisite. This would require very close coordination with the air force and feasibility of achieving local air superiority ensured.
- Such intimate coordination with the Indian Air Force is difficult to achieve when the three services do not have a unified command.

- Suppression of 'anti-air fire' from the enemy's ground forces is difficult. Proliferation of shoulder fired anti-air missiles in addition to other weapons available to the enemy's ground Forces has made helicopters highly vulnerable to ground fire.

Another important aspect is Electronic Warfare. Both sides having AWACS, radars, drones, satellites, it would be very difficult to avoid detection of use of large number of helicopters against an equally well equipped enemy.

Electronic Warfare will play a very important role in jamming/fooling enemy's early warning assets. Again, this would require very close coordination between the IAF and the Army, which has not been buttoned up so far or discussed on paper only perhaps. Helicopters in an Air Cavalry assault are likely to suffer high attrition due to above mentioned threats.

It is easy to plan such operations on a sand model or controlled exercise. In actual war, when pitched against a better or similarly equipped enemy, all above aspects will become reality and possibility of success of such operations will have to be weighed up realistically. On the positive side any offensive thinking is a good sign for Indian Army, which has got bogged down in anti-terrorist operations and guarding every inch of very long borders, in a bunker syndrome.

Maj Gen Anil Sengar
This has been long discussed; to get it going is the need of the hour. In plains sector, where the terrain is getting more urbanized, there will be limited maneuvering space, and the so called the methodology of heavy breakthrough, that is fighting your way through, the attack helicopters will be of immense use in breaking through the areas where mechanized elements are operating. One Attack Helicopter (AH) in the air, skillfully operated will be a force-multiplier.

While this sounds good, there are issues such as safety and logistics of AH launch pads is critical, as in the present day battlefield transparency and the ability of the adversary to destroy these AH bases, a detailed thinking through is required. Peace time lessons need to be understood in the operational environment. In exercise, all assets of the formation, vehicles, manpower, etc., which have some other jobs, are employed in making such facilitates functional. They will not be available in war as they have other jobs. So there is a need to look at it with a fine comb in all its dimensions. The theory is fine, implementation – budget, manpower; vehicles etc are still a grey area.

Col Pradeep Dalvi
Air Cavalry is a must and has been delayed for a really long time. Mechanised Forces need to have Air Cavalry integrated down to CG/CC level. It will add real teeth to the mechanized forces not only in desert terrain but obstacle ridden terrain of Punjab and Rajasthan. We need to produce utility, attack; missiles based helicopters to special ground operations. I have been given to understand that the Army is looking at raising more mechanized units in near future for

terrain based on ORT and semi desert. Air Cavalry as resource should be with Army. There should no fight/debate over it.

Gp Capt T P Srivastava

Until the Indian military, past and present, gets out of the 'ownership syndrome', we are not going anywhere. Indian military leadership (Officers) is shy of propagating the concept of 'mutual inter dependence'. 'Ownership' and successful and pragmatic employment are two entirely different issues.

"Firstly the Air Cavalry concept is not a new and original thinking of recent origin. Way back in 1981 a US Army officer, a student of 37th DSSC, made a presentation on the issue. That was in 1981. Incidentally US and NATO forces no longer advocate this option.

Secondly, the AD environment in TBA has undergone a total metamorphosis and has completely changed due to the advent of shoulder launch SAMs, having a kill range from 500 metre to 4.5 Km. In some case far boundary touches up to 8 km. Hence the Air Cavalry elements, irrespective of who 'owns'/'operates' these, will suffer huge casualties. A 15 kg launcher with four SAMs being carried by the duo has changed the risk in TBA.

Thirdly, the fire power required to knock out/cripple a marauding Armd Division during the break out phase will involve employment of Air Cav elements over a wide frontage.

Fourthly, random attack/armed Heptr strikes coupled with strike fighters with CBUs will give disproportionate and favourable results with minimum casualties to own elements.

Fifthly, I must mention that NATO is actively practicing the concept of lifting, may be dozen two men teams equipped with shoulder launched SAMs by heptrs to TBA, where an air threat is expected. I reiterate that AD environment in TBA has made Air Cav employment and Bn GP Drop etc totally redundant. Indeed if we must learn from our own experience, we must practice it in actual war and regret it later in form of lessons learnt from Indo-Pak Conflict 2020. Total/complete air superiority is a term that is consigned to military text books on air warfare. Total/complete air superiority is unachievable by the mightiest air forces.

Rear Admiral Vineet Bakhshi

Air Cavalry: Obsolete in the twenty first century

> "Cannon to right of them, Cannon to left of them,
> Cannon behind them Volleyed and thundered;
> Stormed at with shot and shell, While horse and hero fell.
> They that had fought so well
> Came through the jaws of Death,
> Back from the mouth of hell,
> All that was left of them, Left of six hundred."
> – From Charge of the Light Brigade, by Alfred Tennyson

The 'Charge' took place in 1854, and was mowed down by technology in the form of Artillery. 170 years later, we seem to become suckers for the Western arms industry, who wish to sell us obsolete systems to keep their factories, and therefore employment, ticking. Today, the shoulder fired missiles, short range vehicle mounted missiles, close support radar and laser controlled guns, and quite possibly in the near future energy weapons like high intensity lasers will make the Air Cavalry a Turkey shoot. The way ahead is the technology of armed drones, with standoff 10 km range missiles. Armed helicopters could only be used in well sanitized areas. The Russians learnt a bitter lesson in Afghanistan 3 decades ago, where their air assets became redundant, once and the Stinger missile was introduced. It became the turning point of the war in 1986. But where is our R&D in this vital area of drone development? As far as Air Cavalry using helicopters is concerned, it's obsolete.

Some Highlights

Air cavalry operations are not a new phenomenon in the world. The US Army successfully used this complex form of combined operations, when 'soldiers in the sky reshaped combat on the ground' in the 1960s in Vietnam. The raising of the 1st Cavalry Division (Airmobile), comprising 15,000 men during 1965 gave flight to the US Air Cavalry Concept when the 1st Cavalry Division was incorporated in the US Army force structure. The Division had its own Infantry, Artillery, logistics and other division support capabilities including own aviation assets assigned to the Division to provide aerial reconnaissance, troop transport, air rocket artillery fire support and logistical transport. It integrated attack, transport and observation aircraft with the fighting elements of the Division. The 'combat air assault' was the zenith of the attack phase of air mobility.

In the Indian context, the air cavalry concept is not new and has been advocated by our military thinkers in the past to gain tactical victory over our adversary in the critical and complex battlefield zones/sectors. This form of operations demands 'great battlefield innovations' with a high degree of specialized training and effective integration of all the key air and ground forces with adequate development of Army's Air Land Battle doctrine. The multiple challenges of 21st century demand the creation of several independent Air Cavalry Divisions and Brigades to improve the cutting edge over our multiple adversaries on our long borders and vast frontiers comprising hostile desert, jungle and rugged mountainous terrain.

A word of caution! How prepared are we actually for this form of operations? Do we really have the entire where withal, backup and inter service integration for it? The views of Rear Admiral Vineet Bakhshi highlight the inherent dangers in this form of operations and expose the hidden agenda of the 'western arms lobby'. The Russian example, where their air assets became redundant in Afghanistan, three decades back due to the introduction of the deadly Stinger missile and consequent Russian withdrawal in 1986 are glaring examples that cannot be ignored and must be analysed for the lessons we should draw from it before venturing into this deadly form of operations and even possible western arms industry/lobby trap!

CONCLUSION

Gp Capt Johnson Chacko

Principles/doctrines governing employment of Air Power and land power are different. Air Cavalry combines the two. A Mechanised Infantry/Armoured Officer may need to unlearn some aspects that have been ingrained in him and learn principles of application of air power to exploit the concept fully and not many can do it at that stage. They need to be groomed from Lt Stage itself. An Armoured Corps officer is considered to be extremely flexible in his concept of operations. An Air Cavalry officer needs to be 10 times more flexible than that, I guess. Army ethos does not provide him that luxury.

If it can be operationalized it will be a good thing for an advancing thrust. It may not do much for operations in depth unless territory is captured and link up takes place. I must admit that I don't have in depth knowledge of Army operations and this opinion is based on my memory of interaction in DSSC where I was a DS. The induction of man portable shoulder fired SAMs will wipe out the air cavalry before it can be brought to bear on the battle field. It will be an extremely expensive affair in terms of operational costs and losses.

The tone for propagating such a concept appears to be for ownership of air assets by the Army rather than the operational benefits that can be derived from air cavalry. The objective needs to be achieved, it does not matter who achieves it.

This has been elaborated in the suggested Indian military doctrine at *http://www.indiandefencereview.com/news/indian-military-doctrine-an-analysis/*

The implementation of the concept was done by the US during Vietnam War.

The account of it is at *http://www.historynet.com/air-cav-how-soldiers-in-the-sky-reshaped-combat-on-theground.htm*

Selective quotes may misguide the decision makers. A comprehensive analysis needs to be carried out before clamoring for implementation of this concept. The US appears to have learnt lessons the hard way or else these Divisions would have been in existence today in the US or NATO. Our officers do Staff College in the US. May check with them as to why this concept has not been implemented by the US Army. We need to learn lessons from those who can afford to try it in combat rather than learn lessons the hard way. We need to optimize our resources so that necessary military power can be brought to bear in time and space without being concerned about who "owns/operates" the asset.

CHAPTER 18

Paramilitary Forces Need Restructuring, Merger and Consolidation

Maj Gen VK Madhok

It is essential that Paramilitary Forces (PMF) is so organised, trained and equipped, that they are in a position to convert to an active operational role at the outbreak of hostilities when placed under the Army. Those forces which are meant for internal security and restoration of law and order should come under the Ministry of Home Affairs and should have a police orientation. In this category will fall the Assam rifles, CRPF, RPF, CISF, Home Guards and the India Reserve Battalions. Maximum use of Ex-Servicemen should be made by employing them in the PMF.

A tax payer is puzzled at the scale and range of our 10 lakh or so Para Military Forces (PMF) – the 4th largest in the world. Though an indispensible requirement, these continue to proliferate at an unrealistic and unimaginable pace. I believe, a decision was taken few years ago to further recruit another 1.23 lakh personnel (nearly 123 Battalions). This would take the strength of central forces to nearly 11 lakhs – more or less equivalent to the regular Army's.

Therefore, crucial questions arise. Why can't we merge those forces which are performing the same tasks? What are the major disadvantages of multiplicity and why have the NSA and the NSC not rationalize this situation? Do we need these forces at this scale when finally, for instance, after Dantewada incident in 2010 (75 jawans of CRPF killed by Maoists), we are still wanting the Army and are now going to recruit Ex Servicemen for the tasks. If that be so, then the PMF need a serious look and total restructuring.

Today, India has 15-16 types of PMFs: CRPF, BSF, NSG, ITBP, CISF, DSC, Assam Rifles, RPF, SSB, India Reserve Battalions, and some more outfits like the Command Battalions for Resolute Action (COBRA), a commando force of nearly 10,000 personnel organised on the lines of Grey Hounds in AP. All this, in addition to the Territorial Army, Rashtriya Rifles and a Garud Force, that the IAF has been planning to raise for defence of airfields and the Army. So the question is, what are we trying to achieve?

A number of proposals are still pending with the government which when implemented, would increase the expenditure. India Reserve Battalions to get 35,000 personnel (sanctioned in Dec 2007). Assam Rifles to get 26 additional Battalions (sanctioned Jan2010), ITBP to get an additional Battalion for NBC warfare and disaster management, CRPF to get 13 additional Battalions for anti-Naxalite operations (sanctioned Jan 2008). That is not all: CRPF has created its own Spy Wing (sanctioned in February 2005). It wants to set up a Disaster Management Institute at Latur, Maharashtra (cost Rs. 100 crore). It wants more institutes: An Internal Security Academy at Mt Abu, an all India Police Academy, an OTS and a recruit training institute (sanctioned Nov 2006).

Now there is a proposal to bifurcate the CRPF, one half to deal with soft targets and the other for dealing with hard targets. RPF is to raise a women's battalion and awaits hi-tech equipment for nearly 100 crores (sanctioned in Oct 2008). ITBP has three training institutes and wants two more and a satellite facility. One can go on and on with the list of demands of each PMF. There cannot be any disagreement on the issue, that when war breaks out, there are many peace time duties mostly of a police nature which are required to be carried out at the border.

Prevention of Smuggling, protection of check posts, patrolling, safeguarding of installations close to the border as well as protection of bridges, railway lines or even tackling dacoits, are just a few of these. If the Army was to undertake such tasks, then it would need two types of units: one for police duties during peace and the other for military operations during war. This would weaken the Army. Accordingly, the PMF are required for protection of the border in peace as well as to restore law and order within the country when the police fail to do so.

The roles of PMF have however been enlarged to include protection of industrial and administrative establishments which are of national importance (by CISF), protection of railways (by RPF), the environment and development of construction work in inaccessible areas like building of roads in northern borders (by BRO) and so on. Most of these PMFs are organised on the Army pattern but do not come under the Army or the Army Act. They carry light weapons and follow separate chains of command, except in sensitive areas like J&K where even during peace, PMF deployed at the LoC are placed under Army's operational command.

It is essential that PMF are so organised, trained and equipped, that they are in a position to convert to an active operational role at the outbreak of hostilities when placed under the Army. This is generally the pattern followed all over the world. No reason why it should not be followed in India. In the last few years or so, a variety of PMF have sprung up. Some raised in a hurry, like the ITBP after the Sino-Indian agreement on trade was signed in 1954. Its task was to provide protection to the border check posts on the Indo-Tibetan border, as the Army was not in a position to spare troops.

After 1962, the ITBP was expanded to operate as a guerrilla force. Its role has since been brought at par with the BSF, raised in 1965. Therefore, a force which should have either merged with the BSF or dispensed with has now acquired a separate identity. In March 2008, a decision was taken to raise 13 additional Battalions to be deployed on the Sino-Indian border. It is also raising a women's Battalion (commando) to be deployed at Natu La in Sikkim, to frisk traders and for protection of VIPs even at Rashtrapati Bhavan.

Multiplicity of forces means a separate Director General and the connected hierarchical structure for each PMF, separate training establishments, separate budget and rules and regulations for service and recruitment and a distinct chain of command under separate ministries. Further, each PMF wants more units, more funds, more officers, better accommodation and weapons and additional transport to perform its tasks. The bureaucracy and ministries under whose control these function, in turn feel justified to get such recommendations through.

As a result, fragmentation of effort and competition with each other for narrow interests cannot be avoided. Assam Rifles, a 31 Battalion force is now raising another 31 Battalions for the Indo-Myanmar border. The raising of each Battalion costs 10-12 crores. Besides, led by regular officers, the Army will find it difficult to provide them officers in view of its own shortage of nearly 50% against its authorization. There are sufficient examples to show that similar tasks are being performed by different PMF. For instance; the ITBP, BSF or the Assam Rifles, but on different channels! In an operational sector controlled by the Army, one may find the BSF, Assam Rifles or the ITBP units deployed side by side in addition to the regular Army units at the international border.

Or there may be Village Guards, CRPF or a medley of state and central intelligence agencies. Besides, there is the DSC for providing protection and security cover to the Army, Navy and IAF installations and Ordnance Depots; CISF for providing security cover to Public Sector Undertakings, BRO for developing road communications in remote areas and RPF for providing security cover to the railways. Now, the issue is that when the NSC became functional and an NSA was appointed, their first important task should have been whether India can afford the luxury or having such a large number of PMF? Further, multiplicity of PMF has created the most serious problem – lack of coordination!

If these forces are to support the Army besides taking on the first shock at the border, then a number of important issues need looking into: their equipment, officer cadre and its age group (an older Colonel will not be in a position to handle stressful assignments at the border) and training. India's current and future security environment requires the conversion of resources to a war time machine in the shortest possible time. Assam Rifles and the Rashtriya Rifles are the only PMF whose units can be treated at par with regular army units except that they do not carry heavy weapons.

The remaining PMF have police officers except the BSF which has a sprinkling of army officers. Units with a police orientation meant for dealing with law and order situations cannot be expected to operate in battlefield conditions. An interesting situation arises when along a single line of communication, say Tezpur-Towang, road in 4 Corps area, a number of PMF units are maintained with each force having its own transit camp, check posts, transport columns, even a small hospital and block timings to move. Therefore, departmental battles at Delhi, duplication of command and control channels has indeed led to unhealthy rivalries between the Army and the PMFs.

In most foreign countries, PMF are designed for employment in four distinct areas: a border defence or a police force patterned on an army culture; a police oriented internal security force; an organisation for training the youth; and a 'People's Militia' to help expand armed forces in an emergency. What stops India from following this concept? Take Russia's example, on which we are dependent for supply of nearly 80% of equipment and weapons for our armed forces. They have Frontier Guards to protect the border which touches nearly a dozen or so countries. When an independent unit of Frontier Guards is located in the same area as army garrison, the former is grouped with it.

Why not in India? As regards internal security forces, their basic training is akin to the Army's. The integration of these PMF with regular forces is far easier. China has its 'Public Security' forces, a people's militia, a protection and construction corps and local forces. Notice; the diversity is minimal and this, their pattern has emerged after trial and error and of course past experience. In both cases, the Border Guards are so designed that they can take the first shock.

The recruitment of their officers, equipment, and state of training are more or less on the army lines. Russia's Frontier Guards are headed by a senior General from the army. We, in India, can take a cue from foreign countries as we can ill afford to have such a large variety of PMF especially where the tasks are duplicated. Accordingly, a national policy should be evolved after reviewing the entire structure of PMF including their equipment, training, officer cadre and the need for quick interaction with the armed forces. The concept evolved would need to keep certain broad principles in view, summarized in the following paragraphs:

Those PMF whose purpose is to guard the international border during peace and which are currently deployed for this purpose should be merged and re-designated as 'Border Guards'. In this category fall the BSF, Coast Guard, ITBP and the state armed police. These forces would need an army orientation except for the Coast Guard, who are meant for the Navy. Each force should be commanded by a senior service officer. The recruitment should be based on the service pattern. The entire PMF should have a single code of conduct and one set of regulations. While it should be primarily officered by regular officers on deputation, its own corps of officers should be recruited on the army pattern.

Above all, this force should come under the Ministry of Defence and not the Ministry of Home Affairs.

Those forces which are meant for internal security and restoration of law and order should come under the Ministry of Home Affairs and should have a police orientation. In this category will fall the Assam rifles, CRPF, RPF, CISF, Home Guards and the India Reserve Battalions. Various land armies like those in Karnataka and Rashtriya Rifles should also be included in the internal security force. The Village and Home Guards should be merged with the TA. This leaves the NSG and SPG at the disposal of the Centre, while the states will have their police and SAP to look after law and order problems specifically related to the states.

Finally, after restructuring, besides the three services, India will have the Border Guards under the Ministry of Defence, an internal security force under the Ministry of Home Affairs, TA – the citizen's volunteer militia to help the armed forces expand immediately at the commencement of hostilities and to relieve them from static duties. BRO for construction purposes in remote areas and the NCC for training the youth. Maximum use of Ex-Servicemen should be made by employing them in the PMF. This is a workable concept in which there can be minor differences of opinion. Obviously, this concept would draw flak from the existing hierarchies of PMF and the bureaucracy due to resistance to change. But unless we take action now, the PMF would continue to proliferate at the tax payer's cost.

To sum up, India is in the thick of terrorism. Multiplicity and resultant lack of coordination are an obstacle and a serious handicap in tackling it. This aspect is slowly but surely dawning on our government. And therefore, we are now asking for the Army to counter it. I am suggesting to the Honourable Prime Minister to consider restructuring the PMF and to tame this monster we have created. Further, the people of India heed to be involved in tackling terrorism. And this can best be done by expanding the Territorial Army (TA).

CONCLUSION

We have created a Monster in the shape of the 4th largest PMF in the world, which are making a big hole in the tax payer's pocket. There is a crucial need to reorganize these. All we need is a Border Security Force and Internal Security Force, TA (Citizen's Militia), NCC and a BRO. It is ardently proposed to the PM to get a detailed briefing from the three Chiefs, Director Generals of PMF, the Home Minister, NSA and so on to take a final call on this proposal.

CHAPTER 19

India's Stakes in a Two-Front War – Analysis

Maj Gen V K Madhok

Currently, India does not have the initiative and is not in a position to simultaneously engage both its adversaries. It doesn't have the intentions, or the resources, nor the political and military will, or the leadership to do so. Paradoxically, both China and Pakistan (combined) have the resources, reasons and will to do so. And as such, the initiative rests with them. Can they do so? The answer is yes. But 'will they do so?' is a million dollar question.

Recently, free and vague talks besides conversations have been doing the rounds regarding the possible involvement of India in a two-front war against China and Pakistan. Nevertheless, the issue is serious and important, and cannot be wished away.

This missive attempts to cautiously deliberate and explore the following questions before drawing worthwhile conclusions. The questions are – can India get involved in a two-front war? And if so, in what capacity? Does our defence policy cater for such a situation? Are we prepared for it? Or, have we taken it for granted that such a situation won't arise? Have our two adversaries the resources and intentions to take this initiative? In which case, what will be their strategic aim, objectives, and targets? Has such a situation risen in the past? Should China and Pakistan take the initiative and India is caught unawares, what could be the scenario? Or, can India take the initiative to engage both our adversaries or will have to contend only with a defensive or offensive-defence posture? Will any reorganization be necessary and possible to counter such a threat?

Currently, India does not have the initiative and is not in a position to simultaneously engage both its adversaries. It doesn't have the intentions, or the resources, nor the political and military will, or the leadership to do so. Neither does the Ministry of Defence visualize such a situation. In fact, we don't have a defence policy. And if there is one, the nation has a right to know it. Paradoxically, both China and Pakistan (combined), have the resources, reasons and will to do so. And as such, the initiative rests with them. Can they do so? The answer is yes. But 'will they do so?' is a million dollar question.

Their strategy aim, objectives, and targets can be spelt out with great precision if they take such recourse. But that is the task for the RAW and IB, who failed miserably in 1962 and the Kargil conflict, and even while forecasting Sheikh Mujibur Rehman and his family's assassination after a military coup was concerned, or for that matter, the assassinations of Indira Gandhi or Rajiv Gandhi.

Was such a contingency visualized earlier on? Take 1971's thirteen day Indo-Pak conflict from 4th December 1971 to 16th December 1971 as an example. When India nearly got involved in a three-front war, i.e. against China, East Pakistan and West Pakistan! Possibility of Chinese intervention was catered for. When India launched operations against East Pakistan and also in the West, it was a risk which paid off. In the West, Lt Gen Candeth, GOC-in-C, Western Command had 11 Divisions, Armoured Divisions, 4 Independent Armoured Brigades, and 3 Artillery and Engineer Brigades, but we fared poorly at great cost to the country. If China, which wanted and still wants a unified Pakistan, had intervened, the scenario would have been different.

If at all, in the next ten years or so, should India be in a position to engage our two adversaries simultaneously, it must never be done. History teaches us about many such instances when a nation failed after indulging in a two-front war. Take Hitler's invasion of Russia 129 years after Napoleon's invasion. After conquering Europe, and still engaged in Africa, Hitler invaded Russia. His forces included 134 Divisions at full strength, 600000 vehicles and 700000 horses, the largest force at that time. But it ended in a disaster – loss of 800000 troops, and Hitler's demise.

What conclusions can we draw from this very brief dissertation is that; China and Pakistan are in a position to jointly invade and cross our borders. India is only in a position to defend itself. But even to do so, some very hard work will be necessary. Some recommendations have been made for our strategic planners:

- India must have an articulate defense policy which is periodically updated.
- Our paramilitary forces must be reorganized, preferably into an internal security force, Border Security Force, TA, and NCC.
- Our Border roads and logistic infrastructures need a major effort and consideration to enable the Armed Forces to move, live and fight.
- Territorial Army must be expanded from its current strength of 40000 to 50000, to at least 1,00,00,000.
- Indigenization needs a major push. We should institute an indigenization council instead of just an acquisition committee for our arms and equipment.
- Reorganize our command structure into two theatre commands – one each for the East against China, and the second one against Pakistan. Both under the command of a full General officer respectively. In which case, India will need a CDS.

- There's a need to conduct exercises against a two-front invasion and our defensive posture to counter it.
- Our intelligence agencies have fared poorly in the past, and they must be monitored and specific questions must be set for them, concerning our adversaries and their intentions.
- Our reservist system specially regarding the officer corps, is nonfunctional. It must be activated. Our senior combat leaders must study those campaigns which ended in disaster, as they have much to teach. Besides, they should also read thoughts on the Art of War, by original military thinkers.
- There is an urgent need to make up officer shortages.
- Students from colleges and training institutions must be encouraged to see our borders.
- We should practice and create wherewithal to move or lift at least a division from one sector to another, when such a contingency for additional troops arises.
- Our military training institutions must make the students familiar with the organizations of Chinese and Pakistani military, and their doctrines.
- Finally, we may have to think of allies in case of a combined invasion by Pakistan and China.

These are but a few brief suggestions. But there are many, many more recommendations which can only be made by the Armed Forces HQ themselves.

CHAPTER 20

Prepare for Three-Front War: India's Security Imperative in 21ST Century! – Possible Scenario

Col Rajinder Kushwaha

Centuries back, great Indian thinker-cum-administrator, 'Chanakya', had listed four dangers to national security. They were: one, emanating from outside and abetted from outside; two, emanating from inside and abetted from inside; three, emanating from outside and abetted from inside; lastly, emanating from inside and abetted from outside. He had also cautioned that a threat emanating from inside and abetted from outside was the most dangerous threat for the integrity of a state. Time has come for India to upgrade her security apparatus to be able to cope concurrently with this three-way pincer.

The security environments of India have undergone diabolic changes in the recent past. As India marches further into the 21st century, it is becoming abundantly clear that threat to her integrity and sovereignty rises from three adversaries, i.e. internal foe in the form of raging insurgencies, inclusive of North East, J&K and Maoists/Naxalite militancy; external foes on the Western and Northern borders. The threat becomes more serious when we consider that all three have begun to seek coordination and mutual support against their common enemy, called India. It becomes imperative for India to develop abilities to face all three adversaries simultaneously and concurrently. And this has to be developed as early as possible as India would enter a major security minefield after 2020. Time is running out for Indian defence planners.

Maoist attacks in Madhya Pradesh, Chhattisgarh and Jharkhand in the recent years provide ample proof of seriousness of the threat arising out of internal foes. It is no doubt they are trained and equipped by India's Northern and Western adversaries. There is enough evidence available of Chinese and ISI connection. Therefore India has to take peace overtures from China and Pakistan with pinch of Salt. Pakistan sees its Jihadis as 'strategic assets' against India.

China's aggressive posture towards India at Dokalam and her hectic activities of 'string of pearls' policy in the Indian ocean, rail-road construction in the Tibet Autonomous Region (TAR) along with positioning of its troops in the FCNA of Pakistan, some two years back, is a sure indicator of her future intentions about India. On April 15, 2013, some 50 PLA troops had intruded into Indian Territory, up to 19 KMs in Daulat Beg Oldi (DBO) Sector of Ladakh and established a tented camp. This was clear provocation and not a friendly act. Though the matter was resolved amicably, it was at a great cost to India, where she had to accept Chinese terms to dismantle Indian look-out post in Chumar.

If one adds to this macabre high-handedness of China, the unfolding schism of Pakistan's military and the poisonous fangs of Maoism/Naxalite violence, now biting 240 districts of 20 Indian states, one finds a classic script for India's planned disintegration by her internal and external foes. Yes, India is likely to be under siege by her internal and external foes, in the ensuing decade.

Read all this in conjunction with an article that appeared in the year 2009 in 'Global Times', an English language Chinese official internet news portal. The article had sought to break up India into 20-30 smaller states to remove India as an impediment to China's global ambitions. It suits the Pakistani military and her Generals, who see a united India, as a potential threat to their rule in Pakistan.

It also suits the sectarian interests of some self-styled guardians of India's poor i.e. tribal, rural and urban, all included. Indian history is full of instances of traitors like Jai Chand, who joined hands with Mohammed Gori against Prithvi Raj Chohan; King Ambhi of Taxila, who sided with Alexander against King Porus and 'Mir Jaffar', who betrayed Nawab Sirajudaula and helped Lord Clive. Do not forget the role of Sikh Generals, Lal Singh and Tez Singh in the first Anglo-Sikh war of 1846? In modern times, they masquerade as Koteshwar Rao, Kishenji and Ganpati or even as Paresh Barua, Syed Gillani, Dawood Ibrahim and Wadhava Singh. Defence and strategic planners in India cannot view these internal mascots of danger, separately or in isolation. Thus, a 'three-pronged' danger to national security emanates in unison from inside and outside.

Centuries back, great Indian thinker-cum-administrator, 'Chanakya', had listed four dangers to national security. They were: one, emanating from outside and abetted from outside; two, emanating from inside and abetted from inside; three, emanating from outside and abetted from inside; lastly, emanating from inside and abetted from outside. He had also cautioned that a threat emanating from inside and abetted from outside was the most dangerous threat for the integrity of a state. Time has come for India to upgrade her security apparatus to be able to cope concurrently with this three way pincer.

In all assessments, the threat to Indian security from China is considered paramount. China had been following a policy of encirclement of India both by sea and land. Its 'string of pearls' spreads from Gwadar in Pakistan, through Hamanbantota in Sri Lanka to deep water port at Sittwe in Myanmar. Her rising interests in Bay of Bengal explain the Dokalam crisis of June-July 2017. Her One Belt One Road (OBOR) or CPEC/CMEC (China Pakistan Economic Corridor/

China Myanmar Economic Corridor) projects to link up by road with Gwadar (Pakistan) on the Persian Gulf in the West and Sittwe (Myanmar) on Bay of Bengal in the East, are attempts to get control of sea lanes in the Indian Ocean. CMEC can threaten India's strategic assets along the eastern coastline along Bay of Bengal.

Besides, China had been busy courting India's neighbours to contain India. It backs up Pakistan. The Maoist Nepal, despite temporary setback, also looks to China as a friend, philosopher and a guide. China might also cultivate Bangladesh by luring her with her surplus funds. It sees Bangladesh (BD) as a key to her OBOR to Bay of Bengal. It might use BD for seeding and supporting separatist movements in India's North East states. It is molly coddling Sri Lanka. In the past, it supported Sri Lanka with weapons and equipment, during its final war with LTTE in the year 2008-09. Besides her CMEC proposal, China has been supporting the military regime in Myanmar to go nuclear through covert assistance from North Korea. If it happens, then India would be fully flanked in the North, East and the West by nuclear states. It would be very dangerous situation for India.

Thus, China's over all military strategy against India has been four pronged:
- Contain and isolate India by making her neighbours hostile and unfriendly.
- Outsource its low-cost proxy war to Pakistan and Maoists/Naxalites
- Supporting and encouraging internal insurgencies brewing in India and thus break-up India through implosion.
- Using Pakistan to the maximum to retard India's military and economic growth.
- Dominate sea-lanes around India through a 'String of Pearls' policy.
- Befool Indian leadership and Indian public through overt goodwill gestures in the interregnum period.

Generals of Pakistan have their own arithmetic on India. Their game is to survive as rulers of Pakistan at all costs. The only way they can do this is by creating a "monster of Hindu India" in the public mind of their country and thus hobnob with anyone who is unhappy with India and her policies, whether it was USA of 50s though 70s or China since 1962. In so doing, if they have to ignore basic Pakistani interests, so is it.

In any case, in Pakistan's military perceptions, interests of the 'Generals' are the national interests of Pakistan. It is, therefore, in their interests to have a continued state of hostility between India and Pakistan. Any attempt to normalize relations must be scuttled with some irreconcilable incidents, like Kargil-99 episode; assault on Indian Parliament on December 13, 2001 or Mumbai 26/11.

Thus, Pakistan military follows five pronged strategy on India, as under:

- Isolate India by enhancing US/West helplessness over Afghanistan by controlling militant network engaging USA/NATO in Afghanistan.
- Act in conjunction with China to not only retard India's economic and military growth but also be an important node of a combined threat in-being to India's security.
- Continued animosity with India by harping about 'unfinished agenda of 1947' and seeking Kashmir.
- Weaken, attrite and balkanize India through her 'War by Other Means' (WOM) by using her so called 'strategic assets'.
- Use nuclear black mail to check mate India from a 'measured military response' and use of 'strategic depth' in case of controlled nuclear exchange. Thus, Afghanistan remains her major worry, if it was hostile to her. This is the Achilles heel in their strategy.

Both China and Pakistan seek to dismember India by an internal explosion triggered by double pronged fuse from the East via China-supported-Maoist/Naxalite insurgency, along with other separatist movements in the North-East states and from the West through Pakistan sponsored trouble in Punjab, J&K and entire North India.

There is no real effort required to find links of Maoists and other terrorist outfits of India with India's Western and Northern adversaries. In fact, while Pakistan treats 'ultra-outfits' as her 'strategic asset'; China covertly supports them with weapons, training and a safe sanctuary for the leadership. Presence of ULFA commander-in-chief, Paresh Barua, in China is not without reason. Certainly, he is not holidaying in China. Thus, prospect of a combined and coordinated threat from three elements, in the near-future, is very much on the cards.

Thus, while a three front 'collusive threat' to Indian security is real and genuine, question arises if India can fight this war on all three fronts concurrently. Answer as on date is NO. It must be noted that defence and security is a most neglected aspect of Indian political leaders. Firstly, political expediency overrides security interests. Secondly, political leaders are ill-informed of matters of national defence and security. Finally, all governments at the centre have been bureaucracy dominated, who have their own axe to grind.

Thus security and defence apparatus has remained neglected. India spends only 1.56 % of the GDP on national security as compared to China and Pakistan – whose defence budgets are many folds of their GDP. In the bargain, armed forces have been only 40% efficient because of 60% deficiency in their equipment and other needs. We need some 45 squadrons (18 AC each) in air force. But we have only 33 squadrons only at 50% strength. To dominate the Indian Ocean we need 30-40 submarines and 3-4 aircraft carriers but have only 12-13 outdated submarines and one real aircraft carrier. This year's budget only catered for 55-60% needs of armed forces. We must modernise armed forces quickly, if India has to acquire capability to face this collusive threat from all three fronts.

Other than strengthening and modernising armed forces what else India must do to counter this combination of three-pronged threat? The first is to recognize internal foes, aided and abetted from the outside. As highlighted above, internal foes can be more damaging than the external enemies. In identifying her internal foe, it is no gainsaying the fact that India was utterly confused. Learned intellectuals and intelligentsia of India considerably add to this confusion by calling insurgents/militants/terrorists as "our misguided boys". How can the killers, extortionists, kidnappers and butchers be termed as "our misguided boys", when they plan and kill innocent people at will? This is the bane of all democratic forms of political systems.

The law of the land is very clear: anyone who has picked up arms against the state is the enemy of the state, whether he/she was a resident of India or otherwise. Thus, the 'enemy' has to be dealt with as 'enemy'. There is nothing 'misguided' about these paid 'stooges' of China and Pakistan. They clearly know what they were doing. If there was confusion, it was in the minds of those who think they would listen to reason. Even if they want to listen to you, their masters across the northern and western borders won't give them this flexibility. This option was long annulled when these so-called "misguided boys" fell into the lap of their foreign patrons.

Let us remember one thing that military option was adopted once all other efforts fail to make the so called "misguided youth" listen to reason. This failure graduates them from so called "misguided youth" to an enemy of India. If the logic of "bullet for a bullet" has to be followed, then, there can be no half-cocked measures.

In order to do so, we ought to delink internal security from law and order problems. We cannot confuse the two, as it leads to dilution of the problem, India faces. Once we do it, we would realize that both need different kind of forces to deal with it. Law and order is essentially to be tackled by police force, trained in dealing with law-breakers of a civilized society, ranging from theft, murder, cheating, forgery, kidnapping, spying and other such like civil offences. Law and order is essentially a term to be used for 'individualized crime' and not for 'organized crime', in whatever form. I would, therefore, even exclude mass protests, resulting into rail/road blockades in organized manner, from the realm of law and order.

Internal security requires a specialized force capable of conducting a military operation to fight well-trained 'irregular soldiers' of our external foes. Besides militancy and insurgency, it would also encompass all acts of mass violence by organized crime mafia, such as communal riots, violent agitations, affecting national progress and development. Drug-trafficking, gun-running and organized extortion must also come under the purview of internal security.

Internal security also needs to be delinked from external security, from the execution point of view and not from overall defence planning and strategy.

The forces dedicated for internal security not only be properly trained, organized and equipped but must also be placed under a unified command on all-India basis. Internal security must have a national security grid and forces dedicated for each grid, depending upon the extent, nature and type of internal threat.

External security must have specialized forces separately, for the defence of mountainous and plain types of terrain, requiring minimum switching of forces from one theatre to another, except emergency. There is a need to raise dedicated area specific and specially trained, organized and equipped troops to effectively ward off any surprise. This is to ensure realistic and measured response to external military threats, individually or combined from China and Pakistan, with nuclear dimensions appropriately debated.

A comprehensive strategy to tackle all three dangers concurrently must be evolved to effectively ward off the dangers. We also need to have an appropriate mix of nuclear defence, both at tactical and strategic level, in our overall strategy of national defence.

I see following six points, though nothing new about them but still worth considering:

1. Unified Command under CDS (Chief of Defence Staff) and Theatre commanders. Vitalize three wings of our armed forces and internal security forces in such a manner that they ought to fight under unified command on a synchronized battlefield with area specific needs, from mountains to desert to plains and riverine terrain. He should also act as the National Security Adviser (NSA). It is time an NSA is appointed who is well versed in matters military and not from the cadres of people who spent their lives, "suited-booted" in the foreign capitals. There is no need for a separate person to be appointed for this purpose.
2. National Grid for Counter Insurgency: To deal with the menacing threat of internal threat, the nation ought to be organized into a grid of sectors and sub-sectors with dedicated force allocated to each sector/sub-sector. Overall command of the National Security Grid be under the CDS and respective theatre commanders.
3. Space and Nuclear Defence Command (SAND-CO): Functioning directly under PM, it should have, scientific adviser to PM, CDS cum NSA, Defence Minister, Home Minister and External affairs Minister along with head of NIA as members. The Vice President of India should be observer with this command.
4. Integrated Intelligence Organization for External & Internal Threats: National Intelligence Agency (NIA) should command all agencies engaged in intelligence gathering and interpretation. All intelligence agencies, such as RAW, SB, SSB, IB and intelligence agencies of various states be place under the command of the NIA for effective coordination and dissemination of intelligence.

5. **National Security Council (NSC):** The National Security Council must be vitalized to include relevant central government ministries, such as Home, External Affairs, Defence, Finance, Commerce etc and Chief Ministers of various Border States. It should be headed by the President of India with Prime Minister as Vice Chairman. It should have external and internal security wings headed by the Defence Minister and Home Minister respectively.
6. **Theatre Specific Organization of Armed Forces:** To deal with external threat from North and West, defensive forces must be organized based on terrain specific requirements. The theatre specific forces must have limited offensive capabilities. Besides, India needs to create double role offensive forces, who can switch rapidly from mountains to plains or deserts. These strike formations must have adequate air support and air defence components. Indian Air Force must develop a capability to carry out deep strikes in the North and West simultaneously. The role of Strategic Missile Forces would be very important in any future conflict. Indian Navy must not only guard her coast line or the sea lanes in her economic zone but develop a capability to transfer a Division sized force on the enemy coast line. It is high time it has an offensive arm like the Marine Corps.

It is imperative for India to be prepared for the worst. And the worst is when internal and external foes join hands to balkanize her. The moral and material support to Maoists and J&K militants from China and Pakistan give enough indications as to what India must expect from her external foes. India doesn't have to not only develop ability to fight on three fronts simultaneously but also be mentally tuned to face such an eventuality. Half the job would be done once India accepts this as a reality of the near-future. Sometimes preparing for war serves as a good deterrent to the adversaries. Preparing meticulously, with worst scenario in mind, often lays the foundation of victory. And ignoring the warning signals is to face military disgrace and humiliation of 1962 type!

CHAPTER 21

Mending Fences – Sino-Indian Détente: A Compelling Necessity for Both

Col Rajinder Kushwaha

China would rethink about its unstinted support to Pakistan which has been India's continued headache since 1947. With China delinked, Pakistan has to cool down about its India policy and might be forced to seek a thaw in its relations with India. Strategic thinkers on both sides of McMahon line must note that the advantage of balance of power, shifting from West to Asia, can come to them only through a meaningful detente. 21st Century can be truly an 'Asian Century' if India and China join hands. Both have much to lose if conflict and confrontation is the option they choose.

The crescent of crisis, from the Middle East to South China Sea and North Korea, is alive with horrifying signatures of conflicts, which threaten to engulf the entire region into an unimaginable catastrophe. Iraq-Syria, Saudi Arabia-Iran, Afghanistan-Pakistan, India-Pakistan, North Korea-South Korea, China-USA over South China Sea and Japan-Australia-China are some of the flash points of this crescent.

India and China hold the key to avoid the catastrophe. A detente between two Asian giants is the first step towards this. However, at the current reckoning, a Sino-Indian detente may seem unthinkable. But as the future unfolds itself, it may be the compelling need of both. There are economic and strategic reasons which cry for a detente between the two Asian giants. It compliments their national interests.

Let us first take China. It must be noted that 80-90% of China's petroleum products are supplied from the Middle East. This is transported over a distance of 12,000 kms through Indian Ocean via Choke points at Malacca Strait and South China Sea. They say China has only 55-60 days reserve petroleum products. Thus, it cannot sustain an intense military conflict for more than 60 days. With sea lanes choked by USA, Japan, Australia and even India, it can run out of steam to sustain a conflict which might involve USA and the West. Also to sustain its reasonable economic growth, china needs continued supply of oil and gas from the Middle East.

Accordingly, China has been thinking of alternatives to sea route for the continued supply of its petroleum product needs. Thus, the Belt Road Initiative (BRI) in the shape of One Belt-One Road (OBOR) is her masked attempt to create alternative land routes. It has thus zeroed in to two land routes, one from Gwadar port in the Baluchistan province of Pakistan and the other at Sittwe port of Myanmar in the Bay of Bengal.

As for as Gwadar port is concerned, it is the nearest land route to China, some 3,000 kms but passing through most hostile region of Pakistan, dominated by tribal militant organisations such as the Tehrik-e-Taliban of Pakistan. Further, the land route passes through the disputed territory of Gilgit-Hunza region, which is claimed by India. But the most dangerous part is within China's own territory, Xinjiang province, dominated by the Uighur Muslim militancy. Thus, this alternative though viable, is going to be cost prohibitive. Although China has committed some $60-75 billion as part of the China Pakistan Economic Corridor (CPEC), within Pakistan there are strong voices opposing it. Do not discount the interference and disruptions that can be caused from Afghanistan by Hostile USA and her allies. Thus, China is going slow on this alternative.

The other alternative route is from Sittwe port of Myanmar in the Bay of Bengal. It may be noted that China had already hired this port on lease in 1992. It has developed two pipelines, one gas and the other oil, from here to China. The bulk of China's oil and gas needs would be pumped through these pipelines. But it is important that the port should be safe and secure. It has thus acquired the Coco Island from Myanmar on lease and developed military facilities including an air strip. All the same, what is significant is that the land route to Bay of Bengal will not only safeguard these assets but also ensure uninterrupted supply of energy needs.

This land route passes through Bhutan's Doko La, India's Siliguri Corridor and North-South length of Bangladesh before touching the Bay of Bengal. This land route enjoys advantages of less distance and less friction through the region. While Bangladesh and Bhutan can be lured through economic doles, it is India which will be a spoilsport. It is therefore essential that China cozy up to India for a detente. It is more of a Chinese need than India.

Let us now review Indian needs. As predicted by Bank of America's financial brokerage arm, Merryl Lynch, India is likely to be the third largest economy of the world by 2028, after USA and China, if it grows at 10% rate of GDP. To do so, India needs total stability both at the borders and within. A detente with China would reduce interruptions both at the border and within.

Most important is that China would rethink about its unstinted support to Pakistan which has been India's continued headache since 1947. With China delinked, Pakistan has to cool down about its India policy and might be forced to seek a thaw in its relations with India.

India must realise strategic disadvantages accruing to her along the Eastern coastline because of a hostile China. One thing must be realised that Bangladesh and Bhutan governments might be friendly today but nothing can be said of the future because both need tremendous funds for their development and economic growth. China, with surplus funds, can fill the void.

Imtiaz K Hussain, a Bangladeshi scholar, notes in his article, in Financial Timeson 28 July 2016 that Bangladesh's core 21st century interest is infrastructure-building, and there are just too many projects for any interested investor-country to be disappointed. He brings out that 100 such mega projects would need $100 billion over the next 5 years. And this can only come from China or India. While India has her own constraints, China is ever ready to chip in through her surplus funds in the Asian Infrastructure and Investment Bank (AIIB). China would attempt this entry, whether India willing or not.

Thus, in a long term perspective, Bangladesh might cave in to lucrative Chinese advances. After all, Sheikh Hasina Wajid and her party might not be in government always. So is the case of Bhutan. China might mend fences with both in the future. Therefore China might have a forced run through from Chumbi valley, through Siliguri Corridor, to Bay of Bengal with the help of ULFA and other militant organisations of North East. A detente may prevent this and also stop severing of entire North East. Further, a hostile China getting entry into the Bay Of Bengal by whatever methods would threaten India's strategic interests along the Eastern coast line from Kolkata to Thiruvananthapuram, along which are located India's missile testing range at Wheeler Island, ship and submarine building facilities at Vishakhapatnam and the Indian Space research Organization's (ISRO) satellite launching facility at Sriharikota. Besides, India's Maoists infected states of Bengal, Odisha, Andhra Pradesh and Tamil Nadu would become vulnerable to a hostile China in Bay of Bengal. Include in this the vulnerability of Andaman & Nicobar group of islands which allows India to dominate Eastern Indian Ocean. Friction between the two is harmful for both from the Andaman group of islands.

Strategic thinkers on both sides of McMahon line must note that the advantage of balance of power, shifting from West to Asia, can come to them only through a meaningful detente. 21st Century can be truly an 'Asian Century' if India and China join hands. Both have much to lose if conflict and confrontation is the option they choose.

SECTION 5

SELECTION AND TRAINING AT THE MILITARY ACADEMIES

CHAPTER 22

Officer Selection and Training System Needs Re-Appraisal and Correlativity – Overhaul Needed

Brig LC Patnaik

Unauthorized punishments often lead to 'cognitive dissonance', which impairs learning, creativity, slowing down problem solving skills and increases forgetfulness, create inhibition in creativity, slow down problem solving skills and increase forgetfulness. Similarly, unauthorized punishments like manhandling, ground swimming or rolling down the stairs can create 'concussion' to the tune of 30-60g force range. Emotionally, above symptoms leads a person to be aggressive, impatient, impulsive and prone to low self-esteem, creating major disruption to an individual's ability to perceive and assimilate. Some of them also suffer from post-traumatic hypopituitarism with reduced muscle mass, decrease exercise capacity and depression.

The policy of officer selection for the Armed Forces is jointly decided by the Chief of Staff Committee and the Defence Institute of Psychological Research (DIPR) under DRDO. Ever since independence, three major revisions have taken place, with the last revision being made in 1998, wherein the screening process was introduced due to substantial increase in the number of applicants. The fourth revision is under consideration by the DIPR and is at the trial stage. The Services Selection Boards (SSBs) conduct one of the finest selection process over a period of five days and recommend potential officers cadets with high trainability factor to the service Training Academies.

The cadets undergo training for a period of one to four years depending upon the type of commission, before they are commissioned to the Armed Forces. Notwithstanding the world class infrastructure and sufficient budgetary support for training of cadets, the National Defence Academy (NDA) has an annual attrition rate of 14-16 %, while the service specific pre-commission training academies have 5-7% attrition rate. Although attrition in terms of withdrawals, medically unfit and physical casualties are unavoidable in any military training establishments all over the world, the high rate of attrition at NDA, one of the premiere military Institution in the world, is a matter of concern.

In this context, Col P K 'Royal' Mehrishi's analysis (Fauji India-Dec 2017) on the evolution of ragging, unauthorized punishments and psychological impact on adolescent minds is highly relevant as regards training of cadets at NDA and other parallel academies in the Armed Forces. The observations provide valuable inputs for re-appraisal of selection and training methods for our future leadership. Hence we need to consider de-novo transformation measures to enhance the quality of our officers.

The psychological impact on adolescent cadets has been adequately analysed by Col Mehrishi in the perspective of mass and excessive punishments leading to cognitive dissonance. In 2011, a study undertaken by the Centre for Disease Control & Prevention in US, found that cognitive dissonance can lead to impairment of the ability to learn, create inhibition in creativity, slow down problem solving skills and increase forgetfulness. The above factors seriously hinder learning ability amongst cadets. Similarly, unauthorized punishments like manhandling, ground swimming or rolling down the stairs can create 'concussion' to the tune of 30-60g force range.

The damage to the brain in such a force is not easy to detect because it is usually not structural in nature and severe enough to interrupt normal functioning and cause physical and cognitive symptoms, some of them immediate, others delayed for weeks, even months. This leads to dizziness, headache, fatigue and change in sleep patterns, which are normally the complaints during 'sick reports' by the cadets at NDA. Emotionally, above symptoms leads a person to be aggressive, impatient, impulsive and prone to low self-esteem, creating major disruption to an individual's ability to perceive and assimilate. Staying amongst peers in a highly competitive environment, many cadets turn to artificial stimulants and drugs, harming their adolescent body and mind.

Some of them also suffer from post-traumatic hypopituitarism with reduced muscle mass, decrease exercise capacity and depression. Hence, it can be surmised that the three essential factors of learning as brought out by Col Mehrishi; attention, retention and re-production are severely compromised through unauthorized and excessive punishments, prevalent in the Academy, for which there is a high rate of exodus in the form of withdrawal, relegations and absconding. To address the issue, we need to follow a '3-S' policy of 'specialization', 'segregation' and 'scientific' physical training at NDA.

Specialization: There is an urgent need to create a new Deptt/Wing for 'Physical Training' controlled and supervised by qualified persons both military and civil, with responsibilities to plan, execute and monitor the complete (360 degrees) aspect of physical training of cadets to include physical exercises, sports, drill physical adventure/co-curricular activities, and also authorised physical punishments as laid down. Physical training as a specialized training component and subject needs serious attention and can no longer be left to inexperienced Divisional Officers or senior cadets. All major military training academies of the world have already incorporated such measures since long. Details of organizational and command structure can be worked out on a functional basis.

Segregation: All new entry cadets to be kept separately in their first two terms; for which one Battalion with 4-5 squadrons could be earmarked. Minimum two terms are recommended considering the time required for the muscles and bones to be set on a scientific basis.

Scientific: The overall weightage of physical training to be enhanced to 60% from the existing 30% for first two terms. Subsequently, scientific monitoring of body mass-muscle ratio bone development, identification of physical strength and weaknesses, spotting of potential sports persons, and scientific and medical treatment with the help of sports medicine specialists, counselors etc could be planned. On completion of two terms, the cadets can be distributed to other squadrons with the physical training ratio gradually reduced to 20% by VIth Term.

Selection

There is also a strong need to review our selection process to assess their cognitive and physical capability and link it with the training at the service Academies. Certain recommendations in the selection system as given below could be considered:

- A fundamental shift required to move from existing personality based selection to a cognitive based selection process for the following reasons:-
- Existing personality variables/Officer Like Qualities (OLQs) focus more on social effectiveness and adjustment, derived from the Freudian concept of behavioral process and observable responses, neglecting the mental process which actually mediates the stimulus and response (Hilgard & Atikson, 1975).
- Cognitive assessment provides time course for information processing, reaction based measurements to provide baseline of assessment and subsequent monitoring.
- Rise of reliable cognitive function assessment tools such as British Army Recruitment Battery (BARB), Cognitive Screen AE (US) and Australian Computerized Cognitive Assessment Tool (ACCAT).

Physical Efficiency Test (PET) can also be introduced at the Services Selection Boards (SSBs), to include:

- One mile shuttle run
- Pushups (30)
- Sit ups (30)
- Chin ups (18)

The above tests should be assessed on a gradation scale and marks obtained to be included in the overall assessment.

- Screening Test (Day 1): Based on Picture Perception & Description Test (PPDT) to be replaced by Cognitive Assessment Test (CAT) and the Physical Efficiency Test (PET).
- The Psychology Test and GTO assessment could be suitably modified on cognitive assessment tools to reduce the scope and duration so as to complete the test in one day; thereby reducing the overall duration to four days, instead of present five days.
- In addition, to reduce the load of non-UPSC entries at the SSBs and reduce the vast rejection on the Screening Day, we could consider their shortlisting through established public examinations like GATE (Tech Entries), SAT/CAT (Non-Tech Entries).

Correlativity Assessment & Training: There is a need to develop software to assess the correlativity between assessment and training to be shared periodically between the assessors and trainers to review their own mechanisms. The existing procedure is outdated and devoid of sincerity in purpose. This aspect, being tri-service in nature, should be under the control of CIDS.

CHAPTER 23

Lessons to Learn
Intro: Public-Private Partnership can be a Way Forward to Military Education and Filling up Officer Shortage

Maj Gen Raj Mehta

The path-breaking, Shemrock School-Armed Forces Preparatory Institute (AFPI), Punjab public-private partnership for imparting quality education to young military aspirants has resulted in a staggering 111 cadets joining India's elite military training academies since 2012; the NDA, being primary among them. This successful 'pilot project' in military-civil education between the Punjab government's AFPI and a forward looking private school in Mohali, Punjab, makes one wonder whether this model cannot be replicated in every state of the Union of India considering that the sainik/military school system nowhere near meets India's need for officer induction into the defence forces. There is need, too, to review military education at the overarching level of the upcoming Indian National Defence University (INDU) as also streamline the current system of officer cadet entry to India's defence academies. The winner in this will obviously be the quality of professional military education (PME) imparted in India.

India has been promoting 'Make in India' as well as changes in Public-Private Partnership to improve our defence outlay since the current government took over in 2014. Whereas both aspirations have met with a modicum of success, it is not certain whether military education was also targeted for such improvement in outlook and content. The INDU remains a three-phase dream project costing Rs. 2,072 crore under construction since December 2015. There have been no public inputs whatsoever on where things stand except the May 2018 news that a bus bay has been sanctioned for its expected 12,000-15,000 student/teacher population. The UPSC exam system for officer entry into the defence forces remains essentially unchanged for decades (ironically, the UPSC exam has undergone radical change for the Civil Services examination regimen with thinking responses being preferred to rote testing).

The PME system run by the defence forces also remains unchanged. At entry level though, the Defence Institute of Psychological Research (DIPR), a

DRDO Laboratory, has been pushing its much-hyped five-years under-formulation *'De Novo'* SSB examination system which has reduced the five-day SSB testing in vogue since 1948 to three days 'without loss of quality or focus' as per DIPR claims. It is on trial since 2016 at SSB Bangalore along with the current system and has invited mixed responses from veterans. Let us examine these issues dispassionately.

Entry Level Officer Induction
We have 26 Sainik Schools (21 more have been proposed and Rs 80 crore earmarked for them, as per a PTI report of 11 August 2017 on Parliamentary proceedings). In a written reply to Parliament, RRM S.R. Bhamre stated that the 26 Sainik Schools in 2016, fed 159 or 29.33 per cent cadets and the five Military Schools fed 31 cadets or 5.1 per cent cadets to the NDA in 2016. In the same year, media reports indicated that 25 cadets from the elite RIMC cleared the NDA UPSC exam with seven of them being in the top 20.

Seen statistically (it is presumed that the figures are for one term for which NDA takes in an average of 355 entries), the figures imply that on an average, each of the 26 Sainik Schools fed a mere six cadets to the NDA despite being tailored for solely feeding cadets to it. The Military Schools likewise fed six cadets each, with the really stand out performance being that of the RIMC. A total of 215 cadets thus came from India's official 'feeder' institutions for NDA entry, leaving the balance 140 (out of 355) to come in from outside the official system.

This is where the Shemrock-AFPI public-private partnership comes in. It has sent 22 cadets to the NDA in June 2018 against a vacancy of 355 which is 6.2 per cent of the NDA batch strength. Also, in the May-June 2018 passing out of commissioned officers from India's defence academies, Shemrock-AFPI had 21 officers passing out from IMA/NAVAC/AFA/OTA... again, a stunning achievement. Even as this reality is accepted, there cannot be but deep concern about why the feeder institutions, which have been set up at great initial and residual cost, aren't doing enough to send more officer candidates to the NDA.

We have a daunting shortage of around 13,100 officers in the defence forces persisting for decades which even limited women officer entry and short-term measures such as increase in Short Service Commission induction has not been able to resolve. Clearly, something more needs to be done and this is where the Shemrock-AFPI pilot project can be viewed as an innovative and effective measure to induct more officers into India's defence academies.

Public-Private 'Pilot Project'
Way back in 2012, the Punjab government worried about the rapidly declining intake from Punjab into the defence forces, had taken concrete steps and built a preparatory training academy that would train boys inducted in class 11 for a two-year cycle of preparation during which the boys would not just clear

class 12 but also be given the military training and skills needed to clear the UPSC/SSB regimen.

This is how the Maharaja Ranjit Singh Armed Forces Preparatory Academy-Shemrock Higher Secondary School partnership came about in 2012. With both based at Mohali, within two kilometers of each other, the well-thought-through partnership has succeeded despite the trials, tribulations and challenges that partnerships generate.

Chairman Shemrock A.S. Bajwa says he is living out a dream he nursed since he started Shemrock in 2002. He points out with quiet pride that the Union ministry of human resource and development's website lists almost 1.1 million (10,9,318) higher secondary schools in India but no other secondary school in India can claim the results his school has shown in partnership with AFPI. Principal Shemrock, Prineet Sohal, feels that it was a momentous task and many hurdles had to be negotiated and intense coaching programmed with IMPACT/FOCUS Math/Science specialists but the results have been worth the sweat, toil and occasional tears.

Founding director Shemrock, Air Cmde S K Sharma (now retired), who steered this programme at Shemrock from 2012 to 2017, says balancing academic excellence with multi-pronged military activities; getting the students to crack the UPSC exams even as the AFPI prepared them to clear the unrelenting SSB regimen was tough but mutually rewarding. This has resulted in Cadets Gosal and Shashank topping the All India UPSC Merit in 2015 and 2017 respectively in an examination where five lakh apply but only 300 make it to the NDA. Maj. Gen. B.S. Grewal, VSM, founding Director AFPI recalls tough times with a wry smile and reinforces the feeling that focused work was needed at both ends of the partnership.

How Tough is NDA Entry?
The NDA is among the oldest and finest joint-service training academies worldwide. Sixteen and a half-nineteen and a half year olds join it after undergoing one of the world's toughest academic, psychological, physical and medical testing systems. How difficult the examination is can also be gauged from the fact that the pass percentage for NEET is 2.8 per cent. Similarly, the acceptance for IIT Delhi is 2.5 per cent after Joint Entrance Examination. Going by 2014 figures of candidates who applied for the NDA examination, actually took it and cleared the UPSC exam, the chances for being called for the interview were 0.02 per cent. In 2014, the total number of candidates who registered for the NDA UPSC Examination was 9, 26, 626 of which 5, 69, 528 actually appeared. 355 were finally cleared per term for joining the NDA or a total of 710 for 2014. Around 6,000 candidates are called for the NDA SSB per term which indicates a pass percentage of roughly 1.7 per cent.

A report suggests that the NDA entry is the eighth toughest in the world as under:

- Harvard University
- Massachusetts Institute of Technology
- California Institute of Technology
- Stanford University
- Indian Institute of Technology, Delhi
- Yale University
- Princeton University
- National Defence Academy, India
- The Julliard School (Julliard), NYC
- Peking University, China

The point being made is stark and clear. If officer deficiency has to be fast-tracked, the Shemrock-AFPI partnership in each state is the way ahead for India.

The INDU Conundrum

Conceived in 1967, the National Defence University's concept was validated by the Kargil Review Committee and Group of Ministers in 2000. Nearly, 205 acres was acquired at **Binola, Gurugram** in September 2012 with construction commencing in December 2015. Coming up 11 km outside Delhi on the Delhi-Jaipur highway at a cost, INDU **will be headed by a serving three-star general/ equivalent rank.**

The fully autonomous university is expected to promote synergy not just between the three armed forces of India but also between other agencies of government, civil bureaucracy, paramilitary forces (PMF), central armed police forces (CAPF), intelligence services, diplomats, academicians, strategic planners, university students and officers from friendly countries.

It will be affiliated to the NDA/DSSC/CDM/NDC and have the following departments:

- Indian Institute of Defence Technology
- Indian Institute of Defence Management
- National College of Defence Studies
- Defence Institute of Distance and Open Learning

Sixty-six per cent of its students will be from the regular armed forces, the balance from PMF/CAPF and civilians. INDU will offer doctoral and post-doctoral research, post-graduate studies through regular and distance learning. Courses will include regional and area country studies, Southeast Asia, Indo-Pacific region and world players. Macro security and strategic issues will be studied as also national strategy, maritime/aerospace strategy, gaming, military simulation, deception, logistics, counter-insurgency and counter-terrorism.

Will INDU Deliver?

One key aim of INDU, going by its draft Bill circulated in 2016 for public comment is to boost macro level 'jointness' involving all players and of the kind the Services display in the Tri-Service NDA/DSSC/CDM/NDC. This is easier said than done. Let us clinically examine why the proposed INDU structure doesn't support this aspiration.

- The stated desire is to have the military/civil faculty (300) in 1:1 ratio. While desirable, few Indian institutions run defence courses and most that do lack PME/trained faculty. Such deficiency also exists in PMF/CAPF. Foreign faculty from bench-marked universities/think-tanks is needed but not enunciated.
- The draft NDU Bill offers no clue on how the National Defence Studies, Defence Management and Defence Technology Departments will run/ their syllabi/ teaching pedagogy.
- Student intake from the regular forces will be a major dampener being 13,100 officers short. Getting deficiencies filled in by PMF/CAPF/civil intake is impractical. And will question the credibility of INDU as an overarching institution promoting overall military synergy and PME.
- INDU tie-ups with our IITs/IIMs are not spelt out nor have tie-ups with IAT/DRDO/Defence PSUs/DIPR/Artificial Intelligence/Cyber Agencies/IDSA/USI/CAFHR/foreign/Indian think tanks been mentioned.
- Private entities like Tata/Reliance/Bharat Forge and industry promoted think tanks such as ORF are left out.

In sum, PME both in pedagogy as well as in its detailing has been left out. Critically, the need for public-private partnership in military education has been left untouched, leaving one to see INDU as a key 'work in progress'.

SSB Testing

The existing Services Selection Board (SSB), in vogue since 1948, is a five-day process for officer selection which includes an interview, group and psychological testing of aspirants. The 'De Novo Selection System' designed by DRDO's Defence Institute of Psychological Research (DIPR) laboratory over five years is being tried at SSB Bangalore since 2016 and will be implemented from 2019 if approved. It is personality and not intelligence-based and focuses on his/her ability to adapt, learn, unlearn and relearn repeatedly and comprehensively. The new DIPR system assesses both conductors and aspirants.

It involves:

Day 1: Online Screening Test, Running 1.6 km and Psychological testing.

Day 2: GTO Tasks, Individual obstacles, Lecturettes.

Day 3: Personal Interview and Conference.

Besides reducing testing from five to three days, the Psychological Screening Tests will now be online. The Thematic Apperception Test shall now have nine pictures rather than 12. The Word Association Test has been reduced to 40 words from 60, with candidates writing three descriptive words which immediately come to mind instead of sentences. Cleared candidates will undertake a timed

1.6 kilometre run (Not Race), which should complete in less than eight minutes; the marks increasing with lesser completion time; zero being awarded beyond eight minutes. In the Situation Reaction Test there will be two tests, in one a situation and a picture will be shown, in the other only a situation will be given. For answers, four optional answers will be provided; candidates being required to prioritise them.

De Novo SSB System?

The jury is still out as the DIPR De Novo programme is shrouded in secrecy with only skeleton information available. Before the question on its efficacy and improvement over the existing regimen is offered, it would be pragmatic to consider the antecedents of SSB testing.

Copied from the pre-World War II German officer-selection system, SSB testing as we follow it was its British adaptation; a legacy we took over in 1948 and which Defence Research and Development Organisation (DRDO) was allotted to conduct for unexplained reasons. DIPR is the DRDO laboratory that runs the testing, keeping it essentially unchanged but for this De Novo pilot project; in sum, 75 years of stasis even as the UK, the US, Germany, Sweden, Russia, have long since evolved selection systems far advanced than what we have on offer.

The reasons for change are (cynically) administrative more than scientific, as veterans once part of the SSB system opine. There are over 6,000 candidates for NDA entry alone who need testing six-monthly and SSBs are few as are DIPR-trained testing officers. To handle the load, a Screening Test (not part of the British system) was created by DIPR which assesses and rejects over 60 per cent SSB candidates after a hasty three-hour psychological assessment. Candidates clearing screening take the SSB tests.

The De Novo system retains the screening test but has made it online. A physical run (not race) has been added to pay a token salute to physical wellness. A few redundancies such as personal details have been scrapped; the tests shortened to fit with reduced time norms and that is the De Novo system awaiting approval effective 2019. Clearly, yet again, PME has been given short shrift in this instance because of poor selection regimen.

RECOMMENDATIONS

The public-private partnership as mentioned earlier is an initiative needing exploitation by the government as one out-of-the-box, cost-effective way of ending the logjam of crippling officer shortages in India's armed forces. At macro levels, a serious review of PME from overarching INDU to UPSC-SSB entry levels is needed.

(The writer is director Shemrock School) The article was published by Force magazine, July 2018 issue.

CHAPTER 24

'De Novo' SSB from 2019: An Analysis

Debate Compiled by Col Vinay Dalvi

Background

The existing Services Selection Board (SSB), in vogue since 1948, is a five-day long process for officer selection which includes an interview, group testing and psychological testing of the aspirants. Indian armed forces are trying out a new system of officer selection to bring the selection process in tune with the changing job requirement of a modern military officer, while allowing them to better assess the newer generation of aspirants. The new selection system, once approved, will be implemented from 2019. Candidates who are called for the SSB after having passed a UPSC written exam are administered a screening test on the first day. Qualifying on the screening test is mandatory for the candidates to take further tests.

The new 'De Novo Selection System', which has been designed by DRDO's Defence Institute of Psychological Research (DIPR) lab over five years, will accomplish the SSB testing in three days. The new system is being trialed at an SSB at Bangalore for two years, running in parallel with the existing tests. According to DRDO, testing trials in the first year will focus on the sub-systems while integration checks will be run in the second year. The SSB testing is personality based and not intelligence based. Our aim with the new tests is to reduce the gap between technological development and human skill development.

Formal education is not as important for a military officer of the future as the ability to adapt, learn, unlearn and relearn repeatedly and comprehensively. It is about the modern mind, not the traditional mindset. The period of generational change has shrunk and the type of aspirants now changes dramatically within a decade, unlike earlier. The post-1990 generation is a post-globalization generation, whose analytical and cognitive abilities have gone up, so have their expectations, and changes in the value system.

Although the prototype tests for interview, group testing and psychological testing have been designed by DIPR, development of additional tests for different entries, training of assessors and creation of infrastructure for parallel run is still taking place. Subject to the outcome of the trials, and its acceptability by the three defence services, the De Novo Selection System is likely to be implemented at all SSBs in 2019.

Technical Analysis of Seven 'De Novo' System Points

1. *Reduction of selection period from 5 days to 3:* Reducing the selection period from 5 days to 3 days will have its drawbacks for the candidates and selectors. For the candidates being observed for only 3 days instead of earlier 5 days, they will be required to prove/display their personality traits, potential and trainability in 2 days lesser time span with fewer tests/ assessments. For the selectors, they will be required to be more focused and observant as they will get 2 days lesser time for their assessments.

2. *Screening/Psychological Test:* The removal of the 'physical screening test' and replacing it with 'online screening test' will have several negative implications not only for the candidates but the selectors as well. Firstly, the candidates who are the outdoor type will not be able to display their physical characteristics/traits and military potential, which will remain hidden/ veiled behind the online screen. Secondly, the candidates who are intellectually/academically more proficient are likely to excel, keeping their physical personality traits and potential hidden/veiled behind the online screen.

3. *Thematic Apperception Test (TAT):* TAT will now have 9 pictures instead of 12. The very premise of this test is projective. Projective tests have limited usage in psychological testing as these are subjective can be manipulated and cannot be standardized. These tests lack validity and reliability important constructs for a psychological test. They also do not have a standard grading scale thus leaving it to the judgment of the analyzer. Where is the guarantee that the psychologist himself is not projecting his personality and accepting only those answers that are close to his world view?

4. *Self-Description (SD):* Is an over inflated bombast, as each candidate knows that they are in for a competition and the aim is to get through the selection procedure. Each person tries to project the best of his personality, hiding/ repressing aspects which later could manifest as neuroticism, delusional disorders or attention seeking syndrome.

5. *Word Association Test (WAT):* Reduced from 60 words to 40 words, no sentences and only three associated words to decipher an individual's psychology. The concept arouses mirth, as the hold of coaching has not been "factored in". Eg: words like 'mother'–'determination'/'motherland'/ 'affection', what does it reveal of an individual's psychology? Nothing. Such answers can be rehearsed and have no test/re-test validity.

6. *The 1.6 km Endurance Test:* The military academies (IMA, NDA, and OTA) for the past 22 years, through their Commandants, have been representing to the DG Recruiting/DGMT/ARTRAC the imperative need of mandatory physical tests in the SSBs for several justified reasons like high wastage rates, resignations, relegations, withdrawals and medical cases. Shockingly

and surprisingly, the COSC/HQ IDS/ARTRAC/DGMT have been unable to convince/persuade the DIPR to accept this simple basic requirement, particularly when they were rejecting two thirds (66%) of the SSB candidates only on the basis of a non-transparent/subjective screening (psychological) test! The purpose of a physical 1.6km run (not race) is defeated when the most physically suited/talented candidates would get screened out in the online screening test. Hence, there is an imperative need of a blend of both physical and psychological tests in the screening process. The requirements of the training academies and the users/three services must be factored in to decide/finalize the De Novo System. A holistic and coordinated approach involving the selectors, trainers and users/services is of paramount importance. Presently it appears to be an exclusive DIPR/DRDO exercise.

7. *Situation Reaction Test (SRT):* This improved test with pictures and without pictures seems to hold ground with four options numbered 1 to 4. Just a few months into the tests in SSB all possible situations will be available with the coaching centres and the entire process will become a charade. The answer keys to such tests have little reliability as they cannot always measure what they are initially set for.

Solution lies in exposing a candidate to a multiple/randomized battery of relevant Psychological Tests online (computerized) at the SSB with immense time pressure, so as to eliminate well thought out/ideated answers.

RESPONSES BY VETERANS

Col Pradeep Dalvi

We have still been following a British legacy officer selection system, which itself has reformed its candidate selection procedure, including many of the NATO countries. Gen Sir Richard Shirreff, Dy supreme commander of NATO forces in Europe said "It is important of an officer candidate training course in Bosnia & Herzegovina brings together young cadets from all ethnic backgrounds. The new selection process takes place over 6 days and tests volunteer candidates in a wide range of physical, academic and intellectual tasks designed to identify leadership potential."

He stressed that continued close supervision and leadership from the government/minister and senior staff is needed for maintaining success of this project and develop a national sense of identity and ethos amongst future military leaders." The British Army till date has had nine important organizational changes (five under labour government, three under conservative government and one under conservative and liberal democrat) since 1963 initiated by MoD, British Armed Forces for greater integration.

The reduction of the testing period from 5 to 3 days will entail the GTO having to assess very large number of candidates and prepare their documents for the final conference. He will have to work minimum 10-11 hrs a day, directly affecting the quality of assessment. In addition the GTOs are deployed on various administrative duties of the SSB/station. The entire process has not been discussed with staff at SSB.

Procedure for carrying out online screening test has not been given out by DIPR. Will aspirants take on line test sitting at their homes or will they visit one of the Armed forces Centre? Can an individual take help of others? How will they monitor use of unfair means? Reducing the TAT from 12 to 9 is nothing but a cosmetic change which will not have any bearing on the change being carried out.

The Self-Description (SD) test is basically related to psychologist and has nothing to do with GTO and IO. The psychologist's views have to be taken into consideration before dropping such test. He generally formulates personality of the candidate by going through the thought process articulated by the candidate in SD. He also confirms the same when he goes through various other tests like WAT, TAT and SRT. The psychologist is also able to weed of coached candidates as they reflect different personality traits vis-à-vis original candidate.

The new WAT involves writing three different words which are similar to its original word. I believe this will favour candidates who are from good English medium schools, as majority of the candidates are from lower middle class background. This test is not recommended until scientific testing and verification is done at SSB.

The physical attributes are tested in all foreign selection Boards with qualification standards. The paper has recommended 1.6 km run to be completed from 4 to 8 minutes. This means the candidates will have to come prepared for the test. Weak candidates can be given more time to qualify without losing their chance to face the SSB. The most important factor of 'potential' and 'trainability' must be kept in mind for candidates and their background.

In the new SRT test there are two phases, in phase 1 only picture will be shown and candidate is expected to write story based on the overall picture. In phase 2, only situations are given and no picture, the candidate will have to write down the priority of the situation as per his preference. The new recommendation has not been tested and without extensive trials it will be difficult to comment upon. The claims of the new test being mentally challenging need to be tested and verified.

In the new SRT test there are two phases; in phase 1 only picture will be shown and candidate is expected to write story based on the overall picture. In phase 2, only situations are given and no picture, the candidate will have to write down the priority of the situation as per his preference. The new recommendation has not been tested and without extensive trials it will be difficult to comment upon. The claims of the new test being mentally challenging need to be tested and verified.

From above comments it is very clear that DIPR on its own cannot formulate De Novo selection system for officer candidates in 'isolation' without taking into consideration all the stake holders. The stake holders are qualified SSB staff, Armed Forces (including 'trainers' and 'users'), MoD and the government. Looking at the examples of USA, UK and other affiliated NATO countries and the trivial importance which continues to being given to this entire process of 'selection' and 'training' future potential military leaders needs no further elaboration.

Lt Col M K Guptaray
I have reservation on using the word 'De novo' which means new as subject is not new. The curriculum must be created by the tri-services with each service peculiarity being retained. Unlike civil services where qualitative requirement of the job is more to implement plan through various agencies than leading the men through most difficult period towards supreme sacrifice. Army requires totally different type of leadership. This needs long observation through different angles. Lesser time span will definitely deprive both the exhibitor and observer to display and observe maximum potentiality.

I do not know the pattern of the depicted pictures but ideally these should be so graduated that these pictures give out complete personality. The 'blank picture' speaks the most. I disagree to remove it. SD is the part of the test which must be retained. It brings out what is the self-assessment by the candidate. How much one may try to cover oneself up but the actual picture will definitely come out. Grit and determination are two very important characteristics that an army man of all ranks must possess.

I do not understand what major benefit the WAT will bring about. This system will have a drawback for the candidates who lack vocabulary. I feel writing sentences will clarify more clearly. 1.6 km is nothing at the entrance age. It could be more. Along with endurance there must certain degree of strength tests too.

Col C M Chavan
Reducing selection days from 5 to 3 would give SSBs time to test more number of candidates. But then having introduced screening test before SSB; would in any case reduce the number of candidates. On the contrary, the candidate will have lesser time to show case their skills and traits and so will the GTOs find it difficult to assess the candidate subjectively.

Regarding screening test, a word of caution! Though it is envisaged that the online screening test cannot be compromised, it needs to be further validated as multi texting on cell phones by few experts sitting at any part of India can intelligently dictate answers to the candidates formed into a node and cheat the system.

Reducing the WAT from 60 to 40 is understandable but not writing sentences will not display power of expression of the candidate with psychological backdrop for meaningful assessment. "Formal education is not important for future generation of officers" is a rather farfetched and will categorize the candidates amongst lesser educated class, which is not desirable. Introduction of 1.6 km endurance test is a very welcome addition as the candidate can be assessed on his ability to endure the training period in the academy successfully. Changes in the SRT are welcome as the candidate will have to remain focused and prioritize their answers.

Col P K 'Royal' Mehrishi

DIPR/DRDO in their exuberance to claim credit for developing a De Novo Selection System has once again waded into unknown waters. Psychologists working in DIPR have little or zero exposure to field/combat conditions. The major stake holders are units/formations and the training institutions, which are always at the receiving end of an intake they have not programmed/prepared themselves for.

Has any authoritative source in the organization defined what is required of a future military officer? Is there a requirement of a man-child with rippling biceps and well defined lats ora scholar-soldier functioning within defined parameters of physical fitness but astute and sharp to seize and create opportunities in combat and win battles? Till what level of physical exhaustion do we need to push the cadets so that they are still alert to assimilate important facets of learning/training? Three days of SSB & saving money is fine, but do the tests designed have test/retest validity, if yes what is the margin of error and probability of leaving out potentially good candidates because of skew/bias due to subjective nature of WAT & SRT?

Out of the box thinking, creative solutions, ability to utilize given resources, initiative, people skills (Emotional Quotient) are some of the mandatory skills required of a leader in this century. Are the tests designed up to it? I reserve my judgment till I get to see the entire content. Solution lies in exposing a candidate to a multiple/randomized battery of relevant Psychological Tests on line (computerized) at the SSB with immense time pressure, so as to eliminate/ideated answers. I have already covered this in my previous article in Fauji India on Military Psychology.

I consider myself a potential consultant to DIPR as I have been for good amount of time with vast exposure been on either side of the divide. Firstly as an Infantry Officer for 28 years and secondly as a practising Psychologist for last 11 years; The De Novo System is still flawed for want of best available inputs from Combat units/Formations/Training Academies. We need not be in perpetual denial about our own inputs and keep harping that DIPR/DRDO knows best.

Unfortunately this change, whatever we see has come about because of Victory India/Fauji India series and some more independent authors. The present system from WW II, though majorly flawed was still being pushed as a tried and tested system. Repeated financial impropriety, breach of discipline over serious issues, burgeoning court cases by serving senior Officers has put the focus back on Officers intake and mechanisms of training/grooming/conduct. We are still far from developing a system wherein the inherent hardiness and native intelligence of a potential cadet is not compromised by some flimsy jargon from Military Psychology such as "Fit to be a Commander without Troops".

Gp Capt Johnson Chacko
Many aspects described in the 'cadet's prayer' are based on psychology. Psychological screening is of utmost importance as, if that is negative, and then we are wasting our time and resources in training him. If an online foolproof process has been developed it is a win-win situation and economical. In fact it should be available for everyone in the formative stage when he decides to appear for NDA entrance examination.

If a candidate does not have 'character', can he change, is it trainable? Can the lack of character displayed at higher ranks be discerned at the SSB stage and weeded out? As for physical strength, the pre-requisite for building strength is lung capacity and efficiency. A 1600 meter run is an excellent idea to weed out the physically weak.

Every officer is supposed to be courageous, mentally and physically. Either he has courage or he doesn't. A seven meter board, unassisted jump into a swimming pool, after the 1600 meter run is more than adequate, even if he does not know how to swim. I have done it at NDA as a non-swimmer. I presume that other aspects such as Situational Awareness, Effective Intelligence, Leadership Potential etc, are tested in the tests that are not mentioned above.

CONCLUSION

The subject of 'selection system' of military officers is technical in nature and can be commented upon only by qualified officers who are educated, trained or experienced in this field. DIPR/SSB qualified officers or/and military psychologists would be the most competent to comment. Additional training experience as instructors in military academies will enable the officers to better comprehend and connect selection with training rather than view selection in isolation.

There has already been tremendous publicity (unofficially) about the De Novo selection system and the likely implementation of 7 points from 2019. Apparently, the DIPR is very secretive and over cautious about their proposals and intentions. Little or no input is coming on this subject from the environment, including the military officers posted in SSBs. Unless there are meaningful interactions between the DIPR and the end users – the SSB and the trainers in military academies – there can be no worthwhile progress. Selection cannot be viewed in 'isolation' for optimum results on ground.

Glaring shortcomings in our selection and training systems have been revealed since Nov 2011, through Maj Gen Raj Mehta's cover story titled 'Grim Portents' in Geopolitics magazine, followed by 'Grim Portents 2' and also book reviews of 'Victory India Series' including Force Magazine, Mar 18 of book review of Volume 4 of Victory India 4. Seven years have lapsed since several weaknesses and shortcomings have been repeatedly exposed by Four Victory India Campaign books from 2013-18 and Fauji India Magazine for last 2yrs from 2016-18.

This is yet another technical debate on 'military officer selection' revealing the glaring shortcomings in the speculated 'De Novo System'. All these are ominous signs which do not augur well for the future. Something has gone drastically wrong with our selection system which is no more relevant and failed to keep up with the times and the needs. Most advanced/modern armies have been regularly reviewing, revising or refining their respective selection and training systems. For most of these countries their manpower selection base is very small. Hencethey immensely value their manpower and remain relevant and keep abreast with new technicalities of selection with frequent review revision and refinement besides linking it adequately with training requirements and actual user needs.

On the contrary, we despite our huge manpower base, do not value it and never even bother about seriously revising our selection and training systems. The huge number of candidates applying to join the military may not be 'qualitatively' as good or suitable as before but 'quantitatively' their numbers have increased manifold. This is one of the chief reasons for our lackadaisical attitude and approach when it comes to some serious review or introspection of our 70 year old and obsolete selection system. Lack of coordination between selection, training and grooming to give the user arms and services the required product as per the need of the times is another main drawback.

If the foundation of our selection and training continues to be weak, consequently the officer product too will be wanting, not only after commissioning but in later service too. There is now an inescapable and imperative need to change that to improve the quality of our military leadership at all levels. Victory India and Fauji India shows the way forward!

Note: This article was published in Fauji India magazine, Sep2018 issue

CHAPTER 25

National Defence Academy Faces Unprecedented Burnout

Parth Satam

A report prepared by the Indian military reveals a huge rate of burnout of cadets at the country's premier military training institution.

A report jointly prepared by the Integrated Defence Staff Headquarters and the NDA, accessed by Asia Times, has revealed the rate of young cadets quitting the institution.

The NDA is arguably the only military training institution of its kind. Sixteen-year-olds join the Pune-based institute as army, navy and air force cadets after passing an entrance exam and a five-day personality, psychological and medical examination. They receive a bachelor's degree at the end of three years and then enrol in their respective service academies – the Indian Military Academy (IMA), the Indian Naval Academy or the Air Force Academy – where they train to be future commissioned officers.

NDA alumni squarely blame ragging; 'unofficial training' and excessive physical punishment for the high attrition rate and describe the torture at the hands of senior cadets as sadistic and misguided.

Col P K Royal Mehrishi, an NDA alumnus, explained how senior cadets ask juniors to roll down staircases of three-story buildings, vault over a wooden horse, do back flips, hand-springs etc without the supervision of any qualified instructor.

"Senior cadets believe they're toughening them for war or better performance in the hard-fought inter-squadron competitions," he said.

A former NDA instructor, Colonel Vinay Dalvi, said senior cadets often justified the punishments as a mode of getting the freshmen into the grind. He said a senior cadet, or the overstudy, often faced punishment from divisional officers for newcomers' mistakes. This, he said, put severe pressure on the freshmen.

Ankur Chaturvedi, a former NDA cadet, reveals that the bulk of the injuries are reported during the initial terms. He sustained a kidney injury during a boxing bout and left the academy in 1996.

Retired Air Marshal P P Rajkumar, a former deputy commandant and alumnus of the NDA, confirmed the long-standing culture of ragging and unstructured training. In 1975, a senior cadet lost his life after juniors assaulted him for all the physical abuse he had put them through, he offers as anecdotal evidence.

"This happened during the run-up to the passing-out [graduation] parade when the departing cadets bury the hatchet with the juniors while parting company in an event called Socials. Here, the junior cadets in the squadron are allowed to rag the sixth-senior cadets in a friendly setting. However, a group of juniors hit him so hard that he died," he said.

Too Exacting
Col Mehrishi suggests that the NDA's revised physical standards are a bit too exacting, even more than that of commissioning academies such as the IMA. Retired Brigadier L C Patnaik points out that even cadet with background in sports; find themselves underperforming in tasks such as a front roll. He pointed out that this is apart from the late-night unofficial punishments, which cause complaints of dizziness, headache, fatigue and changes in sleep patterns.

In his book Quality Military Leadership, Colonel Dalvi quotes a former director and commandant of the Armed Forces Medical College, retired Air Marshal B Keshav Rao, who had carried out an assessment of the NDA's training regimen: "Inadequate rest between periods of intense physical exertion, inadequate sleep, missing meals and inadequate focus on personal hygiene [and] off-syllabus physical activity at the squadron level mitigated attempts at scientific and structured strength and stamina building."

'Relegations,' 'withdrawals' and 'resignations' are the three heads under which departures from the academy are classified, depending on whether the cause was academic failure, rustication, medical fitness or voluntary separation. "Relegations" refers to repeating a semester for failing an academic or outdoor training (ODT) test. Dalvi said that sometimes the reason for relegation might be both, because a cadet is too exhausted to focus on studies, thereby flunking his exams or not having adequately recovered from the grueling physical regimen to crack the ODT.

Two consecutive relegations can lead to a "withdrawal," which is a permanent release from the academy. It can also be on disciplinary or medical grounds. In the case of "resignations," the cadet can choose to leave the academy within two weeks of joining, without paying the NDA the 1.35 million rupees (US$21,250) incurred on his three-year training.

It is not the only armed-forces institute witnessing burnout. According to the Directorate General of the Armed Forces Medical Services, the hospitalization rate among officer cadets across military-training institutes in the country between 2013 and 2015 was 34.14%.

Officials at the NDA did not respond to a detailed e-mail query sent on December 15, citing the absence of officials and staff on account of the mid-term break. This story will be updated if they respond.

Need for Scientific Methodology
Both Colonel Dalvi and Brigadier Patnaik recommend phased training that progressively increases the physical strain. Dalvi said cadets' endurance and strength would have peaked by the time they graduated as officers. Patnaik recommended a scientific assessment of cadets, such as muscle and bone-density testing, before subjecting them to the rigorous regimen at the NDA. He said a dedicated department of physical education should be set up to oversee the cadet for the first year, with the proportion of military training gradually increasing in the last two years.

For retired Admiral Arun Prakash, former navy chief and commandant of the National Defense Academy, the remedies lie in the service headquarters paying greater attention to the training academies and ending the ad hoc methods in appointing the commandants. He said the commandant is a three-star officer, usually slated to retire within a couple of years. He argued that the commandant should ideally be a two-star officer, with another promotion left to go.

"A blue book for academies, prepared by the Chiefs of Staff Committee, with inviolable rules for their functioning, should be introduced. No commandant or instructor can introduce their own ideas," he proposed.

Col Mehrishi advocates a mandatory supervision of all training and punishment by qualified instructors with a "ruthless, zero-tolerance ragging policy." Most military veterans Asia Times spoke to believe that the problem also lies with the outdated officer-selection system.

Brigadier Patnaik says the existing personality and psychological tests that assess "officer-like qualities" only consider the behavioural process and observable responses, neglecting the mental processes that trigger actions and decisions. He points that out tests such as the British Army Recruitment Battery and the Australian Computerized Cognitive Assessment Tool judge the mental processes and not the response.

Medical tests, Patnaik insists, should be revised to include exercises such as 1.6-kilometer shuttle runs, push-ups, chin-ups, sit-ups etc to match with the physical capability required during training.

Dalvi argues that the British Raj-era selection and training system has destroyed the careers of many talented young potential officers.

CHAPTER 26

Excessive Punishments and Ragging Causing High Morbidity and Waste Rates at Premier Military Academies

Col P K 'Royal' Mehrishi

The juniors in fits of rage have in some instances ganged up and beaten some unpopular seniors with hob nailed boots (drill boots) and in a one extreme case, with stones filled in a pillow case. In this particular incident (in the mid-seventies) he died and the issue was a talking point in the Parliament. Most of the unstructured/unauthorized training, punishments/ragging in NDA are well known and have continued uninterruptedly with impunity for decades with Squadrons having their own variations and traditions passed on from course to course. What is common in them is the mistaken belief that these physical and mental sessions actually toughen the cadets to face any grave threat or future eventuality.

Introduction

Ragging, hazing, fagging, bullying, pledging, horse-playing etc. are different terms used in different parts of the world but each signifying the same old practice of welcoming the fresher in a barbaric manner. The word 'ragging' is mainly used in India, Pakistan, Bangladesh, Sri Lanka and Malaysia. It involves existing students baiting or bullying new students and often takes a malignant form wherein the newcomers may be subjected to psychological or physical torture.

Ragging in its present form came into our country via the Public School system set up by the British. A general feeling of exclusivity and elitism permeated the atmosphere in these institutions with a certain amount of connivance from the teachers/staff with the senior students to initiate the so called raw, uncouth or uninitiated into the proper environs of a boarding school.

Like a Frankenstein monster, these childish, at times nonsensical initiation rites in its worst form, have now assumed the proportion of death, suicide, maiming or worse, psychological scarring for many of its victims in the prime of their youth. The worst affected are medical colleges/IIT/engineering colleges and include our military academies like NDA, IMA and OTA where it is often relentlessly pursued with impunity, generally camouflaged as non-structured training and grooming.

Analysis

Between the age of 18-21 years when a boy student enters these institutions, factors like massive hormonal (testosterone)activity, bodily changes, questions regarding identity/personality/height/weight/build/looks etc, basic rebellion against authority, peer pressure to conform, a feeling of superiority after clearing a national level competitive entrance exam, pressure to excel, heightened risk taking behaviour (because of underdeveloped Pre-Frontal Cortex), a feeling of invincibility in seniors after "having been there, seen it all, and a frenetic pace of training/education with little time for introspection/genuine reflection/ personality development are in play.

It can easily be understood that a young boy of this age can never pass off as an expert in any field. Let us for example take the case of a NDA cadet in his third/fourth/fifth semester asking juniors to roll down the staircase of a three-storied squadron building (billets for cadets) as part of the 'Course Initiation' rites or enthusiastically hold PT classes like vaulting over a wooden horse, back flip/handspring etc., in the squadron premises without the supervision of a qualified PT instructor. Injuries/mishaps are waiting to happen. Some of these classes are held in the mistaken belief of extra training to earn points during Inter Squadron competitions. Ragging can get nasty during midterm breaks for juniors or end of term sessions when seniors come requesting for "forget and forgive" sessions before passing out parade (POP). The juniors in fits of rage have in some instances ganged up and beaten some unpopular seniors with hob nailed boots (drill boots) and in a one extreme case, with stones filled in a pillow case. In this particular incident (in the mid-seventies) the senior cadet died and the issue was a talking point in the Parliament.

Most of the unstructured/unauthorized training, punishments/ragging in NDA are well known and have continued uninterruptedly with impunity for decades with Squadrons having their own variations and traditions passed on from course to course. What is common in them is the mistaken belief that these physical and mental sessions actually toughen the cadets to face any grave threat or future eventuality, like being taken prisoner of war by the enemy with serious consequences of actual physical and mental torture during future military life, fraught with severe hardships and uncertainties! **These unofficial punishments meted out to cadets for decades are not being described as it would leave a bad taste and be highly detrimental to the good and positive impression/ image the academy enjoys even today.**

It is pertinent to mention that none of these punishments or so called physical exercises are authorized or structured but assimilated and continued as part of tradition blindly passed on from seniors to juniors. The qualified APTC-PT instructors and AMC doctors would never approve or endorse any such punishments which cause grievous injuries, especially when meted out/conducted by senior semester cadets with little/no expertise or knowledge about life impairing injuries. **Even the 'Geneva Conventions' for 'Prisoners of War' would never endorse/approve them!** Some punishments like hackle order (rolling up all your belongings and reporting to a senior) and changing of rigs can bring a smile to one's face as these are harmless innovations to brighten up an otherwise monotonous routine. Not all seniors are sadistic/cruel in meeting out punishments. Some are true mentors who coach the squadron boxing team (boxers are prestige earners) in spare time, make the team do only push-ups/sit-ups/chin-ups/rope skipping/sparring and running up the stairs toughening exercises. Some are good at academics who coach juniors during study periods. A few are good at drill and worthy of emulation. It is partly ganging up/sadistic pleasure/bludgeoning juniors to servility that is the problem which needs to be addressed. A few cadets carry these psychological scars of humiliation later in their careers with adverse/negative 'psychological impact' on personality.

Psychological Impact

Motivation Crowding Theory: Extrinsic motivators like excessive punishments can undermine intrinsic motivation. Since all punishments in NDA are physical in nature it can lead to a 'zero–error syndrome' wherein a cadet, later an Officer shies away from taking decisions in an ambiguous situation lest he be identified and punished.

Cognitive Dissonance: Change in attitude/behaviour for the better is desired in a cadet, but mass/group punishments cause cognitive dissonance instead of cognitive consistency. Self-concept is threatened when one is punished for the fault of others.

Positioning Theory: For a young impressionable mind, words from a senior like, "I don't care. Beg borrow, steal," to make up the deficiency in kit items focuses on moral orders and their correctness in later life. If a cadet has lost something, his moral courage should be reinforced by asking him to own up and say he has lost such item and will buy it from the Regimental shop (raincoats/cycle valves/FSMO)

Behaviourism (Bandura): Environment causes behaviour, true. But behaviour causes environment as well. This concept is reciprocal determinism. Personality is an interaction among three 'things': the environment, behaviour, and the person's psychological processes. Excessive unstructured physical punishments lead to observational learning or modelling, and his theory is usually called social learning theory. A cadet growing up in this environment will know nothing but this as the only reality. As he grows by the semester, he gives it back to his juniors manifold.

Faulty Learning Process: Leadership is about nature and nurture. A nurturing environment includes associations, reinforcements, punishments (authorized and not demeaning), and observations. Some of the primary learning theories of development include: classical conditioning, operant conditioning and social learning. If one has to learn something, one has to go through this process. In NDA, junior term cadets are perpetually suffering from sleep deprivation because of physical punishments/unstructured training:

- **Attention** – If a cadet has to learn anything, he has to be paying attention. Likewise, anything that puts a damper on attention is going to decrease learning, including observational learning. If, for example, he is sleepy, groggy, drugged, sick, nervous, or "hyper," he will learn less likewise, if he is being distracted by competing stimuli.
- **Retention** – Second, he must be able to retain (remember) what he has paid attention to. This is where imagery and language come in: we store what we have seen the instructor doing in the form of mental images or verbal descriptions. When so stored, a cadet can later "bring up" the image or description, so that he can reproduce it with his own behavior.
- **Reproduction** – A cadet has to translate the images or descriptions into actual behavior. He has to have the ability to reproduce the behavior in the first place. A cadet learns by watching his instructors/peers perform. Performance of difficult tests in PT/riding/drill would in fact improve if he watches cadets who are better than him. Another important tidbit about reproduction is that our ability to imitate improves with practice at the behaviors involved. And one more tidbit: Our abilities improve even when we just imagine ourselves performing! Many athletes, for example, imagine their performance in their mind's eye prior to actually performing.
- **Motivation** – And yet, with all this, a cadet is still not going to do anything unless he is motivated to imitate, i.e. until he has some reason for doing it.

An environment of excessive punishments/unstructured training will create tendencies of harm avoidance that develop in the cadet. A defence mechanism to cope with this kind of forced/unstructured/illogical training develops, which involves cutting corners or 'shamming' which is undesirable during training as the cadet is in the prime of youth having volunteered for progressive military training and become a responsible Officer.

Morbidity (Hospital Admissions)
The morbidity/hospital admissions rate of military cadets per 1000 strength for all causes (injuries and sickness) of cadets and recruits given below indicate the rate of cadets to be 3-4 times that of recruits. This clearly indicates that the physical fitness parameters for selected SSB candidates do not meet the actual

training schedule or training curriculum to meet high bench marks set by Academies. Clearly, there is a mismatch between SSB selection standards and actual physical bench marks of Academies, especially NDA, which traditionally has raised their physical bench marks even beyond the finishing academy (IMA) with several negative/serious implications to the cadets, academies (both basic and finishing) and consequently, the three services!

Year	2013	2014	2015
Cadets	280.98	351.74	391.39
Recruits	109.65	92.62	105.21

Relegations, Withdrawal & Resignations at NDA

The total number of relegations, withdrawals and resignations of NDA cadets for the past 10 years (2008-2017) are approximately 1260 (average 126 per year or 63 per term). The average relegations, withdrawals and resignations per term have been 38, 10 and 15 respectively and the yearly average is 76, 20 and 30 respectively. The strength of the cadets varied from 1800 to 1920 during this period (2008-2017).

Financial Implication/Loss to Tax Payer

The expenditure per cadet at the NDA was about Rs. 9000 per week. From 01 July 2017, it has been increased to Rs. 10247. Hence for one term/semester of 22 weeks what was earlier Rs. 1,98,000 will now be Rs. 2,25,434 from 01 July 2017. So for six terms, what worked out to 12 lakh earlier would be Rs. 13.5 lakh from 01 July 2017. The average relegations for the last 10 years has been 38 which means 76 lakh additional expenditure per term and 152 lakh per year have been incurred. From 01July 2017, it would amount to approximately Rs. 85 lakh per term and Rs 170 lakh per year for the same number of relegations/semester repetitions. The financial loss on account of withdrawal of cadets on 'medical' or 'disciplinary grounds' and 'resignations' have not been included. In case of 'resignations', the parents of cadets have to pay for the cost of training incurred on the cadet as per the above rates.

Aim of Furnishing Statistical Data

The above statistical data is to mainly reiterate/highlight the imperative and urgent need to address the underlying root causes for the high number of relegations, withdrawals and resignations for the last ten years. The figures for earlier ten years too would be similar. The chief cause for it is undoubtedly the non-structured training, excessive punishments and ragging which must now be corrected/rectified on a war footing. The DIPR Study report of 2000/2001 for ten NDA courses (96-106) highlighted this same cause which led to a wastage rate of 18%. It is believed to have later dropped to 16-20 % and probably the same now?

THE WAY FORWARD

The way forward is sensitization, education, example, persuasion and in rare cases punishment/rustication:

- Before the beginning of the academic/training session all cadets to be briefed regarding zero tolerance of the management towards unauthorized punishments/training.
- Any training related activity without an authorized expert/instructor with Qualified for Instructor (QFI) badge to be viewed as a serious breach of discipline.
- Ragging/unauthorized punishments in any form to be banned. Instead, cadets should be exposed to survival and outdoor camps/martial arts/adventure activities.
- Availability of psychological counselors (one every 400 cadets).
- Foreign exchange programs during term breaks with cadets from friendly foreign countries.
- Constant sensitization during roll calls/parades regarding ill effects of ragging.
- Wholesome entertainment and freedom of expression via sports/art/culture/outdoor activity/drama/debate/declamation to the trainee and enhancing all aspects to develop a well-rounded personality.

CONCLUSION

The medical statistics of for the past three years (2013-15) of cadets and recruits highlight the 'high morbidity' of cadets which is 3-4 times that of recruits and consequently leads to their high wastage/attrition rates vis-à-vis recruits.

Serious issues like military training and PT are best left to experts in the field. Many of them have spent a lifetime pursuing physical training/education, sports medicine/sciences and its effects on training young minds. Military training is a highly complex and specialized field.

Novices can never even dream to come near the level of professionalism exhibited by weapon/drill/PT/commando/parachute/high altitude/jungle warfare instructors. Since all learning is progressive and cumulative, it is best done under supervision of those who wear the Qualified for Instructor (QFI) badge.

Our military training pamphlets issued by DGMT/ARTRAC and training instructions by concerned training institutions/centers lay down the training methodology and guidelines. These must be implemented uniformly both in letter and spirit, without any deviations due to individual views or perceptions on the subject during entire official raining curriculum/training periods.

Unofficial and non-structured training, including excessive punishments, conducted after official training time by novices or young/inexperienced instructors or senior cadets without any valid qualification must cease forthwith.

This single factor is the chief cause for high 'wastage' rate of cadets besides serious negative psychological impact during their critical formative years leading to imbibing and inculcating negative personality traits detrimental to bold, efficient and effective military leadership in their later service life.

VALIDATIONS

Brig LC Patnaik

Despite numerous initiatives by erstwhile Commandants of the training institutions and the Recruiting Directorate, the qualitative output of Officers has been a major concern at the unit/subunit level. Hence we need to consider de-novo transformation measures to achieve our desired goal at the functional level. The psychological impact on adolescent cadets has been adequately analyzed by the author. Unauthorized training leads to dizziness, headache, fatigue and change in sleep patterns, which are normally the complaints during 'sick reports' by the cadets at NDA. Emotionally above symptoms leads a person to be aggressive, impatient, impulsive and prone to low self esteem, creating major disruption to an individual's ability to perceive and assimilate.

Hence, it can be surmised that the three essential factors of learning as brought out by the author; attention, retention and re-production are severely compromised through unauthorized and excessive punishments, prevalent in the Academy, for which there is a high rate of exodus in the form of withdrawal, relegations and absconding. To address the issue, we need to follow a '3-S' policy of 'specialization', 'segregation' and 'scientific' physical training at NDA.

Professor Emeritus S S Nathawat, ex-HOD (Psychology) University of Rajasthan.

Col P K 'Royal' Mehrishi attempts to trace the genesis and psychological impact of this undesirable behaviour citing various psychological theories. The problem of ragging behaviour appears to be multi dimensional and not uncommon in higher education institutions around the world. Despite the Government's ban on it since the late 1970s and thereafter interventions by the Supreme Court (1999 and 2006) issuing guidelines to eradicate ragging, it is still prevalent. We are still not clear whether the incidence and severity of ragging has declined or increased in last few decades.

On the directions of the Supreme Court (1999), the UGC formed a four member committee under Prof KPS Unny, which defined ragging and outlined its 'positive' and negative impacts. While pointing out 'positive' impacts of ragging, it observed that its negative impacts had become more prevalent. However, the Raghavan Committee, constituted by the Supreme Court in 2006 took a more serious view of the problem. The Committee observed: "If education, and particularly Higher Education, is to serve as the lever to the great surge forward of the Indian nation, the scourge of ragging which corrodes the vitals of our campuses needs to be curbed"(Raghavan Committee Report, 2007, p. i) In the late 70s, in the aftermath of the death of two fresher's in a Regional Engineering College that the Government of India for the first time issued a notification banning ragging in the country. However, despite the national ban, incidents did not come down, prompting several universities to bring ordinances and state governments to issue executive orders or bring modifications in their state education act or initiate legislation against ragging. Surfing the internet disclosed that educational institutions in several countries had practices like ragging that functioned primarily to initiate newcomers into the institution's student community.

Col C M Chavan

We have failed to analyze and rectify the physical harm and negative psychological impact caused to cadets by excessive punishments and ragging. The entire system in the academies should be structured and coordinated to progressively build up the physical endurance and academic intellect of cadets, dovetailed to meet needs of present day warfare and future eventualities. There should be a common code of conduct for junior and senior cadets as well as instructors as for all dealings with cadets. The Battalion and Squadron Commanders should be made accountable and responsible to ensure strict implementation of the code. Those found wanting, especially Division Officers and Senior cadets must be dealt with ruthlessly.

Cdr Mukund Yeolekar, *ex-Principal INS Shivaji*

The academy should set up a Centre for Professional Military Ethics tasked to lead and coordinate the planning, synchronization, execution and assessment of the character program so that every graduate is a commissioned leader of Character. The core functions of this Centre should be as follows:

- Assist in the synchronization and assessment of the character development strategy.
- Design and administer the Cadet Character development program (CCDP).
- Educate, train and inspire cadets with a focus on honorable living, building trust and respect and to desist from sexual harassment/assault.

The CCDP provides the conceptual and inspirational content to support the individual and collective development of Cadets into commissioned leaders of character, and is the foundation of character education efforts. The CCDP will be responsible for instruction and structured reflection on the concepts central to professional and ethical standards of behaviour for the Indian Armed Forces. Cadets should put these standards of behaviour into practice through their participation in the academic, military and physical programs. We should take a leaf from academies in the developed countries which have gone through this phase.

CHAPTER 27

Incorporation of Scientific Approaches in Military Training Methodology – New-Age Science

Col Vinay Dalvi

This is an abstract of a talk delivered by Col Vinay Dalvi, an athlete and physical trainer, at the Sports Authority of India Conference (SAICON) at New Delhi in December 2017.

Reproduced here for the larger benefit of the Indian military fraternity!

'Enhancement of Training Curriculum in Armed Forces Training Institutes' was a subject of discussion at the apex military level and a joint decision being taken to make military physical training more scientific by incorporating 'Sports Medicine' in the training methodology of cadets, recruits and combat soldiers. The effective implementation of this decision on ground can bring immense benefits of sports/fitness medicine with systematic, progressive and scientific physical training, especially for the officer trainees, where the physical training activities form 70% of their average daily 24-hour training period.

The entire physical training syllabus, curriculum and tests rest on three great principles of PT (harmonious development, systematic progression and continuity) evident in the training pamphlets. The inclusion of sports/fitness medicine can bring scientific orientation to the entire physical development. The aim of physical training in the military is to make and keep a soldier fit both physically and mentally to perform his assigned task effectively and efficiently. The training methodology must consider the 24-hour daily routine of a trainee and cater for adequate rest, recovery, recuperation, diet and nutrition with physical load being administered progressively to improve fitness levels methodically and scientifically to attain optimum results as per individual potential or capacity. The knowledge of physical and recreational training and sports/fitness medicine must be promoted amongst officers and junior leaders with a practical vision plan and road map.

Definition of Sports Medicine

'Sports science' (also sports and exercise science, sports medicine or exercise physiology) is a discipline that studies how the healthy human body works during exercise, and how sport and physical activity promote health and performance from cellular to whole body perspectives. The study of sports science incorporates areas of exercise physiology, sports psychology, sports nutrition, anatomy, biomechanics, and bio kinetics.

Sports medicine, also known as sport and exercise medicine (SEM), is a branch of medicine that deals with physical fitness and the treatment and prevention of sports and exercise related injuries. Although most sports teams have employed team physicians for many years, it is only since the late 20th century that sports medicine has emerged as a distinct field of health care.

Background

Sports medicine as a subject was introduced in the military in 1980s by our pioneer sports medicine doctors to a few select sportsmen, coaches, physical trainers, managers and administrators in the field of sports, especially individual and team sports like athletics, weight lifting, boxing, and hockey; subsequently spread to few other sports discipline. This new knowledge and its technical application was not adequately understood or taken seriously due to our rigid/status quo mind set and laid down training concepts and methodology.

Review of the Army PT tables for recruits/cadets/combatants and PPT and BPET for all ranks of the Army was done during late 1980s by a Review Committee under Commandant AIPT/ASPT including a sports medicine doctor and most qualified and experienced APTC officers. The trials on the new PT tables and tests were conducted and comparisons drawn with the old system. The new system of PT tables and tests were approved and adopted from 1992 and continue till date. Based on these changes, the officer pre-commission military academies and recruit training centres adopted the new system with their existing ones to meet the new service requirements of trained officers and soldiers.

Relevance of Subject

The importance and relevance of this subject in the field of overall physical training methodology of military training for cadets, recruits and combatants was strongly felt by me due to my all round exposure to not only several sports disciplines at national level but also my deep and sustained involvement of training officer cadets, recruits and testing all ranks through laid down PT tests.

The old, obsolete and outdated system of physical training methodology repeatedly came to my notice besides the unsupervised non-structured unofficial training by senior cadets and unqualified or inexperienced service officers especially at our elite military academies disturbed me tremendously. The damage that they had caused and continued to cause gave me many sleepless nights. The only way to address these issues was through debate and discussion and subsequent penning down, initially as discussion points, articles, responses or debates and papers, leading to compilation of full volumes. 'Role Model',

'Sun Tzu', 'Victory India' – 1,2,3 and 4 involving over 60 reputed/renowned military Veterans and others.

Our sustained and combined efforts to convert our penned down recommendations into realistic transformation on ground slowly but surely started 'bearing fruit' through better and wider awareness of the entire subject of quality military manpower, especially the elite officer leadership and the ways and means to improve it. The decision of the UCC to incorporate sports medicine in the physical training methodology of military training of cadets, recruits and combatants in July 2017 came after one year of consideration by the three services and joint acceptance for implementation on ground.

Army Physical Training Syllabus, PT Tables & Tests

These are based on the training pamphlets issued by DGMT/ARTRAC and the PT doctrine and training methodology but finally left to the concerned training academies and recruit training centres. The trained manpower is left to the unit and formation commanders with supervisory role by concerned staff/tech/line directorates depending on the unit or establishment.

The immediate problem for incorporating sports medicine in training will be the imperative need to understand the laid down system of training as per the training pamphlets and guidelines. The correct/better understanding of this is a dire need as the training concepts and philosophy is personality based, not only in units but also training institutions. Other than APTC staff or PT Course qualified personnel, hardly anybody knows about the technicalities and principles of PT and the link with recreational training. Hence, this knowledge must be taken seriously first. Thereafter, the introduction/incorporation of sports medicine/fitness medicine should be done. Sports and fitness medicine are two sides of the same coin. Similarly the military training encapsulating the entire 24 physical training curriculum must be viewed holistically and a vision plan and road map made for systematic, methodological and coordinated implementation at all levels including training academies and recruit centres.

Entry Level Physical Fitness Needs Revision

Entry level physical fitness tests/parameters and selection system needs immediate review especially for the officer cadre with transparent/objective mandatory tests. The recruit entry tests are basically physical oriented with less scope for other talented/technical candidates for selection. This needs review and dovetailed to meet different/varied requirements of multifarious trades of all arms and services, especially technical arms.

For the officer entries, the minimum physical take off level required/demanded by the military academies must be met. The high wastage rate of cadets is partly due this 20-year-old demand of academies not being met. 'Trainability' and 'potentiality' are the two key words that have been 'subjectively' deciding the selection of SSB candidates. Objective and mandatory physical tests at the SSB selection centers will raise the entry level physical standard of officer cadets and positively impact the overall fitness standard of cadets besides drastically reducing wastage rates and training injuries.

Fitness Enhancement with Scientific Methodology

The entire physical training methodology should be imparted progressively and scientifically to enable systematic and harmonious development of the cadets and recruits right from the beginning with small and progressive doses for all round steady development. Violent and irregular doses of physical training in any form without rest, recuperation and recovery cause more damage than gain. The cadets and recruits must be made constantly aware of the drawbacks and adverse effects of following the wrong methods through official/structured or unofficial/non-structured training.

Awareness and education will bring in a desire to avoid wrong doings and misguided methods in both the trainers and the trained. Interaction between seniors and juniors cannot be avoided for effective team work and leadership development. However, it can be modified, refined and improved through awareness of scientific methodology for enhanced fitness.

Benefits & Gains of Effective Implementation

The cumulative and collective benefits that will accrue with incorporation of sports medicine in physical training methodology of military training of cadets, recruits and combatants will consequentially achieve the following:

- Enhance physical and mental fitness of trainees and combatants.
- Spread technical knowledge and scientific methodology of PT/sports/fitness medicine.
- Lead to more systematic, scientific and methodological training of combatants.
- Will reduce training related injuries and even consequent disabilities of combatants.
- Will reduce wastage and morbidity rates of trainees.
- Enable and facilitate better health and physical fitness of all trainees and combatants.

CHAPTER 28

Selection and Role of NDA Academic Staff: A Debate

Col Vinay B Dalvi

Background

Recent (June 2018) CBI raids at NDA, Khadakwasla and filing of FIR against the Principal and few members of academic teaching staff for submitting false documents in support of their qualifications for employment/appointment in various posts in academic department at NDA during 2012 prove that something is grossly wrong with the system of selection and appointment of the academic teaching staff and calls for the immediate review of the system and fixing the faults with a holistic approach and practical vision plan to address them with the involvement of all concerned agencies, viz; – NDA,HQ IDS/ CISC,COSC,MOD & UPSC.

Article by Air Vice Mshl Arjun Subramaniam, on this subject, triggered due to CBI raids, available on the net and circulating on social media is reproduced below. The article is relevant and timely on this subject which has once again caught the attention of the print media. Ironically, this subject and several other issues, pertaining to NDA have been in the print media very often for past 5-6 years, during which a campaign called 'Victory India' for the improvement of the quality of our military leadership at all levels not only took birth but has widely spread in the environment with full knowledge and awareness of our three services and all concerned training institutions and selection agencies.

Four volumes published during 2013, 2014, 2016 & 2018 of the 'Victory India Campaign' by Pentagon Press, New Delhi, encapsulating 175 articles, essays, papers, letters and responses by over sixty (60) military contributors and academicians have amply and elaborately covered this issue (with a holistic approach and practical vision plan) and also entire system of selection, training and grooming of military officers, including NDA and the current issue confronting them.

Trigger

Article below has throws up several critical issues on the existing system of selection and highlights the imperative need to review and revise this system with a view to improve the quality of academic staff and consequently the quality of the academics of the cadets, which has obviously suffered for many years and adversely affected the quality of the cadets fed to the finishing academies and loss to the three services.

Kindly examine the points now raised in the article in the backdrop of the Victory India Campaign reference material and forward your responses with views, comments and recommendations to address the issue which has once again brought NDA into media focus, unfortunately for the wrong reasons.

Article by Air Vice Marshal Arjun Subramaniam

Preoccupied with immediate organisational and operational challenges, the services have ignored military education for too long.

The recent news about CBI raids on the principal of the National Defence Academy and a few other civilian faculty members is not surprising because the whole education system in our military academies has been suspect, and such aberrations were waiting to happen.

Addressing this as an isolated occurrence will not provide a holistic solution to the problem – how do we produce well-educated and not just well-trained officers in India's armed forces?

Having thoroughly studied the Indian system of how we go about educating military officers for almost 30 years, served as a faculty member at various Indian institutions for nine years in a 35-year career, and visited the United States Air Force Academy (USAFA) and several war colleges in the US recently as a guest speaker, I am convinced that we are still confused about the difference between education and training.

Consequently, whenever confronted with problems regarding professional military education at various levels, our military leadership prefers to showcase our highly efficient and effective training systems as an adequate alternative for a poor education ecosystem.

Lack of Upgrade

Much attention is paid to keep the education-training cycle for the civil services at institutions like the IAS Academy at Mussoorie contemporary. But the MoD is least interested in facilitating the same at institutions like the National Defence Academy or individual service academies such as the Indian Military Academy (IMA), the Indian Naval Academy, or the Air Force Academy (AFA).

Why should they really be interested when service leadership itself has invariably been preoccupied with immediate organisational and operational challenges and never really demanded a stake in education?

The archaic and inefficient UPSC system has been entrusted with the task of selecting teachers for Sainik/military schools, NDA and all academies. Selection of faculty members, monitoring their performance and academic calibre and, most importantly, frequent upgrading of academic syllabi have been weak areas that need attention.

Killing Interest in Education

During the 1970s and 1980s, we had dedicated teachers and lecturers at military schools and the NDA, who could sow the spark of creativity or plant latent seeds of intellectual curiosity in the minds of cadets.

The writing skills imparted by G.M. Khan, an English teacher of mine at the Rashtriya Indian Military College, have stood me in good stead over the years. Similarly, Professor Rajan, the HoD of the IR, geopolitics and military history department at NDA Khadakwasla, was an inspiring and committed teacher whose lectures many of us never missed.

Now, when I speak to cadets at the NDA and other institutions, they have no civilian or military educators to look up to; they have many trainers though (military instructors on the drill and PT field, or weapons and flying or sailing instructors). This is the point where mediocre or ad hoc educators kill any interest in education.

Commandants at institutions like the NDA are powerful leaders with vast resources and immense scope to make an impact on both education and training. However, barring a few exceptions, very rarely have they been positioned there because they are considered expert educators or trainers.

It is a routine, stand-in-line post where either the three-star officer is positioned as a stop-gap arrangement till an operational post falls vacant, or because it is the turn of a particular service to tenet the joint establishment vacancy, or the officer has insufficient residual service to assume a C-in-Cs post. Consequently, their interest in education and academics is at best superficial, and at worst indifferent.

Solving the Problem

This problem can be overcome if all these institutions have a dean of academics and faculty, who is either an accomplished academic or a practitioner scholar, to oversee a combination of civilian and military faculty and report to the commandant.

For example, I met the dean of faculty at the USAFA, Brigadier General Andrew Armacost, a PhD from MIT, who was selected from several applicants. The selection was not based on his rank or operational profile, but on his understanding and commitment to both training and education. The first question he bounced on me was: How are our academies addressing the challenges of offering a holistic education for officer cadets that offers opportunities for combining a technological focus with adequate awareness of the humanities and /or pure sciences?

Clearing the rot is not a difficult proposition. But it needs a willingness on the part of the military to acknowledge the need for better education as a critical tool for producing officers and men, who will fit into the rapidly changing milieu of contemporary security landscapes and the constantly changing character of warfare in the 21st century.

It also needs support from the bureaucracy and the political leadership, which should not see hidden demons in a well-educated and intellectually empowered military. Not many know that the Goldwater Nichols Act that reformed the US military included sweeping reforms in professional military education.

(Arjun Subramaniam is a retired Air Vice Marshal of the IAF, and currently, a visiting fellow at Oxford)

RESPONSES

Air Cmde Suryakant N Bal

If the CBI has to conduct raids to uncover malpractices in the selection of academic staff, then the entire system has failed – all the checks and counter – checks: no individual involved in the selection process can offer an excuse. Every system has checks and counter-checks: and any system is as effective as it is allowed to be. What has happened is a reflection of the general situation in society. However, that does not make a valid case for the military to follow such trends. We must stand tall and be above board – not an easy task, but not an impossible one either. The rot has to be stopped – from the ground up. Any deviation has to be managed ruthlessly – and without pity. For the military this is a debt of honour – to the Nation. The Nation is supreme, and anyone who does not fall in line must be ruthlessly eliminated.

Cdr Ravindra Pathak

To my mind the whole system at the NDA started to crumble the day the emphasis shifted more towards academics. I have been a cadet at NDA and as a squadron Cdr, my experience has been of deterioration of standards since 1982 when I was a faculty there. I was fortunate to still have some of the stalwart civilian instructors from cadet's days around but I was also unfortunate to see the new breed of civilians who stood distinctly apart as nondescript. The author is right there are no iconic figures today at NDA from among the civilian staff.

When I was a cadet we had a mathematic instructor who would sum up the entire purpose of the existence of the NDA in his statement "Gentleman you are here to become soldiers and not mathematicians" I do feel that soldiering and academic are two entirely different aspects of a military man's life. Many scholars at NDA did not become good soldiers but many not so good in studies at NDA went on to achieve high ranks and excellent academic qualifications later in life.

NDA was set up so that it became the single institute where bonds were built from among course mates and ex NDA alumni for better inter service functionality. I am not sure if that aim has been entirely met but to me more fundamentally NDA converted boys into men in the 3 years one spent there. Academics was then considered secondary. To this end the entire staffs at NDA was responsible and the staff – cadet interaction was phenomenal.

As science progressed and modern equipment came into services the need was probably felt to change intake level to a higher age. I do feel that was the biggest mistake that was made as by then the incoming cadet had seen some life and it then became more difficult to mould him into a soldier man.

The need for higher education with changing times was inevitable but the stage at which this would start was probably wrong. One can always impart that higher education post NDA. As it is there are enumerable examples of NDA cadets without a degree who excelled in technical field and rose to highest level in the technical branches and even went on to become Professor Emeritus (Research) of Engineering Marconi Society Fellow Department of Electrical Engineering, Stanford University.

It is this shift to higher science oriented education at NDA level and the need to ensure that the cadets got a degree that led to ingress of university culture in NDA and it became more a college that an academy. This brought about external interference in the running of the education in NDA and then scholarly professors and academicians with Ph D and M Phil who could contribute to the academic side of the cadet's life but not the character building of the cadets. Icons vanished and there were no role models left. The experience of years of moulding a cadet with total dedication was lost and you merely had people whose sole job was to teach and thus the outlook changed more towards the cadet's academic excellence rather than his overall growth.

The solution lies probably in going back to the old system of appointing civilian instructors rather than academics alone and lay emphasis on converting the boy into a man with some basic knowledge of military related subjects. Now that he comes with science background he can always pursue higher education in his later life as and when required.

One must look at the fact that no academician became a soldier but many soldiers went on to become an academician.

Nixon Fernando

The point that needs to be made to the people who think it is all about 'unofficial' is that 70% education training and 30% otherwise is there for a reason. This article by Air Mshl Arjun Subramaniam, emphasizes it. The NDA should stop making soldiers and start making leaders and statesmen. Soldiers they will become when they go to their respective pre-commissioning academies (IMA/INA/AFA) and later on in their units/sqns/ships. But to be useful leaders in the modern era they should be intellectually head and shoulders above the men by the way of their education, and they must be scholars who can match wits with the best in the world; Soldiers none the less !

The issues raised by Cdr Ravindra Pathak has already been debated threadbare in the Victory India Series. Consider the following points and the thinking will become clear.

1) The first principal was handpicked by PM Nehru; was a known educationist at the high school level. The aim was to groom the native Indian cadets to have adequate sophistication to be able to lead a British Indian Army. This principal (gentleman) was not an Indian.

2) The other civilians inducted were paid a salary 1.5 times the salary an equivalent instructor received outside (they did this by giving a NDA special allowance of Rs150, that was equivalent to if not more than the entry basic salary for instructors) NDA got the cream of educationists available in the country.

3) The experience from the wars (62, 65 and 71) was that officers in the armed forces who were injured in war were at a disadvantage in being absorbed in civilian life because they did not have a basic educational degree. It was decided that Officers should have at least a basic degree and that was why it was introduced in the NDA in the early 70's.

4) This brought in a new thinking into the NDA and my HOD used to say "I am here for Physics-nothing else". So you see the 'grooming' part was gone. Apparently that mathematics teacher was the new breed. He should have instead said 'Mathematics is not about the subject, it is about the abilities that are instilled in your mind when you study mathematical techniques'. 'There are certain tribes who do not know how to count beyond 10. Everything more than 10 is 'a lot'. They too live their lives and happy ones too! But they are at a great disadvantage in the modern world.

5) The pay and perks of the officers did not get upgraded with time, keeping the status of the NDA in mind. Eventually it was not even on par with other institutions outside. One officer who came to NDA, found that his teaching 12th class students was a far better proposition and more rewarding and went back from where he came.

6) The pay and perks position was messy for some time and there was politics, skirmishes with the uniformed fraternity and among the faculty themselves. Ultimately the UGC scale was accepted for academicians in the academy and NDA made on par with any other college anywhere else.

7) When the story of the 2007 recruitment unfolded, the terms of recruitment were altered in such a way that the older lot of the NDA could not apply because while the best of them were participating in the NDA activities related to cadet grooming they were neglecting their academic research. The new rules asked for research credentials and the old timers did not have it.

The problem is that like Cdr Ravindra there are many others who simply believe that education amounts to nothing. The point is that NDA is supposed to represent 'excellence', but rather you are insisting on paying on parity if not peanuts to educators. The Special NDA allowance of Rs. 150 remained the same for close to half a century. It was upgraded as late as in the 21st century and that too to some paltry amount and it must still be the same? You don't have a vision on excellence; you don't have a vision on how you are going to groom your officers and to what level. You are not rewarding those who actually participate in that process. You are aiming for the mind set of foot soldiers rather than leaders of a modern military. Make up your mind, you want the vision of Cdr Ravindra or of Air Mshl Arjun Subramaniam ? Either ways it can be executed, but decide none the less.

And in the meanwhile if it is 70% education, let it be 70% education. If it is not good change it the other way round. But this idea of saying something on paper and doing something else on ground puts a week foundation in the minds of future leaders. How would they respect their officer instructors who say something and do something else? Is that how they should command in the future?

As for me I am sure a sound education is required for our cadets, to set up the intellectual base on which they can build for sure. The arts must be introduced substantially to the science people and vice versa so that a more holistic leader can emerge. Scientific thinking and a humanist appreciation of life are both required for good leadership in the modern age. And this has to be done with the same passion with which an excellent sportsman, artist, soldier pursue their respective interests. Bring in the best of instructors. Say that the NDA is a temple of modern India and demand that its instructors be paid a significant step higher than his equivalents outside. It is a way of recognizing that the instructor in NDA is to deliver a notch above the rest.

Truly speaking even a small change in attitude in the environment of the NDA can make even the civilian officers presently there deliver their 100% to the academy. It can transform. Give them a broad canvass to work on and you will see how they rise up to the challenge. Give them a small tiny space and they will shrink to fit into it – a disgruntled lot! But yes, when an individual becomes free of the external and is committed to excellence, from within he will shine come what may and may leave the academy if he finds it too stifling. The best of them just go into their shell as time goes by. And as Dr Ali, the outstanding HoD of Foreign Languages department replied in his send-off speech, when asked if he had the chance to come back to the NDA were he to start all over again. 'NO' was his answer. 'People with lesser promise and credentials than me did much better outside' he said.

This temple of modern India is in a mess. It will take another Jawaharlal Nehru to put it on track

Gp Capt T P Srivastava

We, in military, have become adept at RE-INVENTING THE WHEEL and MISSING WOODS FOR TREES.

We deliberate on 'EFFECT' part with amazing brilliance as post event specialists. Let us look back. Our course saw two commandants; AVM S N Goel, a YOGA enthusiast 45 years before Swami Ramdev, and served as Commandant for three years. Rear Admiral R N Batra served for 38 months, i.e. after our passing out on 6th June, 1970.

Let us look nearer times; Arjun has brought out, albeit with tongue in cheek, that NDA commandant post is a mere 'PARKING' for a THREE STAR. Our eccentricity with 'TENURE' for each service has destroyed and continues to destroy vital institutions/appointments. My info is not complete but I would like to be educated on as to how many commandants have completed THREE YEAR TENURE as commandant during the past 40 years. Each service changes at least two, if not three individuals as commandants during its turn.

Worse is the fact that a THREE STAR not considered fit to hold appointments in field/service HQ is shunted to NDA. No wonder then that the outstanding institution of yesteryears is facing issues that will/are impinging on the very existence and quality of training.

An indifferent and/or poorly motivated Commandant, who reaches Khadakvasla as a 'brides maid' in waiting can do very little towards making the institution regain its lost glory.

Now the solution; Do we have it in us to appoint, a genuinely motivated officer and make him stay for three years as Commandant? Sadly the answer would be "NO".

Why then are we cribbing? Self inflicted injuries have no cure.

Prof S P Sharma

1) Till 2007, selection of civilian professors was done by NDA and they were selected as Assistant Professor, the lowest rung and grew in the system getting promoted to Associate Professor, Professor and Head of Department. They were true ex NDAs who followed NDA ethos and values. Cadets loved them as they were involved in all activities of cadets.
2) In 2007 Government changed the rules and selection responsibility was given to UPSC and done directly to Principal, HOD, Professor, etc., as vacancy occurred. So, suddenly people landed up who were totally new to NDA and viewed it as a college.

Earlier Lecturer/Assistant Professors were recruited through UPSC. Readers/Professors were selected in house. I spent 30 years as faculty member and retired as Prof and HOD (English). Service Chiefs have been my boys. The damage was done when a rank outsider was hoisted on NDA who wasn't qualified to teach any subject in our syllabus. He wasn't concerned about the NDA or the Faculty. The cancer continued to grow. The rapport between the teachers and students builds the spirit which is the Soul of an institution. Meeting an ex NDA product is 'joy de vivre' for me. I feel very sad; heartbroken, like a child whose beautiful sand castle has been washed away by a tidal wave. God please save the NDA!

Col P K 'Royal' Mehrishi

Dysfunctional Academic Ecosystem: NDA

1) Recent raid by CBI at NDA & subsequent questioning of the Principal Mr OP Shukla for fraud & falsifying documents is part of a greater malaise that has stricken the premier Institution now with certain regularity. Gone are the days of stalwarts like Prof Kuldip Singh, Prof Bhatnagar, Prof Rajan & their ilk. Now there are civilian Instructors who have problems with spellings & the English language (the medium of Instruction) There are Permanent Instructors who stay within the campus & Ad hoc ones who commute from Pune to teach & rush back home without getting much involved in the Academy routine, thus having little or no affiliation with the Cadets or the Academy.

2) UPSC has no stake in the quality of Instructors that are desirable for a premier Institution like NDA. Matters have come to light where money has exchanged hands for posting Associate Professors to this Institution. A general deterioration of standards for pecuniary benefits. To aggravate the problem, the posting of Commandants from either of the Service Wings at times takes months with the post left vacant for long. Once a Commandant is in place he has his own ideas to run the curriculum thus negating continuity & hampering the academic eco-system. Corruption has also been an issue in this revered Institution, with one previous Commandant facing a barrage of corruption charges in the recruitment of class IV employees. Imagine The dichotomy wherein the cadets are being taught values of a Gentleman & an Officer & the head of the same Institution is under a cloud facing charges of corruption. The message to the Cadets is confusing, Follow the rules when you are a junior, break them at will when a senior. I agree with the recommendation of AVM Arjun Subramaniam (we are Course-mates NDA/59) Have a Military academic dean or head who scrutinizes the intake of Civilian Instructors & maybe head hunts them from across Universities in the Country. There is no room for any ad hocism (that includes ad hoc Instructors). Academic education & training are two different streams of learning; a Cadet has to go through both. An Institution like NDA has produced distinguished alumni. Let the fair name of the Institution be restored to its pristine glory by visionaries & dedicated Staff who are above small & mundane pursuits of personal aggrandizement.

Let my Guru be my leading Light!!

Dr Syed Ehsan Ali, ex HoD, Foreign Languages, NDA

The selection of NDA academic staff as rightly mentioned has all along been done through UPSC. Besides UPSC chairman/member, subject expert etc., there used to be a rep. of services who would interview and find the suitability of the candidate they were to select for NDA.

Though there was a post graduate degree required as a minimum qualification, Credit was given to the sports, extracurricular activities of the candidates. I was selected as a lecturer at 22 yrs plus without any Ph. D (there were 2 Ph. Ds as candidates for the same post). Prof AN Jha (Former VC of Allahabad University) committee had drafted a very comprehensive syllabus for NDA. There used to be a cross stream subject for Science as well as Arts students, and learning of a foreign language & culture as a part of syllabus was yet another unique vision. NDA lecturers were offered a superior pay scale compared to their counterparts in Indian universities & colleges till about late sixties. But gradually it was reversed. Now the NDA Academic staff which; was required to stay on the campus and be available for duty right from 0600hrs to 2300 hrs at times. They were not recruited to merely teach their subject but were detailed for duties connected with the overall training of NDA cadets. Many of us performed the duties of OIC games, hobby clubs, referred matches, be official in sports, members of various boards and help cadets in extracurricular activities such as organising cultural evening programmes etc. In other words the job of an NDA lecturer was not merely to teach his/her subject only but to involve himself with all subjects of cadets training oriented activities. It was all working well till NDA was affiliated to JNU which started putting UGC conditions for award of degrees, recruitment policy for NDA staff. NDA demanded UGC scales, slightly superior to the existing NDA scale. Till then; there used to be only lecturers and a Head of the Department as Reader. MoD somehow took the decision of implementing UGC guidelines in toto, in other words UGC scales to be implemented at the NDA with UGC qualifications and recruitment method for Readers/Professors, and that perhaps, in my personal opinion, was not in the interest of this premier institution. NDA should have asked for an independent DEEMED UNIVERSITY status. Out of the then 9 faculty departments only six professor's posts were sanctioned for NDA, three depts. viz. Foreign Languages, Hindi and Workshop were declared minor subjects, hence to be headed by a Reader only. This was in total contradiction of UGC rules and not followed by any college or university where the entire subject taught are given same status. MoD could NOT convene any DPC between 1981 and 1989, for more than 8 long years which affected most of the NDA lecturers adversely. Some of the faculty members, very talented and dedicated to their duties had to superannuate without a single promotion at NDA. Dr Verma, Reader I/C Social Sciences was promoted to the post of NDA Principal, in late sixties but after him the senior most NDA Reader Mr G D Bhavnani was not promoted, could only officiate as principal and after him all the Principals were recruited directly from purely civil background colleges, ignoring several, very competent, highly dedicated and fully involved insiders. The practice continues till date. Now I understand they have recruited Readers/ Professors also directly as per UGC rules and moulding such a lot to a particular ethos is extremely difficult, if not impossible. In other words the MoD is not concerned with the NDA "Ethos", etc., while selecting its Principal. Right from mid seventies some of the faculty members preferred to stay outside NDA campus and they were perhaps encouraged to do so. They would come only for their teaching related duties and their interaction with cadets will be negligible. Whereas in our early days; we found our seniors fully involved with the cadets training and grooming by way of teaching them high values of life which was never restricted to class rooms. As a Couselor I realized that some cadets would confide more in their academic officers than their Squadron officers in uniform. Academic officers would always watch the cadets wherever possible, monitor their discipline and behaviour in the market, at the bus stop or the railway station. Mr Keswani was well known in NDA as a "civilian Adjutant" Even after having served this great institution for nearly 38 years, having seen 75 courses pass out (26th to 100 course), my wife looking after NDA welfare center and working as Treasurer for NDA Ladies club for over 18 years we have truly learnt the "Art of good Living" at the NDA, much more of pleasantries to relish than a few adversities. Long Live NDA, God help it regain its glory as seen by us.

Dr M K Nagpal

I have liked the response by Gp Capt Johnson Chacko very much, written in a very lucid manner regarding the training and education of military leaders at the initial stages. I am endorsing his views fully. In fact if someone reads carefully in between the lines what I have written in the chapter of the book Victory India, Volume 1 (2013), touch many of these points although very briefly as I wanted to confine myself to the 'civil-military relationship', 'Academics' and 'Environment' at NDA only, without going into the detailed justifications, leaving much to the wisdom of individuals who read it.

CONCLUDING REMARKS & WAY FORWARD

Gp Capt Johnson Chacko

I was posted as the Battalion Commander at NDA from 2001 to 2003. I asked my seniors as to what I am expected to do. I couldn't get a reply that satisfied me. So the thinking process started. I analysed the system of training, why it is being done and how NDA grooms leaders for the Armed Forces fit to lead the soldiers in the Army up to Platoon level, in the navy to lead sailors at the lower level and in the Air Force for no particular reason, as Ex-NDAs are not expected to lead airmen till they become Wing Commanders NDA has been termed as the 'Cradle for Military Leadership'. There are various types of leadership that was taught to me while undergoing the Long Defence Management Course at the College of Defence Management. NDA trains 'Situational Leadership'. What is required to be taught for this type of leadership? This leadership is needed by almost all leaders for success in a situation. Leaders are expected to lead a team or group or whatever comprising of men and women. The leader needs to be aware of the situation that his team is in, ideate as to how to overcome the situation in favour of his team using the skill sets of the members of the team and execute it to achieve success. In a military situation that is victory. A leader provides one victory to his team and his team will follow him wherever he takes them. This principle is valid for any domain. To lead them the foremost requirement is to analyse the 'Situation' that the team is in. This can be termed as 'Situational Awareness'. He needs to grasp this in quick time in military situations. Academics broaden his horizon and enable him in this context. His awareness level of what is happening around him is of great importance and academic training plays a very important part in it. Ideation is also extremely important and without academic exposure he will be found wanting.

Analysing the skill sets or strengths and weaknesses of his team members also needs analytical skills that are honed by academics. Outdoor training enhances the physical capability of the trainee to the level that is required to perform the expected tasks at par or even better than the soldier. Besides these Character building, directing the Morals and Ethics are also very important and I found myself heading this branch of training by real time corrections through Squadron Commanders and Divisional Officers. The overall development of leadership abilities also fell under my purview. Giving a pat on his back when he does well, shifting it slightly lower; converting it to a kick when he doesn't and knowing the difference was also under my realm. There is no classroom exposure to leadership of any consequence. True leadership is learned by the Cadets on the playing fields of NDA. Innumerable number of situations is created for the Cadets where he can excel in all the aspects stated above in the form of competitions. This was also monitored by my staff and the Cadets are told where they have gone wrong so that they can improve. Unfortunately, even academics and physical training has been converted to competitions to transfer the onus of training to the senior cadets who are not adept as trainers or educators.

Every branch has its role to play and there are shortcomings in every branch. Academic branch has come into limelight recently. We need to study the present policy and compare it the older policy of selection and recruitment of the staff and pay them well, at least 1.5 times of what is given to other college staff so that he grows with the institution.

There are scholarly Armed Forces veterans with tremendous administrative experience who are Vice Chancellors of Universities and I wonder why similar officers are not inducted for the Principal's post. Is research mandatory for the academic staff to impart education? Why saddle him with that?

As per ancient Indian wisdom, an educated person is supposed to be a useful member of the society and is expected to be the fountainhead of knowledge. The Guru is morally bound to quench the thirst for knowledge of his Shishyas.

He cannot avoid it. It is the moral right of the Shishyas to seek answers for his doubts of 'Why' and 'How' from the Guru. If he does not know the answers he is supposed to find it out and let the student know. Are the Cadets encouraged to ask questions to their academic staff? Do they give the required clarity? Should we not select the staff as per his capability and attitude to do this? If we can kindle the spirit of inquisitiveness among the Cadets by providing the right environment that enables this, then the major task of generating Scholar-Warriors would have been mostly achieved. They will do the rest.

It is not difficult to do. As a Flight Commander who had about 12 flying instructors and 36 Flight Cadets I have done it. In the briefing, which is attended by both the Flight Cadets and the Instructors, I announced that any Flight Cadet who has a doubt in any subject in aviation is free to ask his Instructor and Instructor will not punish him but provide the answer. If he does not get clarity, he is free to ask me at any time, day or night. If I don't know the answer, I will find out and let him know. The knowledge level of the Instructors shot up and professionalism went sky high as reveled by the subsequent tests conducted by external examiners. The spirit of inquisitiveness has guided me to derive a mathematical formula worthy of a patent, as there was no Guru. This may answer the question asked by Brigadier General Andrew Armacost, Dean of USAFA to AVM Arjun Subramaniam "How are our academies addressing the challenges of offering a holistic education for officer cadets that offers opportunities for combining a technological focus with adequate awareness of the humanities and/or pure sciences?"

The British system of education imposed on us is not delivering the required results as it is based on 'One size fits all'. Syllabus is defined and the Cadet has to go through that syllabus. His passion to excel in the field that he wants to has no consideration. The condition that he has to be a graduate has been imposed for his re-employment in a second career. Why make it co-terminus with his passing out date? He can continue to graduate in a few years after his commissioning. We need to reduce pressure on him at NDA so that his scholarly abilities can bloom.

Military History should be a mandatory core subject as history does not repeat itself to people who know history and it will be essential for future Officers in the profession of Arms. Technology can assist him, especially the operational aspects but that by itself does not make him a warrior. Subject of his passion should be the second subject that he should be enabled to pursue as he can fall back on it if he cannot continue his career as a warrior.

The members of the academic staff at NDA need to be fountainheads of knowledge with vast knowledge and specialisation in his subject, capable of quenching the thirst for knowledge of the Cadets. It goes without saying that the pay scales should be good to attract the best and retain them. Besides qualifications, attitude is very, important. Attitude can be gauged only by those in the institution over a period of time.

This debate was published in Fauji India magazine, Aug 2018 issue.

CHAPTER 29

Cradle of Leadership Fallen on Hard Times

Brig I S Gakhal

Expecting a 19-20 year old to survive 3 years of high octane physical activity, and graduate with good grades academically is expecting too much. A cadet very soon learns when to work and when not to. Thus, from the very basic, we have taught him the value of showmanship and shamming. NDA products are exceptionally competitive always wanting to head the pack, not always by fair means, There is an element of 'self' that NDA trains you to focus on.

'Victory India Campaign' and Col Vinay Dalvi are synonym with seeking constructive change. It's only recently that I chanced upon two volumes of Victory India and delved on issues it raises. Col Dalvi and myself go back to school days and on cursory discussion asked if I had served in NDA and on my confirmation, asked me to pen my opinion of the training at NDA. I was one of the first few non-ex-NDA Divisional Officers (Div O) posted at NDA in 1980-82. Col Vinay Dalvi in his capacity as PTO has served in most academies and seen things up close, his prodding and persistence on the subject is therefore knowledge based.

My personal experience of training at NDA as Div O and consequent study and analysis of issues involved have led me to following observations and conclusions:

An institute conceived and tailor-made as a tri-services training establishment modelled on the lines of US Military academy, West Point. NDA began operations at Khadakwasla on 07 December 1954 on a campus that covers 28.39 square kilometers. The half yearly course intake varies between 300-350 cadets that are selected after a written UPSC exam followed by a Services Selection Board series of tests designed to gauge the military potential of a candidate. A three year residential undergraduate course follows after successful completion of which the cadets move for specialized training to their respective service academies.

As a non-ex-NDA Officer, I was possibly in the first batch that served as Instructors at NDA, called Div O. My impressions are therefore unbiased and undiluted. NDA is undoubtedly producing very smart and intelligent Officers, many of whom have risen to top the pyramid in their respective service. An NDA officer carries niche value for his grooming, communication skills, timing, ability to showcase, awareness levels and above all the networking he brings by virtue of being at NDA. For the rest there is little difference among officers from other academies.

Intake Evaluation: The social environment has undergone a drastic change since 1954 where values have considerably diluted, attitudes have hardened, and social malice is rampant though awareness and intellect has improved considerably. The social status of the intake has also changed and intake is now from middle or lower middle class. The fact that hardly any wards of tri-service Officers join NDA points to the changed intake. The services as a profession has diluted in popularity coming fairly low in the pecking order. All this has a direct effect on the intake level of the trainee, however the training has continued on the pattern since the Academy started, remains largely unchanged, functioning with minor tinkering.

The experience of the ex-NDA Div O during his training days becomes the template for training cadets. What was good for the goose is good for the gander. The ground reality and changed intake environment go unaccounted. The bullying that a Div O underwent as a cadet is considered the norm and often encouraged. The over emphasis on physical activity and the instructors allowing it to continue as so, often results for an instructors lathery to change status quo. To treat a cadet as commodity rather than a mouldable young man is often at fault. Thus there is no formalized review system undertaken at a regular periodicity, if there is one in place it's doing a perfunctory job.

Instructor Intake: Elite are shortlisted as instructors, based on their service profile, not based on their ability as trainers. Till the late 70s only ex-NDA were privileged to this hallowed place, many returning to the academy within three years of commissioning. Fresh cadet memory and youthful exuberance took them back to their front-rolling days. They end up replicating their times oblivious of the changed environment or intake quality. Non-service or Academic instructors I found were largely poor specimens as role models. Their dedication, communication skills and social behaviour left a lot to be desired.

I was aghast to receive a charge against one of my cadets which read "giving meaningful looks" from an overweight lady professor. Their selection process through the UPSC is to blame. The first batch of academic instructors in 1954 comprised role models and their stories abound, alas they are all long gone. Thus careless selection of trainers is equally to blame for the decline as is the altered intake.

Tailoring Training Needs: It's imperative that periodic review of training content is undertaken after establishing training needs of the trainees. Such reviews are critical to developing a dynamic training content to prepare the trainees for their envisaged role over the next 20-25 years. If this exercise in not periodically undertaken then we are resorting to train tomorrow's leaders with tools of yesterday. Here in lies the flaw. A review in 1986-87 with the limited aim of increasing technical training content and inter-service interaction could only have its recommendations partially implemented in 1991; such has been our approach to training next generation of leaders.

Vice Admiral Suresh Bangara (now retired) on taking over as Commandant NDA in 2003, got sanction to constitute two review committees, one for military training and the other for educational training reforms. In July 2004 the Vice Admiral moved out on promotion and the reviews took a perfunctory turn. Such has been our approach to systematic review and updating our future leaders training. In the absence of a formalized and periodic training review, we have continued with our "all is well" and 'status quo' approach!

NDA & Faulty Values: Expecting a 19-20 year old to survive 3 years of high octane physical activity, and graduate with good grades academically is expecting too much. A cadet very soon learns when to work and when not to. Thus, from the very basic, we have taught him the value of showmanship and shamming. His menial treatment, often abusive and physical, teaches him that it's the done thing. Imagine if he tries to mete out the same treatment to his Platoon, troop, or equivalent body of troops. Many officers have tried this and got into trouble. NDA also teaches that some amount of dishonesty helps in self-preservation, lies and fabricated stories abound, all harmless but habit forming.

Competitiveness is a good virtue, if executed by fair means, but if practiced by 'hook or by crook' it leads to discord. NDA products are exceptionally competitive in professional activity, always wanting to head the pack, not always by fair means, these results in friction and often trouble. The Alma Mater network is excellent for inter-service operability when used for operational results. However, when used for forming groups within a unit, they have dangerous proportions. There is an element of 'self' that NDA trains you to focus on. Cadets in their third term start to plan DSSC entrance exam.

Professionalism is good, but obsession on ticking the right boxes for personal elevation is not what you want to inculcate in a leader. Another behavioural flaw results from the unbridled power that senior cadets enjoy at the academy, mostly misused for personal good or enmity. All done in the name of enforcing discipline! For a young man, it's a heady power but when he moves into the next academy or into his unit post commissioning it creates adjustment problems. Training at NDA does not promote its motto of 'service before self' but it does its reversed version. Is this what we designed NDA to be?

Behavioural Aspects of Training: How you are treated impacts your personality later, especially during formative years. The ragging, bulling and bullshitting are medal winners at NDA. Despite the orders to the contrary, these are practiced clandestinely. My personal experience at IMA was that those appointments that resorted to such behaviour largely had NDA background. The others direct entry ones were far mature in this aspect. The menial treatment of cadets must stop for their even growth. Physical fitness is not lifelong – thus the over emphasis on this aspect is misplaced. Creating awareness that a soldier must be fit is all that is required.

'Ragda' just removes the enthusiasm in training. Values of comradeship, standing up for your subordinates, being truthful to your command, honesty, team spirit and sacrifice need more emphasis than just physical ragda. Stories of the entire Academy front rolling from the Cadets' Mess to Gol Market and back, for someone pinching Asha Parekh's (an actor) bottom abound and are narrated with pride, but no one has really questioned why a cadet had the audacity to do what he did. Self-discipline is certainly not a virtue inculcated at NDA. Ask a cadet who has been made to roll down the central staircase, in full view of the cadet orderlies, about his prestige and one will get his reply. Raids on the café may be an act of momentary bravado but it's a break in after all and punishable under the law. Are we training leaders to be cheats?

Tunnel Vision Promoted: Training at NDA promoted tunnel vision, dissent and alternate thinking is never encouraged in the name of discipline. Even debates are censored and free flow of ideas curbed. This gravely impacts the future thinking pattern of the product. My experience as a Div O was that given half a chance the cadet will sleep off the entire tactical training schedule. We made his learning even more remote by making him sprint round some land mark trees. One or two cadets would have knowledge of the subject rest would rely on the prompting whispers to impress the instructor. If a live tactical situation was painted their application would be bookish with little innovative options coming forth. We were really creating a tunnel vision among our trainees.

Under-Utilized Infrastructure: NDA has the infrastructure and acreage to turnout commissioned officers, who can then move to their basic professional Young Officer courses. This will eliminate further service level training in service academies. Having experience of the Army training at NDA, I can say with conviction that IMA is repetitive for NDA cadets. This can result to considerable saving to the exchequer.

Training at this premier institute must have an inbuilt periodic review to make it dynamic to environmental needs. The academic/professional and physical training need a rationale mix, over emphasis on physical training has long term ramifications on the quality of the product. Behavioural training must inculcate self-discipline, honestly and comradeship. The emphasis must shift from survival to learning and self to us. Then and only then will we have set our basic officers training on course.

Note: The article was published in Fauji India magazine, November 2018 issue.

CHAPTER 30

'NDA' The Raging Debate and Way Out

Cdr Mukund Yeolekar

Raging Debate

I think it is over a decade now that a debate over NDA is raging. The matter has reached highest echelons and attracted the attention of RM, bureaucrats, former chiefs, Commandants and legions of veterans. The writing on the wall is clear that any honest and concerned officer serving or retired will have an urge to analyse the present scenario in this cradle for Leadership and suggest measures to improve the quality of training at NDA. With the dedicated efforts of past incumbents and veterans a detailed study was undertaken regarding NDA encompassing all aspects such as Selection, Medical fitness standards, Training Syllabus, Physical activities, Grooming as officers, Civilian Academic staff and Feed-back from field units on completion of training. This has revealed startling facts which demand immediate corrective actions in order to stem the downward slide in quality of officers. The efforts were lauded but no tangible action was initiated. It also needs to be noted that the downward slide or 'incorrect alteration of course' has not happened in a day, but over a long period and no single individual or a group of officers of a particular Service/Branch can be held culpable for the same.

Detailed Analysis & Conclusions

Reams of paper have been written on shortcomings in the Academy, its administration, infrastructure maintenance, staffing by Service and Civilians. Umpteen veterans have rued and expressed their anguish over the deteriorating standards of present training.

However this has remained only on paper and not been discussed candidly in a formal forum in order to evolve a solution. The primary problem is seemingly in the line of thinking and a hesitation among the incumbents to be a whistle blower. There is a large percentage of officers who think it right to follow the beaten track and they presume that what was being done for the last few decades cannot be wrong. So why disturb the Apple cart? There is also a tendency to assume that one who is critical and cynical about the organization is not a well-wisher and is not patriotic. Such people get isolated and treated with disdain.

On the contrary, if these people are taken into confidence and their views understood a new out 'of the box' idea can be generated to solve a problem. Most Commanders at the helm however want 'Yes Men' as subordinates who will comply with orders without arguments and will help to ensure their smooth rise up the hierarchy. One has to accept that we are a 'promotion conscious rank-centric' organization.

This is as a result of grooming of each of us over decades. Those in the post-independence era and till the early seventies were heavily steeped in British traditions and customs. Later we had British trained Indian officers to train our officers. Surely, sometime in this transition period there has been a slight, seemingly innocuous 'alteration' of course and unknowingly, unwittingly we veered off the right path.

We reached a stage when the goals of the organization and that of the individual are on skewed paths. We need to ponder over the observations of many veterans, discuss frankly in a forum and conclude whether the observations are merely a perception or a fact. We have to be very honest in this and concede mistakes if any, so that they can be rectified. There should be no fear of recrimination. One should have moral courage to accept errors for the larger good of the organization. Denying that there is indeed something wrong only to save the skin would amount to being myopic and will have long term adverse consequences.

WAY OUT

Therefore there is a need to take the following actions on priority:

(a) Form a committee of three former service Chiefs, three former Commandants and one co-opted member as per discretion of the Chiefs.
(b) Committee to pore over all books written on the subject and peruse all relevant reports submitted during the last decade.
(c) Committee to brain-storm, debate, argues, conclude and summarise the essence of the books, condensing them to few pages (10-12 pages). These should list clearly and unambiguously the shortcomings of the Academy and the probable reasons behind them.
(d) Committee to interact with the present incumbents at NDA, other academies and also visit renowned Academies of other countries and ascertain exactly the present scenario.
(e) Committee to draw up a revised 'job specification' of an officer for the future – coming 30 years, keeping in view the advances in technology and threat scenario in view of Geo-political/strategic developments.
(f) Committee to draft a plan to resolve each of the shortcomings and propose a master plan for enhancement in functioning of NDA in all aspects such as –selection, administration, training methodology, Evaluation, career planning of civilian staff, pre-joining study capsule

and instruction to Trainers, infrastructure management, training feedback and corrective actions etc.
(g) Assess the financial impact of all changes recommended and propose phased implementation in every fiscal in order of priority.
(h) In consultation with present incumbents of all three Services (Chiefs, Vice Chiefs/C-in-Cs/COP/DGMT/CIDS/ARTRAC/PDNT) draw up an Action Plan for implementation along with Time Line with a rational and finite limit.

CHAPTER 31

Reforming NDA for Leadership Challenges of 21st Century

Nixon Fernando

The National Defence Academy (NDA) was conceived as one of the temples of modern India. It became one of just a handful of institutions and monuments which got that special designation and that speaks volumes for its importance. The Prime Minister took personal interest in its setting up. And the central government, through executive action at the highest level, handpicked military leaders and educationists to do the honours. There is no doubt that the attempt was to truly create a 'cradle of military leadership'.

And why was the NDA necessary? The nation had just attained independence and could not risk handing over the British Indian Army to military leaders with sub-regional mind-sets; it needed young men with a cosmopolitan and global world view. So, besides the fact that the NDA had to train these would-be leaders in the skill and the science of the arms, it also had to transform indigenous hopefuls into the kind of gentlemen who could represent an integrated British Indian Armed forces.

Military skills were to be imparted to the cadets by military men. A proper military bearing was to be taught in the hostels and drill square. Leadership was to be taught through life in the academy and in its dozens of playfields. Military Strategy, Leadership theory and Military History were to be taught by both military and civilian experts and finally the bearing of a cosmopolitan global gentleman had to be instilled by distinguished teachers pulled out of the top public schools from all over the country.

70 years on: A lot has happened over the decades and today, seven decades after independence it makes immense sense to ask some very basic questions. Is NDA a temple of Modern India anymore? Is a temple of that kind required anymore? If yes, is it doing that job, if no then why spend all that money?

Giving due honour to the remarkable leaders who have passed through NDA's portals, without hesitating to salute the brave young alumni who have led from the front even to the extent of offering the ultimate sacrifice for the nation, one must still critically assess the 'delta factor' that the institution stands for; 'delta factor' meaning the transformation that happens in a cadet which can be directly credited to the NDA.

Is The Delta factor large enough? It is very easy for an alumnus to remember his pre-NDA days, long hairs and all, and think of the young would-be officer he had transformed into when he passed out of the academy. The difference would be remarkable, and surely a lot of it he would credit to the Academy.

But that is not the correct estimate of how excellent his alma mater has been. Proper scientific analysis of this phenomenon can be made only if we have an 'experimental group' and a 'control group' and measure the difference in impact. In lay man's terms we can say that the real delta factor can be estimated if we know how much the NDA cadet has transformed in those three years in comparison to his twelfth standard classmates who had their education in a normal three year college outside. After three years of training is there a difference between the delta factor for the NDA alumni and his other classmates of the control group? Can we justify the difference in delta factors in the two groups to be worth the investment?

Still another relevant delta factor would pertain to members of the control group that are being trained in other academies abroad and in India. Are we sure that the delta factor at the NDA is really better. One can never be sure unless a credible scientific study is conducted by someone who genuinely wants to know the truth. But one thing is for sure, there are not many prospective cadets from the developed nations of the world actually falling head over heels to get trained at the NDA.

May be it is unfair to hold NDA to such a high standard but then, putting it in another way, maybe there is a lot of opportunity for NDA to grow, to improve on its delta factor, and that opportunity needs to be tapped.

Alarmingly, given the bullying that happens in the academies, given the burnout that happens, the man handling by instructors and senior cadets, the shamming that is required for some to survive at the NDA, given the hypocrisy that is practiced in saying one thing officially and doing something else unofficially, the reckless physical training supervised by un-trained cadets, one can cast serious doubts as to whether the delta factor of the NDA is even positive in certain areas.

The intake into the academy has changed: The British military officers of pre-independence India were considered on par with their civilian counterparts from the civil services if not higher. The elite among the Indians were therefore vying for the opportunities open in the military officialdom. So in the earlier decades the NDA got the real cream of the young lot. The cadets were from the premier public schools of the nation. They came in from the higher echelons of society—even royals. This was not necessarily a job-seeker class. These were mostly inspired by the military ethos and wanted to be part of almost royalty.

Seventy years down the line times have changed. The prestige which the pre-independence military officers enjoyed has been considerably eroded. Even officers' children most often opt for lucrative private sector and foreign employment rather than join the armed forces. The cadets increasingly come from the middle and lower middle classes. However, despite the inadequacies in the selection system, these cadets are some of the smartest ones from across the country. And many if not most are indeed driven by the noble aspirations of soldiering (when they join at least).

The requirement of the armed forces has changed: Over the seven decades has the military remained the same old British Indian Armed forces or has it changed and become more of an Indianized Armed Forces? Does the military need a cosmopolitan minded leadership that is well versed in English anymore?

Considering war effort, are the present war requirements the same as that which existed 70 years back? Is it the same in terms of technology, platform of operations and even in dimension of warfare? For example, a digital world never even existed seventy years ago and space war was out of question but now both are serious considerations. Bayonet charging of the past gave way to trigger pulling and that in turn is increasingly giving way to button pushing as the way to fight wars. The soldier leader has to lead increasingly well informed men. He has to understand global dynamics in the socio-political-economic planes and link it with the micro picture in his immediate vicinity. He needs to learn to handle PR and media elegantly, has to answer for Human Rights abuses and soldier rights and deal with nucleated soldier-families. And not to forget, he must be able to hold his own in this democracy where the politicians and bureaucrats rule the roost; most of the latter kind, in turn, does not realize the difference between putting one's sweat on the line and putting one's life on the line.

The delta requirement has increased: From where the cadets begin when they join the academy to where they need to be at the end of their training, that gap has widened. And by that estimate NDA must deliver much more than it did decades ago. So, as on this day, is the NDA up to task of providing the delta factor that is needed to transform the cadets?

Training cadets in the early decades at the NDA should have been far easier surely. And even at that time the visionary leadership went that extra mile to bring in the most positive of influences to make the young recruits capable of leading the Indian military.

Today the cadets are brilliant and committed but come in from a less elite class. As such the cadet needs extra grooming on matters related to nobility and gentlemanliness. These attributes are necessary for them to be at home with the roles they are expected to play later on. And since the requirements of war have drastically changed, the leadership must be nimble enough to adapt. Taking a cue from the corporate arena, the soldier leader, besides being all that a military leader of the past needed to be, must be more innovative, better informed, much more nimble and he must be tech-savvy in order to be effective.

The task has become more difficult but the academy is not moving in the direction in which these challenges can be overcome. In fact the academy is drifting the other way. While cadets have increased in number over these seventy years, the number of instructors has dropped. The mandate for the civilian instructors has been watered down to lecturing for degree classes only. Many of the cadets now come from sainik and military schools who, according to Victory India findings, bring forward a good dose of bullying and ragging into the academy. The cadets must now additionally complete a degree and the intensity of physical and military training has also been increased. Each of these and more has placed additional strain on the training at the NDA and there is consequent dilution in standards. There is now a general feeling that the NDA is but an exalted college in which the military training and the related physical training takes up 70% of the time and energy. And more or less the concept of 'Temple of Modern India' and 'Cradle of Military Leadership' seem to have drifted into becoming mere marketing 'jhumlas'.

Delivering the delta factor: How hard the cadets work is to be seen to be believed. If you have instances of cadets who ran when unfit-to their deaths- then you can imagine how committed they can be. How focused they are you realize when the Habibullah Hall packed with 3000+ cadets of the academy drops to pin drop silence when the story of a martyr, their own senior, is narrated in its details. So there is no question of finding fault with the quality of men passing through the NDA. And yet there is an issue!

The ground reality is that there is no vision operating in the NDA anymore. Why does NDA exist? Each instructor, cadet, staff member will have a unique answer to this question. And most of the times he would think that the others 'don't know anything'. Everything has been reduced to routines and traditions. The best of the best come here alright but eventually most of them pass through the motions doing the best they can (or what is humanely possible) and avoiding getting into any form of trouble for the sake of surviving.

Taking charge and looking into the future: So back to the question: What is NDA's mandate? Is NDA a Temple of Modern India anymore? Is it relevant to the times or is it training solders for past wars? What is the delta factor? How much of it is positive for a cadet and what are the negative aspects? What is the relative delta factor in comparison with the degree holders who join the armed forces after they complete their graduation outside NDA or trained at other institutions with same duration of training? What is the delta factor in comparison with academies the world over? What leadership traits get imparted to the cadets? Do they evolve as Self-Start or Kick-Start leaders? Do they pass out of the academy as 'burnt out' or 'raring to go'? Do they remain still idealistic or are they gone sceptic by the time they pass out?

If one hears what late Capt Vikram Batra's a relative have to say, the opinions they hold and the attitude they bear, it becomes evident that bravery was written into the blood of this inspirational son of India in his home environment itself. NDA had definitely not sullied it (I am sure it would have put Vikram to the test though). And just like him surely there are countless others who pass through the portals of the academy who are already raw diamonds before they step into the NDA. Time may not have highlighted them as in Vikram's or Col Nair's, or Capt Pandey's case. As such NDA continues to be a meeting point of such men of extraordinary calibre. The critical question for us though is to determine whether such outstanding officer materials as these are gaining from the NDA delta factor. Is there a team effort ensuring that the delta factor remains positive in all aspects of training and that nothing negative gets inducted?

Somehow the response of the academy to its mandate or to the requirements of time is not encouraging. For example, how many genuine experts on leadership operate in the academy right now? How can a cradle of military leadership not even have a department for leadership studies and research? How many of the instructors there are trained leadership experts? How many cutting edge research papers on leadership and leadership training have come out of this academy?

The original mandate of the NDA has definitely not been downgraded consciously by any fiat by any government in the past. If there is a down grade then it is because its initial mandate was not pursued relentlessly. Time and ignorance have let things drift. Over the years the orders that have been passed have been creating flip flops and on an average have resulted in eroding the system rather than holding it up to the original mandate.

On the contrary, if we are serious about the NDA continuing to be a temple of Modern India, then this idea in turn must resonate as a core vision living within all those who are direct stake holders in the academy. If there is something that is best in the world in the area of training leaders then the NDA must have it—that must be the attitude. NDA must retain its nimbleness to adapt to the times and at the same time have a sense of historicity and continuity of staying relevant to the highest purpose.

It is the Military's job: Sad as one my feel when saying it, the civilian leadership and the bureaucracy that is in control have neither the vision nor the energy or the desire to see the National Defence Academy flourish and stay relevant. It must be a task which has to be shouldered by the military leadership itself. But those executives in the armed forces, who have limited training in the specialization of education, and who are dealing with more important executive matters in their respective offices are unlikely to give it the detailed attention that the academy may require – it is very often considered low priority. Even Commandants of the Academy who have two year tenures at the academy and who wield ultimate control within the academy could be at a loss. By the time a Commandant (or any directing staff for that matter) gets acclimatized and appraised of the said and un-said nitty-gritties of the academy, it is time for him to leave. The permanent faculty who know the nitty-gritties unfortunately are never groomed into a role of trainers and are merely considered as teachers of the various subjects. No one among them is ever expected to rise in the academy to the highest level and in that sense certain continuity is out of the cards.

Solution Recommended: The only remaining way out is to create a Board of Directors as Advisors for the Commandant on behalf of the Chiefs of Staff Committee. The board should be composed of experts who have served the academy at the highest level. They must have a six year term with a third of them being replaced every two years. Their basic responsibility would be to understand the primary mandate of the National Defence Academy and ensure that it sustains in continuity. The board must therefore carry the vision of the academy forward, work on its continued relevance, bring in experts to make critical self-analysis and advise the controlling authorities of the NDA about decisions and steps that need to be taken to keep NDA relevant to its original high mandate.

The alumni of this majestic institution are numerous at the highest levels in the military hierarchy, maybe it is a duty on their part to do something for the academy at the present moment. The institution has suffered down grading due to no fault of its own. It makes a lot of sense to take the present status as an opportunity to convert it into a contemporary and relevant institution which offers huge delta factor of the positive kind: a genuine cradle of military leadership.

CHAPTER 32

Why the NDA must be Reformed and Reviewed? A Debate

Col Vinay B. Dalvi

Trigger for Debate

A recent article by Nixon Fernando on NDA has once again sparked a debate as the issues raised consequently impacts the quality of our military leadership at all levels. As amply and elaborately revealed through 4 volumes of Victory India Campaign books (with over 175 articles, essays, papers and reviews) and several articles of Fauji India magazine during past 25 issues, holistic coverage has been given to all aspects of training at NDA. One of the main conclusions drawn on which consensus was reached was/is the inescapable need for reforms at NDA to meet leadership challenges of 21st century.

Lt Gen Ashok Joshi, (ex-9th Course NDA) and former DGMT had aptly said, "If the Gangotri of military leadership (NDA) itself has been polluted, the leadership at all levels is bound to be negatively impacted!" Maj Gen VK Madhok, 1st Course NDA/JSW, said in his 'Foreword' to Victory India-1 (2013), "Thousands of military officers and Veterans who passed out from NDA, have failed to fulfil their responsibility to keep their alma mater relevant and contemporary to the times for past 70 years (despite occupying the highest posts of the three services) leading to present urgency for review and reform for 21st century challenges." A few relevant extracts from the article titled 'Reforming NDA for leadership challenges of 21st century' by Nixon Fernando are highlighted below.

"The National Defence Academy (NDA) was conceived as one of the temples of modern India. Military skills were to be imparted to the cadets by military men...A lot has happened over the decades and today, seven decades after independence it makes immense sense to ask some very basic questions. Is NDA a temple of modern India anymore? Is a temple of that kind required anymore? If yes, is it doing that job, if no then why spend all that money?

"Giving due honour to the remarkable leaders who have passed through NDA's portals, without hesitating to salute the brave young alumni who have (offered) the ultimate sacrifice for the nation, one must still critically assess the 'delta factor' that the institution stands for; 'delta factor' meaning the transformation that happens in a cadet which can be directly credited to the NDA.

"In lay man's terms we can say that the real delta factor can be estimated if we know how much the NDA cadet has transformed in those three years in comparison to his twelfth standard classmates. Alarmingly, given the bullying that happens in the academies, given the burnout that happens, the man handling by instructors and senior cadets, the shamming that is required for some to survive at the NDA, given the hypocrisy that is practiced in saying one thing officially and doing something else unofficially, the reckless physical training supervised by un-trained cadets, one can cast serious doubts as to whether the delta factor of the NDA is even positive in certain areas."

"The ground reality is that there is no vision operating in the NDA anymore. Why does NDA exist? Each instructor, cadet, staff member will have a unique answer to this question. And most of the times he would think that the others 'don't know anything'. Everything has been reduced to routines and traditions. The best of the best come here alright but eventually most of them pass through the motions doing the best they can (or what is humanely possible) and avoiding getting into any form of trouble for the sake of surviving.

RESPONSES

Lt Gen Harbhajan Singh

Educational Training: The original concept of education training at NDA was formulated by renowned but 'civil educationalists'. The education curriculum of NDA has been revised many times but those reviewing have again been civil educationalists, following age old system of learning by rote! Also the powers that be have been obsessed with cadets getting BSc degree from JNU, which over shadows the planning of whole training curriculum at NDA.

The Indian education system is in a mess and way behind that in the West. It does not prepare students for any vocation. The emphasis there is on doing reading and thinking about various topics of current and futuristic value, applied projects and not cramming facts and figures. The Indian system of education percolates to our bones and even as commissioned officers our thinking by and large is so conventional and narrow. Status quo is the passing time Mantra.

We should prepare NDA cadets for degree in military science, with former uniformed officers guiding preparation of the curriculum. Inputs from all the Arms and Services and training institutions should be taken and studied. Serving officers are denied foreign interaction and experience while in service, which some of us, who do not wear uniform any more have had the opportunity to experience/observe. We can also examine curriculum of military academies of USA, Russia, and China. The emphasis should be on studying geography and history, particularly of India and neighbouring countries, military history, psychology of religions, nations, terrorism, combatants and foreign affairs/diplomacy and so on.

Knowledge about electronics, applied mathematics, some physics and chemistry would also need to be imparted. Information Technology would be a core subject. Above is a first list which would need to be gone into in detail and deliberated upon.

Physical Training: Future wars are going to be driven by technology but physical combat will remain important basic component. None the less, the debate about 'brain and brawn' is important. I often still think, did my entire physical prowess make me a better Young Officer, Field Officer and later a General? What if I was not so physically endowed? The answer that comes to my mind is that it did make me a better Young Officer when I rubbed shoulders with men, but in later years, it was more of brain than physical prowess that mattered.

Should the PT be conducted as taught by the British even before WW-2 and Western countries or new subjects like Yoga, Karate and so on brought in? Should cadets going to Services like ASC, Ordnance (Material Management), EME be expected to have similar standards as those joining arms like Infantry and if so why?

Family Background: Personality of a person is about 70% or so based on his genes. Any training can hence have effect on about 30% of qualities/performance. What a child learns/experiences as a child has profound effect on his thinking, values and actions throughout his life. When people buy horses for racing, they go back 6-7 generations! Here we are selecting and training leaders for a contest which is bloody, most dangerous and where there are no runners up! Should we not look at the family background of cadets we select for training? This may be a very unpopular suggestion particularly in a democracy but it has scientific basis.

Adverse Effects of Prolonged Regimented Schooling: If you ask non-NDA officers about NDA Officers, oft heard remark is that they are "shirkers", "clever" and know "how and when to be seen performing!" I am convinced those 4 years pre-commission training is too long. It should be reduced to 3 years. Imagine the state of mind of cadets coming from Sainik and other Military schools. The adverse effects of a school child growing up in regimented and uniformed environment need to be studied. Some of the ills that are being highlighted in NDA may be having their base in cadets growing up in military type schools.

Maj Gen Anil Sengar

There is no denying, every institution needs a review of its purpose of existence in the context of the changing environment. So much has changed in the RMA, human factor, weaponry that the needs of leadership too have changed, even though the basics do not change. NDA undoubtedly needs a review. Unfortunately, the senior serving hierarchy lacks the commitment, as it involves extra work with no immediate short term gains.

The approach has to be top down and on the lines suggested by many learned Veterans. Lack of intellectualism is a major weakness of the Indian officers which goes right to the top. The foundation must be laid in the academy. NDA and all other training academies need a review due to this major shortcoming and many other reasons too. In the selection process, we need to understand, it is the officer like qualities and trainability that we are looking at. For the foreseeable future, the intake will come from middle and lower middle class and therefore, there is greater need to review what the academies are doing.

The army is partly about technology and mainly about humanities and leadership of people who have aspirations, challenges and obligations. Thus, too much emphasis on technology at the expense of sociological and human aspect of personality may not be in order, where your battle winning element is the man and not the machine. Three years in NDA is too long, but then one will have to look at the issue of graduation. Is that a necessity? It was not till 1975 and yet they made excellent commanders.

The need is to change the culture of NDA from physical driven to intellectual and ethics driven. How many cadets ever go to the NDA library? How many read anything beyond the academic syllabus? Majority only read enough to get through! I think the services training as is being done in the two terms – 4th and 6th – is adequate at this stage. The sole purpose of the NDA should be to produce a cadet of character and integrity driven by intellectual pursuits. Physical fitness has its place, and the training must take care that no weak cadets go through. Practices that encourage telling lies, cheating or so called smart acts to survive must be curbed.

Cdr Ravindra Pathak
I doubt teaching military strategy, leadership theory and military history could be achieved in the last two terms of the NDA since the first four terms were actually used to break the civil attitude of the boy who came and take him up to the inter-science level in academics. Yes, it did give him a glimpse of some military history and geography in the last two terms but that certainly did not make him a Gentlemen Cadet with profuse knowledge of either Military Strategy, leadership theory and military history. I do feel that after 70 years there is a need to relook at the aims and purpose of NDA and to study if it has achieved its original aims.

Col C M Chavan
There is no doubt that there is an urgent need to review the entire curriculum at NDA, keeping in mind the present day requirement of an Officer. The students in Sainik and military schools are from the lower middle and lower class, as

also the intake in the academies. But most of them are not fluent in English language which is also our official language and is our medium of instruction at NDA. However there is no denying the fact that they are driven by noble aspirations. It has been seen that the Sainik and Military schools have not been able to feed the academy as expected which also needs to be looked into.

Talking about the present day requirement of an officer, he should be technically well versed; as he is to handle highly advanced weapon systems. So, he has to be given technical education and for that purpose the mandate for NDA should be XII class with science subjects, so that he does not face hardship while being further trained at NDA. There is also a necessity of grooming the cadets in nobility, chivalry and gentle-manliness. It is also necessary that when our intake is from class XII, that we give them a degree of plus three i.e. graduation, as it is the basic qualification expected of an individual for any job, be it government or in the market.

The basic fault of training at NDA and other academies is the bullying and burn out happening at the hands of instructors and senior cadets, which needs to be controlled. The training should be tough to make a street smart youth to a man in uniform with obedience to be inculcated, but not by demeaning or bullying a cadet.

Talking about the delta factor, I think the performance of our officers and troops has never been wanting as seen, from their participation in international exercises. For that matter, the performance in IS duties in J&K and NE sectors has been commendable. However, the same can be fine-tuned further. If we compare the 'delta factor' of the cadets to those who have graduated side by side outside, I think the cadets stand out.

The negative delta factors must not be probed in the NDA alone; other academies suffer from it too. There was for instance this video of one cadet being thrashed with a hockey stick that became viral in 2017. It was from one of the premier academies but not from the NDA. I would recommend that a team of eminent psychologists and psychiatrists at least some of whom have association with military service, should make a comprehensive study of how these practices impact the cadet. Worst part is people develop nostalgia for the bad things they meted out and faced when they were at the academy and start gloating about it later! They go back as Divisional Officers and think this is normal.

The other related point is that I do not think that the status of the military officer has dropped substantially due to external factors. I would say the military fraternity itself is primarily responsible. Providence will conspire to give parity and justice to the armed forces officer and a rightful status. The question therefore is whether a fresh NDA alumnus can hold his own in a rational one-on-one conversation with a youngster who has passed his Civil Services exams.

The youngsters joining the NDA are smart kids. One can count on them to 'perform' when a challenge is thrown at them. But they are to spend most of their three years running around from pillar to post with hardly any time to develop personal interests and their intellects. If the average aptitude of the tribe goes up then it will be increasingly difficult to look down upon military officers.

CONCLUSION

The debate on selection and training of military officers has been going on seriously amongst military Veterans for the past 15 years. NDA has been in the centre of this debate and maximum time and effort has been dedicated towards reviewing, refining and reforming NDA. The preparation of NDA Vision Paper during 2002/03 by Vice Admiral SCS Bangara, the then Commandant, was the main trigger for the start of long and endless debates, which continue till date without any real solution being accepted.

In fact, things have only gone from bad to worse! Maj Gen Raj Mehta, ex-Instructor NDA, was the first 'General' ranking military officer who dedicatedly analysed the vast subject and covered all the intricate and complex issues of selection, training and education of military officers with the main thrust being on NDA. For the past two years, Fauji India magazine has provided a stable platform for ample and sustained coverage.

Sadly and surprisingly, the military hierarchy remains unmoved or pays only lip service. We are unable to get our own house (NDA) in order, despite heaps of evidence by our own. How and why should we complain about our politicians or bureaucrats? Have the three service academies and their respective services been content with the quality of products received by them from NDA? Ask the NAVAC, AFA and IMA and the Navy, Air Force and Army! The answers lie to a great extent in the individual services 'taking charge' of their cadets at the NDA itself.

Jointmanship requirement/tri-service integration should be a second priority and not be at the cost of the individual service imperatives. There is also an imperative need for the three services to clearly define what they want in the cadets and be directly be involved in meeting it. The Army too should clearly define what they need in their cadets for all Arms and Services and be directly/indirectly involved to get it. The selection of suitable cadets for different Arms and Services could possibly be decided at NDA itself, based on aptitude and interest.

WAY FORWARD

Brig LC Patnaik

My views on the imperative need for transformation of NDA stems from the desire to restore it's fame and glory. NDA, like many other civil and military organizations in the country has fallen behind to evolve itself for many reasons, of which some are emotional, while many are organizational and directional in nature. Despite many limitations, NDA continues to remain a pride of the nation and is of one of the preferred destinations for visit of foreign political/military dignitaries.

The lessons learnt from '62, '65 and '71, did not raise any shortcomings on the young leadership of the Armed Forces. On the contrary, many of our war heroes like Arun Khetrapal, Amarjit Singh Shekhon etc who were alumnus of NDA, became the symbols of leadership and bravery. In the last five decades since the '71 ops, the nature of warfare has shifted exponentially to hybrid, non-conventional and technological platforms. The education sector underwent major reforms towards privatization. Many government organizations restructured themselves to meet the new liberalization era. The civil services undertook four cadre reviews while the Armed Forces remained committed in unconventional warfare, aid to civil authorities and border management.

The Kargil war was short and didn't utilize the full potential of the Armed Forces. Due to economic crunch, modernization remained marginal. In the process, the Armed Forces as a whole missed many opportunities to evolve themselves except for two cadre reviews and few operational raisings like the Rashtriya Rifles and development of ship building. Despite the changing dynamics of threat perception, RMA, technological prowess, cyber and space war, our basic training philosophies remained of the pre and post-Independence era.

For any training institute to excel, it must have the best quality students, trainers, professors and administrative staff. To ensure quality students, my article 'Transformative Approach to Selection Process', earlier published in Fauji India, deals extensively on the subject. For quality trainers, the Service HQs have stream lined procedures to select the best Divisional Officers and Squadron Commanders. However, selection criteria get diluted in the upper ranks.

Service HQs intervention is essential to restore the anomaly. Our dependence on UPSC to provide civilian teaching faculty must shift to the affiliated University which also must shift from JNU to some reputed University in Pune/Mumbai. We also need to have a balanced composition of qualified serving/retired officers and civilian faculty. The Service element of training must commence early, preferably in the 2nd term. The syllabus must have a combination of compulsory and optional elective subjects having relevance for all three services like strategy, intelligence, military history, cyber warfare etc.

The basic military training consisting of physical training, drill and orientation must get over in first two terms, with roll over for weak cadets only to maximum fourth term; beyond which cadets not meeting basic QRs being withdrawn. This aspect needs to be included in the statutory rules to avoid legal complications. The modern scientific physical training must replace the archaic methods.

Sports should be optional and available for cadets in all terms and must form part of the overall assessment. Swimming and equestrian training can be shifted to co-curricular activities. The academic training needs to focus on International Relations, Constitution, relevant military and civil laws, military psychology, geography, military history, cyber security with both compulsory and elective options. The division of science and arts stream must cease forthwith to avoid repetition of class XII science subjects (presently 40%), and not overload the curriculum.

The academic wing must excel in a few chosen subjects like military strategy, military psychology and military history etc with world class research facilities. The infrastructure at NDA needs to be improved with bulk grants in similar lines as being done for the IITs and IIMs. It is recommended that a National Committee duly approved by the Cabinet to be established with members from Services, MoD, MHA, MHRD, MoD and few retired officers with domain knowledge, to prepare a blue print for transformation of NDA. Such an initiative can be undertaken by the Study Team of Victory India to present it to COSC and the RM for considering the above proposals.

Note: The Debate was published in Fauji India magazine, November 2018 issue.

SECTION 6

INSPIRATIONAL LEADERSHIP – LIVE EXAMPLES

CHAPTER 33

A Tribute to Lt Col J J Fonseca, the Pioneering Army Sports Specialist

Col Vinay B Dalvi

Lt Col John Joseph Fonseca was born in Pune on 11 June 1918 to Dr Ignatius and Lily Fonseca (original residents Goa). After commission he served with the British Army in the Second World War in the King's Own Royal Regiment. After partition, he was transferred to the Mahar Regt (Infantry) and Army Physical Training Corps (APTC) in 1959. During early 60s, he served as Secretary, Army Sports Control Board/MT-8 at the Army HQ.

He was posted as Commandant, Army School of Physical Training (now Army Institute of Physical Training), Pune in 1963. For six years from 1963 to 1969, his sterling role/performance as Commandant ASPT, undoubtedly left an indelible impression in the minds of all those who were fortunate to witness it or be a part of those six eventful years which were later known as the 'golden era' of ASPT and the APTC, Pune.

During that nostalgic era of the 1960s, Pune city did not have any sports infrastructure of the kind you see today. There was no Balewadi sports complex, Sahara sports complex or the synthetic (astro turf) hockey stadium of the Pimpri/Chinchwad Municipal Corporation. BEG, Kirkee; CME, Dapodi and NDA, Khadakwasla had sports facilities, utilized exclusively for military training and not available to the civil world outside their campuses.

In fact, even local clubs, schools and colleges had very limited facilities. During that period, under Lt Col Fonseca's able directions, the few multi discipline sports facilities that existed in ASPT Pune, were optimally developed and judiciously utilized, both for military training as well as the outside civil world of sports of schools and colleges. This provided a great opportunity and rich exposure to the young and budding youth/talent of local (Pune) schools, colleges and clubs.

That vintage period of the 1960s had very few cars and scooters and the most popular conveyance/transportation was the 'bicycle'. In fact, Pune was then known as the 'bicycle city'. It was then that ASPT, Pune became the central point and hub of several important army and national level sports events/meets.

During these events, all roads in Pune city led to ASPT as very little was available in Pune in terms of entertainment and sports extravaganza not only for the military world but also the civil side.

The notable events and achievements of Lt Col J J Fonseca are that many sports activities received a great boost. In athletics, several Southern Command, Services and National Open Championships were held besides All India Police Meets. National Hockey Championship for the prestigious Rangaswamy Cup was held in 1966 and followed by the Women's Hockey Nationals. National Gymnastics Championship was also held during this period. Besides the sports events, services and national coaching camps in gymnastics, boxing, athletics and hockey were held at ASPT.

During this period, the Principal of National Model School, N D Nagarvala handed over the reins of President MHA (Maharashtra Hockey Association) to O P Bahl, GM of Ammunition Factory, Kirkee with Abel David, founder editor of Poona Herald (Maharashtra Herald) taking over as Secretary MHA. The new team developed symbiotic relations with the ASPT Commandant Lt Col Fonseca, resulting in the first Senior National Hockey Championship being jointly conducted by them. This was one of the most memorable times in the history of ASPT, when the sporting public of Pune got the opportunity to watch not only the national championship, but also see legends like Major Dhyanchand, brother Roopsingh, and KD Singh Babu in action to play during an exhibition match.

The husband and wife team of Lt Col Fonseca too took active interest in sports. The conduct of the senior national hockey championship saw them providing boarding and lodging facilities for the teams participating in the championship. In those days when 'rationing' was in force in Pune, this magnanimous couple looked after the basic amenities for the teams residing in ASPT.

There was also excellent rapport between ASPT and adjacent SRPF (located at foothills of Ramtekdi) for mutual benefit for military training and sports activities. The National Gymnastics Coaching camp for 1964 Tokyo Olympics was held at ASPT, Pune and the entire six-member national team which participated in these games comprised of Army personnel, four from APTC and two from BEG, Kirkee. A rare feat indeed! Later, Lt Col Fonseca also accompanied the National Gymnastics team to Russia for international participation/exposure.

Lt Col Fonseca was also instrumental in showcasing ASPT and APTC through the brilliant physical performances and displays of their physical and recreational training instructors in many fields of military training, especially PT and gymnastics exercises. At his behest, several PT and gymnastics displays were held not only during the yearly APTC Corps Day Tattoo shows at ASPT, where all local schools and colleges were invited but, also at many schools, colleges and even cinema halls (prior to the movie shows). This great initiative in that era not only earned accolades for the ASPT and APTC but also for the Army.

Consequently, there was a great demand for Army APTC instructors in many convent/public schools not only in Pune, but also in nearby Nasik, Devlali, Mumbai, Ahmednagar and Panchgani. This demand for APTC instructors spread to other reputed convent/public schools in the country, especially in Delhi, Dehradun, Shimla, Lovedale, Darjeeling etc. All these initiatives cumulatively resulted in many post retirement jobs/avenues being opened for the Army PT qualified instructors and which continue till date. Hence, the APTC veterans who have since benefitted and continue to benefit even today, feel highly obliged and ever grateful to this great visionary father figure that the ASPT and APTC was fortunate to have at the helm of affairs at ASPT Pune.

The above contributions of Lt Col J J Fonseca and many more(which cannot be penned down due to space constraints) earned for him and the APTC, first Vishisht Seva Medal (VSM) and remain etched in the memory of all those who were witness or part of these activities. ASPT and APTC will remain ever grateful to him and his family.

In 1969, Lt Col Fonseca took premature retirement. He served with Kirloskar Oil Engines till Dec 1972 and migrated to Australia, where he spent the rest of his life. His last visit was to Pune during 2008/09 when he came to attend the APTC Diamond Jubilee & Reunion at ASPT Pune. He was based in South Lake, Western Australia where he died on 03 Mar 2018. His private cremation ceremony was held in South Fremantle on 07 Mar 2018.

The sudden and premature retirement of Lt Col Fonseca from the Army in 1969 was a big setback and great loss for the APTC and Army. His continuation in APTC/ASPT would surely have yielded many more gains for the Army and the nation. These sentiments are being echoed by several military veterans around the country.

I am one of the fortunate few to have seen Col Fonseca in flesh and blood during that golden era of ASPT, Pune as I was studying in the nearby 'Bishop's School' from 1960-68, which had access to the ASPT, Race Course and Command PT School.

Being from an army family, I had the opportunity of witnessing several services and national sports events at ASPT. Besides that, Col Fonseca was often the chief guest for select sports events like boxing and athletics in our school. Like me, many school and college going youngsters of that period in Pune were positively influenced in the development of leadership qualities through witnessing and active participation in competitive sports activities. Many of them, especially children of military personnel joined the NDA, IMA, OTA and AFMC.

Note: This article was published by G T Panaji Goa, TOI & Sakal Times, Pune & Fauji India May 2018.

GRACIOUS ACKNOWLEDGEMENT FOR TRIBUTE

Dear Col Dalvi,

I have been meaning to thank you sincerely for your kind words describing the dedication and effort my husband John put into the Institution of Sports and physical fitness in general, in the article you wrote. It was his love in life, and he gave 110 percent to promote in to Schools & Colleges. When he came to Australia he was overcome by the level of sports in the Schools and Colleges here, but he could not sit quiet, he volunteered to coach Girls in our daughter's School in hockey, he taught young children to ride horses! He was glued to the television to watch every sporting event. He was so taken with Carl Lewis' start in every race he competed in, that he had numerous tapes and watched it over and over! He was so proud of his grandchildren's love of sport, and was even more impressed with our great grandchildren's participation in Athletics, hockey, football cricket and now Soccer! Bringing home medals and cups and winning "champion" "Best Sportsman" "Best sportswoman" in their respective schools. Thank you once again. Our 5 children, 10 grandchildren and 10 great grandchildren join me in wishing you and your family the very best of health and joy in the future.

Yours sincerely,
Blossom Fonseca, Perth, Australia
23rd. March 2018.

CHAPTER 34

Sam Bahadur: Leader Par Excellence

Shashwat Gupta Ray

Late Field Marshal Sam Manekshaw is not just a name. It is the identity of a legend, India's First Field Marshal and arguably the greatest Army chief of India. Born on April 3, 1914, the first Field Marshal of Indian Army passed away in his sleep 10 years ago on June 27, 2008.

Born as Sam Hormusji Framji Jamshedji Manekshaw, he was famously referred as Sam Bahadur.

He began his service in the British Indian Army in World War II, for which he won the Military Cross for gallantry. Known for his commanding leadership, Sam Manekshaw's distinguished military career spanned four decades in which he participated in five wars.

His valour and wit is folklore. But he will be always remembered for standing up to one of the most powerful leaders of our times, the then prime minister Indira Gandhi.

The Indo-Pakistani conflict was sparked by the Bangladesh Liberation war, a conflict between the traditionally dominant West Pakistanis (Punjabi Muslims) and the majority East Pakistanis (Bengali Muslims).

In March, 1971 the Pakistan Armed Forces launched a fierce campaign to curb the protests in East Pakistan. Thousands of East Pakistanis died, and nearly ten million refugees fled to West Bengal and adjoining North East states. In April, India decided to assist in the formation of the new nation of Bangladesh. During a cabinet meeting towards the end of April, Prime Minister Indira Gandhi asked Manekshaw if he was prepared to go to war with Pakistan immediately. He refused to do so saying replied that most of his armoured and infantry divisions were deployed elsewhere and would take time to assemble them and go into war at such a short notice.

Moreover, he Himalayan passes would soon open up with the forthcoming monsoon, which would result in heavy flooding. Indian tanks won't be able to proceed through the swampy paddy fields. Moreover China would have also activated its troops for helping Pakistan. He guaranteed victory provided he was allowed him to handle the conflict on his own terms, and set a date for it. PM agreed. The rest is history.

As Chief of Army Staff, General Sam Manekshaw led India to victory against East Pakistan army in 14 days. Total 90,000 Pakistani troops surrendered before India, the biggest victory achieved by any independent army in one battle theatre, post victory of Allied forces in Second World War.

In the capacity of COAS, Manekshaw once visited a Gorkha unit. He asked an orderly if he knew the name of his chief. The orderly replied that he did, and on being asked to name the chief, he said "Sam Bahadur". This eventually became Manekshaw's nickname.

What made Sam Bahadur so special was not only his self-belief and courage but also the quality of putting nation before self. He could have easily buckled under the genuine pressure of refugee influx in lakhs teeming in from East Pakistan. A leader like Indira Gandhi was adding more pressure on him to wage war on Pakistan immediately. But as true leader and military strategist, he had a foresight and made no bones about it despite knowing the consequences of defying political establishment.

Even after leading the country to such a morale boosting massive victory over Pakistan, like a true leader, he never hogged the limelight. Rather he allowed his juniors – Eastern Army Commander Lt Gen Jagjit Singh Arora presides over the signing of Instrument of Surrender with East Pakistan Army commander Lt Gen AAK Niazi. Another junior ranking officer, Major General JFR Jacob (former Goa governor) was allowed to seek Pakistan's surrender.

This is very unlike today's scenario where the senior leadership wants to take all the credit at the expense of their junior colleagues, indulge in corrupt act and are even ready to bend before the political masters. The number of senior ranking officers getting post retirement positions like Lieutenant Governors and Governors is very high.

Nowadays, we have Army chief who speaks like a politician, without having any innovative strategy to offer. The top military brass plays ball with politicians while meritorious officers are opting out of Services. There is a lack of clarity in the thought process of military leadership. Today such is the scenario that even veterans are questioning the top leadership, selection and training system of the armed forces' officer cadre and the promotion policy.

The golden era of having military leadership of impeccable quality has long gone. It will require another Sam Bahadur who will have the courage to set the wrong right. However, looking at the scheme of things it will be a far-fetched dream.

Nepotism and unprofessionalism has become a deep rooted problem in the society today. Armed Forces are no different. There is a leadership crisis at the middle and top level. We are already seeing how political interference and lack of astute leadership has already resulted in bungling with the Kashmir situation, which has spiralled out of control.

The Indian military has never been so politicised as now. The Central government, especially BJP and its affiliates have been milking one surgical strike against Pakistan since last two years for political gains. But the fact that it has failed to deter Pakistan from continuing with its terror activities inside Kashmir Valley has not been understood or has been ignored conveniently. Sadly enough, even the senior military brass is playing ball. The result is high amount of civilian and military casualties.

According to the South Asia terrorism Portal, in 2009 there were 381 deaths in Kashmir valley due to terror attacks, which came down drastically to 99 in 2012. In contrast, the three years of BJP-PDP rule saw surge in casualties from 164 in 2015, 247 in 2016 and 333 in 2017. This clearly shows that the hard-line approach advocated by Modi government at Centre has not paid off. Having an Army chief toeing the Centre's aggressive stance has not helped the cause.

India does not need a loud mouth Chief who shoots from his mouth more, when he should be actually brainstorming with his commanders to find a way for salvaging the situation in J&K and North East. I am sure had Field Marshal Sam Manekshaw would have been the Army Chief today; he would have come out with some out-of-the-box solution to the problem and not make bones about it. It is unfortunate that the system does not allow astute officers to take up positions of leadership.

The 'Victory India' book series by military experts points out several lacunae in the system. The essays and news reports compiled in the series is exhaustive enough for the authorities to accept them and get down to the business of plugging the gaping holes. Out of the three Services, Army has shown the least keenness in changing its colonial era mind-set.

Time has come for a complete overhaul of the system if we have to produce more military commanders like Sam Manekshaw. Only then we will be a true military power.

Courtesy – Gomantak Times, Panaji Goa.

SECTION 7

COMPREHENSIVE MEDIA COVERAGE: GOMANTAK TIMES, GOA

CHAPTER 35

Integration of Tri-Services is Need of the Hour

By Shashwat Gupta Ray & Nibedita Sen

The above news story was published by Gomantak Times, Goa on 16 Dec 18 on occasion of 47th Anniversary of Vijay Diwas (1971 War with Pakistan).

On December 16, the country will be celebrating the 47th anniversary of Vijay Diwas to mark the stupendous victory of our armed forces over Pakistan in 1971, leading to creation of Bangladesh. This victory was achieved due to the gallant officers and men of Indian tri-services who forced the enemy to bite the dust. One such name is of former Chief of Naval Staff, **Admiral Arun Prakash**, who participated in the IAF 'counter-air campaign' that repeatedly targeted Pakistani air bases with accurate aerial attacks and inflicted heavy attrition on Pakistan Air Force. In an exclusive interaction with **Shashwat Gupta Ray & Nibedita Sen,** the former Navy chief shares his memories of the war, the changing nature of combat and his concerns regarding the quality of leadership in the armed forces.

Admiral Arun Prakash is a specialised Navy fighter pilot, who flew from the aircraft carrier INS Vikrant in 1968. In the 1971 Indo-Pakistan War, Admiral (then Lieutenant) Prakash flew Hawker Hunter aircraft for the 20th Squadron Lightnings. For his gallantry in air action over West Pakistan, he was awarded with the Vir Chakra (VrC).

"I was a young Lieutenant, relatively inexperienced and I played a very minor role during 1971 Liberation war. But I was very fortunate as few months before the war started, I was sent on deputation from Navy to the Air Force. Little realising how events would turn out in 1971, I left INS Vikrant where I was learning how to operate from the aircraft carrier. I was posted to 20 Squadron, which was one of the frontline IAF squadrons," narrated Adm Prakash.

Sharing his war memories he continued by saying, "My squadron commander Wing Commander Cecil Parker was worried that if war broke out we would be falling prey to Pakistani bombers because, in 1965, our air base (Pathankot, which was just 12 miles away from the international border) had been targeted and many aircraft destroyed on the ground, by the Pakistan Air Force (PAF). In late November 1971, as a precautionary measure, our squadron moved to Ambala and then to Hindon near Delhi)."

"By now, the war clouds were building up, and we were watching things happening in East Pakistan. In the evening of 3 December 1971 around 5:30 pm the PAF carried out 'pre-emptive attacks' on 8-9 Indian Air Force bases. The then incumbent Prime Minister Indira Gandhi addressed the nation through radio and declared that the nation was at war. At about 4 am, all our aircraft took off from Hindon, and headed back to Pathankot. There was dense fog all over Punjab and North India. Our commanding officers gave us the targets, as soon as we landed in Pathankot" he described. Speaking about India's preparations he mentioned, "We had been practicing for quite a few months. We knew the likely targets, the airbases, radar stations, ammunition dumps in Pakistan. We had intelligence, photographs etc."

Demolishing Chaklala Base

"On the first mission, on December 4, 1971, myself and my fellow officer were assigned the responsibility of attacking Pakistani Air Force base called Chaklala, near Rawalpindi. As we took off and crossed the border, we found the dense fog was continuing. We had to fly at 500 ft above ground level to avoid radar detection but as we pulled up to 2000 ft before attack, we couldn't see much, the runway was covered with fog. Then we came down and found the tail of a large aircraft hidden in a mango grove near a hangar. We went and fired on it and smoke started coming out. As we were pulling out of the dive we saw few more small aircrafts lined up and attacked them also. We finished our ammunition and came back. At that point we didn't know what we had attacked. But later on it was revealed that there was a Hercules transport aircraft hidden which was attacked," Adm Arun Prakash said.

"We also learnt that an aircraft belonging to the US Military attaché had been destroyed".

"In subsequent days from December 3-16, we attacked around eight Pakistani Air Force bases and Pak troops in Chhamb sector and our Squadron in totality managed to inflict pretty heavy damage on Pakistan. We destroyed the aircrafts, oil dumps, refineries, radar stations, troops and tanks" he said. Two of his Squadron pilots were shot down over Pakistan territory. His Squadron commander came back from mission with bullet holes in his aircraft and earned a Maha Vir Chakra.

Blurb

"In subsequent days from December 3-16, we attacked around eight PAF bases and Pak troops in Chhamb sector and our Squadron in totality managed to inflict pretty heavy damage."

Integrated Approach Helped

The coordination and integrated approach by chiefs of all the three services was the key to our victory in 1971. He said, "Fortunately, the three chiefs, at that juncture, had a good understanding with each other, and due to coordinated planning, everything worked out well. Regrettably, we have rarely been able to replicate the 1971 synergy."

No Integration Now
"The nature of combat has changed tremendously from 1971, which was a purely conventional war. Now we have fifth generation warfare, where nuclear warfare is a possibility. But the armed forces have not adapted themselves because successive governments have failed to integrate the armed forces with the MoD and with each other – for want of resolve – and is a major shortcoming. A Chief of Defence Staff (CDS) should have been created long, long ago. He would have been the single point of contact between the three armed forces and source of cohesive advice to the government and vice versa," he said.

According to him, even though the political leadership is indifferent regarding appointment of CDS, there is much that the armed forces can do internally without seeking help from the government; but unfortunately the three Services don't agree with each other (this is an universal problem that can only be resolved through political intervention/wisdom).

One or the other of the three services doesn't agree with this integration. Unfortunately it is the Air Force that feels most threatened by integration. Since both the Army and Navy, both have aviation wings, the IAF feels that if put under a single commander, possibly their role will be diluted," he said.

Traditionally it is for the political leadership to have the foresight to understand that if the armed forces don't have integrated approach the country's security would suffer. He can push it through, even against the wishes of the armed forces. It has happened in USA, UK, and China. Unfortunately that is not happening in India.

"The three service chiefs need to sit together and discuss amongst themselves how the integration can be done at their level. However, it must be remembered that when the services integrate with each other, and adopt the 'Theatre Command' system the operational command functions will be taken away from the three chiefs. That is possibly a factor for not favouring any change" he said.

Blurb
"The three service chiefs need to sit together and discuss amongst themselves how the integration can be done at their level."

Leadership Quality:
"Perhaps we are not providing the right inputs to our budding officer material, during basic training, and this tends to manifest itself 20-30 years later, at the higher levels of leadership. We need to introspect about the system of training being followed in our academies where young men and women are moulded. If we are not producing good leaders after three to four years of training then

there is some problem with our system. This is exactly what Col Vinay Dalvi from Pune has been campaigning in his four volumes of 'Victory India' book series," he said.

"We need to relook at our system of selection and training and identify what is going wrong. Unfortunately though this issue has been noted by many senior Service officers, but to my knowledge nothing has really moved forward. This will require an overhaul of the full system. While we ensure physical qualities like stamina and, physical fitness, we need to mould the boys and girls intellectually as moral, upright and ethical individuals. We need to strike a new balance," he said. "The ethics part has been forgotten and young boys and girls whom we pick up from schools and colleges, go to the academies and unfortunately indulge in stealing, physical abuse of cadets, lying, impersonation, cheating in examination have become acceptable traits. This is because of the belief that young officer who has to fight terrorists, some these traits are acceptable. They are not acceptable. The ethical moorings must not be allowed to get eroded," he said.

Blurb:
"While we ensure physical qualities like stamina and, physical fitness, we need to mould the boys and girls intellectually as moral, upright and ethical individuals."

Reforms at NDA:
Being a former Commandant of the prestigious tri-services military training institution the National Defence Academy (NDA), Adm Prakash emphasised on the need to begin reforms starting with the NDA, which is the apex institution meant for converting young boys into future officers.

"NDA is one of the finest academies, in the world, but unfortunately we have allowed the environment to degenerate over the years and hence we are producing officers with certain flaws which erode their moral fibre in later years. This trend must be nipped at the bud," he said.

CHAPTER 36

Media Coverage of 'Victory India Campaign'

Gomantak Times, Panjim Goa – 30 Dec 2018

'Ignoring Military Leadership Issues can Become Himalayan Blunder'
Being former instructor at the Indian Military Academy (IMA), Dehradun and the National Defence Academy (NDA), senior Army veteran Colonel Vinay Dalvi (Retd) found to his dismay that the outdated selection and training process in military academies would have a direct bearing on the quality of leadership in the officer cadre of Indian armed forces. The veteran officer decided to identify the gaps and plug it himself through recommendations with the help of other like-minded veterans, which were compiled by him in a book titled 'Quality Leadership – Key to Victory India' in 2013.

The book, which was a collection of essays written by military experts, was a deep insight into flaws in military officers' selection and training. The positive response evoked by the book led to publication of three more volumes and now the fifth part is in the process of getting published. In an exclusive interaction with Col Dalvi, SHASHWAT GUPTA RAY charts the journey of Victory India series, which has now become a campaign.

Q 1. What is Victory India campaign all about?
Ans. The Victory India Campaign is about improving the quality of our military leadership at all levels by studying, analysing and researching about all our processes of nurturing, selection, training and grooming our military officers from the lowest rank to the highest. In any conflict, proxy war or even peace time scenario the quality of our leadership, especially in the Army is of critical importance for success or victory. The better the quality of leadership at the decisive point or levels better are the chances of Victory.

Q 2. Why and when was this started?
Ans. The campaign was sparked off after release of my first book 'Role Model' in 2010 and the subsequent articles and debates initiated by me and fervent plea to our learned veteran fraternity and academicians (who had vast knowledge and experience on several complex subjects of leadership and personality development) during 2011-1, leading to the compilation of articles,

papers, reviews and debates into the first volume. The campaign, per se, took off after release of this first volume by Air Chief Marshal NAK Browne, then Chief of Air Staff and Chairman Chief of Staff Committee (COSC) in New Delhi during November 2012.

Q 3. Why did you come up with 5 volumes of the book series?
Ans. The main reason why five volumes have come up during last 8 years is that the subject of military leadership is vast and unlimited. If the aim of the exercise was to improve the quality of the military leadership at all levels, detailed study and analysis perforce has to be done in all the relevant subjects concerning selection, training and grooming including physical education, fitness/sports medicine, relevance of sports competitions, human psychology, training methodology, academics personality development as per qualitative requirements of the three services. Besides this, other vital issues of assessment and promotion policies of officers, subjects of professional military education, revolution in military affairs and even military doctrines and national defence strategy were covered by eminent military writers.

Q 4. What have been the key findings of experts in the series?
Ans. The key findings of experts are that there has been no worthwhile review /analysis of our Army centric 70 years obsolete systems of selection, training and grooming which are primarily a legacy of the British Army. While the British and the western world have moved ahead and refined all their obsolete systems we are rigidly continuing to maintain the status quo believing them to be still valid or relevant in this 21st century warfare.

The prime reason for this is that unlike the western world which has limited manpower we despite a huge manpower base in the required young age group for recruitment have failed to optimally tap the right and most suitable manpower for the the military. There is vast scope to improve on this front as amply elaborated in nearly 200 chapters of the five volumes of our Victory India book series.

Q 5. Considering that armed forces in India is hallowed institution, how challenging was it to pick holes in this image?
Ans. It was indeed a great challenge to pick holes in the image enjoyed by the armed forces. But detailed study and research of the systems of selection and training revealed glaring faults in the existing policies and implementation methodology that was causing great and unrepairble harm to the military. My personal findings and suggestions for improving the quality of our military leadership were circulated by me to several senior veterans for comments, validation and authentication besides inviting their personal views and opinions on different subjects issues.

This consequently led to several well considered views and

recommendations on almost all complex issues of selection and training leading to conclusions and even consensus on most issues. These were frequently raised with our apex military hierarchy from time to time.

Q 6. What has been the response to your endeavour?
Ans. The responses to my endeavour all along have been quite encouraging at all levels. I have received several letters from even Prime Minister's Office (PMO). Letters of acknowledgement and appreciation have been received from four Raksha Mantris, Several chiefs of three services, Army Commanders and Commandants of several officer training institutions.

These responses over the years have directly or indirectly acted as a catalyst to continue with our mission relentlessly. However, sadly there has been no serious or worthwhile positive action on ground to transfer our recommendations on ground to actually improve the future quality of our military leadership. The serving hierarchy, due to several inexplicable reasons has only been paying lip service to our advice and recommendations and prefers to maintain status quo.

This could be due to several reasons. The problem mainly lies with the Army hierarchy which is unable to study, analyse our findings and recommendations and reach conclusions or consensus within their own arms and services. The reason for this is the strong regimentation and their traditions followed rigidly by them in their respective arms, services and regiments in this 21st century. Uniform implementation of selection systems and training methodologies has therefore become very difficult.

Whenever simple or complex issues were raised with Chief of Staff Committee (COSC) and CISC rather than attempt to understand the technicalities of the issues with an open mind the serving incumbents sadly preferred to avoid or evade the issues by claiming that all was well and claimed the best way forward was to maintain the status quo. Consequently, there has been no worthwhile review, refinement or reform on our recommendations.

It is pertinent to mention that several senior serving officers at apex level have personally confided in me that the issues raised by us were valid and even treated our books as reference manuals and even Bible. But could not officially accept the same as the higher leadership especially of the Army was not relenting and rigidly defending the indefensible.

Q 7. What do the findings mean to common people and how should they react to the findings?
Ans. The findings of our Victory India Campaign books mean that the issues raised by us are very serious national issues concerning the quality of our future military leadership at all levels and will surely impact the fate and destiny of our nation. If serious heed is paid to our findings and recommendations the chances of victory in future conflicts are definitely going to be brighter. If ignored

or brushed under the carpet as being done for past few years, the chances of Himalayan blunder are most likely.

Q 8. What is your message to the policy makers, armed forces fraternity and the common tax payers?
Ans. My message to the policy makers and armed forces fraternity especially commanders at all levels and all tax payers is that unless we focus on improving the quality of our military leadership and intricately linked political leadership including critical bureaucratic link up, the fate and destiny of our nation is heading on the treacherous path of 'Himalayan Blunder'. Unless, we the people of India wake up and rally collectively and relentlessly for the cause of Victory India we shall continue to tread on this fateful path.

Blurb
"While the British and the western world have moved ahead and refined all their obsolete systems we are rigidly continuing to maintain the status quo believing them to be still valid or relevant in this 21st century warfare."

"If serious heed is paid to our findings and recommendations the chances of victory in future conflicts are definitely going to be brighter."

HIGHLIGHTS OF 5 VOLUMES VICTORY INDIA CAMPAIGN BOOKS
Victory India – 1: A Key to Quality Military Leadership (2013)

It was released during Nov 2012 by Air Chief Marshal NAK Browne, then Air Force chief and Chairman COSC Committee.

This book was triggered due to Col Dalvi's first book 'Role Model' a key to character development which was released in NDA in March 2010 and second edition by Lt Gen VS Tonk, Deputy Chief of Army Staff (T&C) on behalf of Chief of Army Staff (COAS), Gen V K Singh at Army Headquarters in September 2010. Focus of book was selection and training processes of cadets of all military academies, especially NDA. Over 20 veterans and academicians contributed articles and responses to them. The conclusions reached were highlighted indicating the dire need to address the identified short comings and weaknesses. Consensus was reached on several key points and highlighted at the end of the book.

Victory India – 2: Quality Leadership a Key (2104)
This book was a continuation of volume 1 with maximum focus on NDA, highlighting the glaring shortcomings in the 70 years old training methodology with the imperative need to address them on priority. Issues and shortcomings of Defence Institute of Psychological Research (DIPR) based Services Selection Board (SSB) selection system are covered in greater detail in this volume through contributory articles and responses from over 20 veterans and academicians.

Victory India – 3: A Campaign (2016)

This book was a further follow up and relentless pursuit of earlier issues especially after my personal briefing of of full 40 minutes of then Raksha Mantri Manohar Parrikar on 28 Mar 2015, appraising him about the need to improve the future quality of our military leadership by comprehensively addressing the issues raised and fully documented with a vision plan and road map. This volume too has over 20 contributors with focus on improving the quality of our military leadership at all levels.

Victory India – 4: Beyond the Campaign (2018)

This volume also comprises essays articles and debates on several subjects / issues concerning military officers and their professional military education, revolution in military affairs, besides selection, training and grooming of military officers. The campaign had been intermittently receiving recognition from all three Chiefs, Army Commanders, especially of ARTRAC, being the main custodian for training the military. The official letter of acknowledgement and appreciation of the campaign by present Chief of Air Staff (CAS), Air Chief Marshal B S Dhanoa and Chief of Naval Staff (CNS), Admiral Sunil Lanba are part of this book. The official endorsement of Commandants of Defence Services Staff College (DSSC) and Indian Military Academy (IMA) are also included.

Victory India – 5: A Key to Quality Combat Leadership (upcoming in 2019)

This volume is the fifth and possibly last volume of the campaign which is likely to be released in early 2019. It has articles, papers, letters and debates on several subjects being debated by military fraternity and of significant national importance. They also include the key selection and training issues with clear solutions and suggestions to address them befittingly. This volume has a stern message (for military hierarchy) from Admiral Arun Prakash (Retd), ex-Navy chief and former Commandant National Defence Academy (NDA).

CHAPTER 37

'Victory India' Campaign Gets Overwhelming Support

Gomantak Times, Panjim Goa – 06 Jan 2019

Through his 5-part book series 'Victory India', senior Army veteran Col Vinay Dalvi (Retd) with help from senior military veterans, has relentlessly pursued and given recommendations for resolving issues of outdated selection and training of officer cadre process at entry level; gaps in promotion policy of Services and numerous other lacunae which has direct bearing on quality of leadership in the tri-services. These observations have received endorsement from important personalities ranging from Goa Chief Minister and former Defence Minister Manohar Parrikar, former Navy Chief Admiral Arun Prakash to present Chief of Naval Staff Admiral Sunil Lanba and Chief of Air Staff, Air Chief Marshal B S Dhanoa. Shashwat Gupta Ray chronicles some these endorsements to the campaign, which shows that the issues taken up in this campaign are true and need urgent intervention from the country's policy makers and military top brass.

Admiral Arun Prakash (Retd)
Having enlisted the support of a galaxy of military luminaries, with tremendous experience and interest in training matters, Col Vinay Dalvi's indefatigable endeavours have turned 'Victory India' into a veritable campaign for introspection and reform. It has delivered, over the past decade, five comprehensive compendiums of essays, focusing on every aspect of selection and training of our young combat leadership.

The thrust of Col Dalvi's campaign has been that the onus for stemming progressive deterioration of 'quality leadership' in the armed forces rests squarely on the senior hierarchy; the Service Chiefs as well as the Commanders-in-Chief. Only their intervention and directions can bring necessary focus on the military's basic training academies and on introduction of a Military Education Programme that runs in a continuum from subaltern to general.

While my admiration for Col Dalvi's single-minded perseverance and tenacity is boundless, equally deep is my distress at the lack of any response from Service HQs. The plausible reason, that comes to mind, for this stasis, is the intense preoccupation of HQ staff with multiple routine issues as well as crises requiring immediate action, and the low priority accorded to training issues.

But a far more disturbing thought is the likelihood of a belief, at higher levels, that the current emphasis on brawn over brains, that delivers a 'rough-and-ready' brand of leadership, is good enough for counter-insurgency forces.

I sincerely hope that my fears are unfounded, and that the Chiefs of Staff will address this issue in all seriousness, by constituting a high-level committee to study all issues related to selection and training of officers and report to them in a time-bound manner.

Air Marshal Raj Kumar (Retd)
Every organisation generally tends to improve over time. The Armed Forces very survival depends on such improvements. So, they do take this aspect seriously. There certainly has been an improvement in all aspects of military training over the years.

In many exercises with foreign forces, our personnel have done exceedingly well. That goes to show that we are on the right track as far as our selection and training are concerned. Evolutionary changes may be indicated but no revolutionary changes are needed.

However, like in other countries, it is important to pick holes in the functioning of the military to keep them rooted. Lest the Services start believing themselves to be infallible! Criticism is important to progress. Most times it is painful but leads to improvement.

Air Marshal Narayan Menon (Retd)
The essence of Victory India campaign has been to transform the Indian Military into a modern, well-trained, technologically competent fighting force with superior leadership skills and qualities.

Over a period of time, due to environmental changes which include the ecosystems of technology, education, finance, politics and social milieu, there are reasons to suspect a disconnect or discord between the various levels of hierarchy, leading to reduced effectiveness of the military. The entire mission, aim or objective was to bring in improvement in the military, especially the officer corps.

Rear Admiral Vineet Bakshi (Retd)
It is quality military leadership that is the cutting edge of the bulwark to our peace and progress. The focus on the development of military leadership to achieve peace and prosperity by an assurance of being victorious in war, is the essence of Victory India campaign.

It is the primary task of senior leadership to develop more and better leaders. Nonetheless, a recent phenomenon is the lack of in-depth reading and awareness, as a consequence of the ascendancy of the electronic media and the demise of the book. This is suggestive of leaders who aren't learning or are not curious. How would they develop vision?

'Victory India' suggests tweaking of various processes to enhance its efficiency. The onus of doing so lies with the serving leadership.

Brig L C Patnaik (Retd)

The junior leadership is highly motivated, aspires rapid transformation, seeks faster decision desires to grow in a corporate style and accords low priority to social and regimental issues. The senior leadership in contrast develops a cautious approach, prefers procrastination on contentious issues, and tends to shift from his erstwhile deep organisational interest to more personal interest and remains very critical of the system if professional growth gets halted for any reason.

Picking holes in the image of the armed forces is a positive social trend which entails a matured response and thoughtful corrective actions at appropriate levels.

Col Rajinder Kushwaha (Retd)

'Victory India Campaign' seeks internal audit of the functioning of military leadership with a view to make suggestions to introduce new methodology and training procedures to suit the emergent forms of war. It is directed at the breeding centres, like NDA, for producing modern military leaders to ensure that young leaders were not square pegs in round holes.

Five volumes has identified the problem areas and recommended adjustments to be made in grooming young leadership. It is not condemnation of army leadership but a self-correcting mechanism.

The contributing authors have identified that military leadership training in the academies was outdated and outmoded for present day socio-military environments.

Group Captain Johnson Chacko (Retd)

The essence of the Victory India Campaign is to transform the quality of military leadership with the knowledge of how it has been trained in the past, what is happening now and what direction it should take for the future, culled from the experience and views of the Veterans.

Leadership is essentially the art of achieving success for the group that the leader is leading. He needs to assess the situation that the group is in, ideate on overcoming the situation in favour of the group, using the strengths of the members of the group.

At grassroots level the junior officers are expected to do this and the training in academies if imbibed correctly provide the solution. At the senior levels, the focus on the group gets diluted and the interests of the self take over ending up with the focus of his immediate superior. This transformation is entirely a matter of the environment of the service he is in and appraisal reports play a prominent role in such a deviation.

Nixon Fernando, *former lecturer at National Defence Academy, Pune*
Victory India campaign is about pursuit of excellence. The nation can rise to greater heights and the armed forces are a cut above the rest and yet there are heights to climb. Every institution must fight to stem the rot and Victory India is the way the armed forces must take to its own reform.

The way we select, train, groom, promote officers, can it be better? Yes it can be and we must be assured that we are getting the best of the boys, making them the optimum best they can be so that our men can have the best of leaders at all levels.

Can the grooming be faulty, can the selection process bring in lesser then the best candidate? Indeed all are possible. An attempt is needed to stop the degradation and continue targeting excellence—to make the organization worthy of an even greater halo.

ACTION POINTS FOR SERVICES/ACADEMIES

Gomantak Times, Panjim Goa – 07 Jan 2019

Critical Weaknesses (W) & Solutions (S)

W 1. SSB Selection system not linked with training methodology especially NDA, resulting in high wastage/attrition viz. relegation, withdrawal, resignation & medical cases.

S 1. Link actual training content of 24 hours schedule (high physical load) by introducing physical tests to assess physical suitability and robustness to cope with sudden high physical load on cadets most unscientifically against basic principles of PT.

W 2. Combining 3 year academic degree course at NDA with basic military training does justice neither to academics nor military training.

S 2. Imperative need to change or modify this impractical combination to give respite and breathing space to cadets who mostly doze off during academic classes and consequently suffer in their academic grades nor gain much in military training.

W 3. At NDA combined training for all cadets, including non structured Squadron training is harmful for specific service needs. Consequently, cadets perforce change service from Air Force and Navy to Army or within Army from Science to Non-Science stream.

S 3. Parent service must take charge of respective cadets during full three year training and be primarily responsible to their service for their training, grooming and performance before joining their finishing academies.

W 4. At NDA in the 24 hours cycle routine, 16 hrs are spent in non-structured training under unqualified senior cadets or officers.

S 4. The conduct of training and grooming under unqualified / inexperienced senior cadets and officers should stop. Unreasonable raising of physical standards must stop as they have been causing high attrition and burn outs through premature, high and unscientific physical doses to young cadets.

W 5. DIPR based officer selection system at SSBs not reviewed objectively for decades to meet actual training content and methodology at our military academies.

S 5. Army DG Recruiting must get involved with selection process of officer cadets for military academies with introduction of Army screening field tests, similar to recruits. The screening tests must be conducted prior to actual SSB interview and could be held at select regimental training centres where adequate staff and facilities exist.

W 6. There is no vision in the overall selection, training and grooming of officer cadets especially for NDA. All cadets are basically put through same training schedule for three years.

S 6. Cadets of three services must be trained as per vision and actual service needs after commissioning or requirement of finishing academies. Unnecessary and unwanted physical load in name of military training for future possible confrontation with terrorists/insurgents by over enthusiastic Divisional officers must stop. All training must be done Service wise under respective service teams only.

W 7. Incorporation of sports medicine in physical training methodology of cadets, recruits and combatants is a joint United Commanders Conference (UCC) decision in Mar 2017. However, on ground there has been no worthwhile change on this aspect. There is a need to effectively implement this point with a vision plan.

S 7. Armed Forces Medical College (AFMC) Pune has been tasked to produce sports medicine specialists in greater numbers. This is being done with six months duration/short courses and posting the Sports Medicine Officers (SMOs) to academies and recruit training centres.

There is a need to integrate the sports medicine aspect with Officers Physical Training Course at AIPT, Pune for optimum results as the actual conduct of PT & Sports activities is done by the service officers of Arms & Services. SMOs are only the technical advisers in sports/fitness medicine and sports sciences aspect.

CHAPTER 38

Mission Victory India – Six Part Series

Gomantak Times 3-8 Jan, 2019

MISSION VICTORY INDIA – I
'Government mustn't dilute Army's power by revoking AFSPA'

'Mission Victory India', 5th in the 'Victory India' series of books (2010-2018), examines the human resource aspects of personnel management, military leadership, training and selection, all of which go a long way in deciding the quality and calibre of a nation's military forces. In a six-part series SHASHWAT GUPTA RAY explores some of the important issues taken up in this book by various senior military experts, which have been compiled and edited by senior Army veteran Col Vinay B Dalvi (Retd) and can be 'Key to Combat Leadership'.

The Government of India must not dilute the Army's power by revoking the Armed Forces Special Powers Act (AFSPA) considering that the country's internal and external security situation is still volatile and the neighbouring nations are always on a lookout for a chance to disturb country's integrity, writes former Division Commander Major General Anil Senegar (Retd).

"The decision whether to revoke or dilute the Armed Forces Special Powers Act (AFSPA) will solely be taken after analysing the present and future complications that will crop up after its removal. It is also important for the Centre to not dilute the Army's power in today's environment when our neighbouring nations are always on a lookout for a chance to disturb our integrity," Maj Gen Senegar states in the book.

Heed the Dangers

Taking a dig at human rights activists questioning Indian Army's actions in Kashmir and North East where AFSPA has been imposed.

"The champions of human rights may question the Sri Lankan Military for war crime and human rights violations. In reality, common people there are grateful to their Army for getting them rid of the LTTE menace and bring peace to the country," he writes.

Questioning the intentions of political leadership, the former Indian Army Division Commander said, "The Army has restored normalcy in the Valley many a times. What has the government done to leverage that stability and achieve lasting peace? Even today, the government has no clear long-term strategy for resolving the Kashmir issue. This delay is really making the situation even worse," he says.

He further adds that the Army will not get into a confrontation with the judiciary over repealing of AFSPA.

"It is not part of Army's DNA. It will continue to serve the country, but not the way they have been. The real danger comes in the form of loss of morale, passion, commitment and trust in the leadership. All of these are capable of destroying the core pillar of our army that is unity," the retired Major General writes.

The Way Ahead
According to him, asymmetric warfare (counter-terrorism) is not about rules; it is about fighting without rules. It is about neutralizing the advantage of the stronger adversary by any means. And that is exactly happening in Kashmir.

"At the same time, the Army is not above the law or the Constitution. There is a serious need to understand the difference between actions done in good faith and those done with bad intent.

Thus, for our forces to remain effective, the judiciary should keep out of the combat space and leave it to the government to address the balance," he adds.

MISSION VICTORY INDIA – II
'Army permanently employed in armed constabulary role'
Pakistan may not have achieved cutting away Kashmir from the Indian Union but the three decade employment of the Army in its sponsored proxy war has resulted in the Army being permanently employed in an armed constabulary role.

At the same time, the 1.4 million strong Central Armed Police Forces and Para Military has practically relinquished their primary internal security mandate, writes former Deputy Chief of Integrated Defence Staff (DCIDS), LT Gen N S Brar (Retd) writes in the upcoming 'Mission Victory India – Key to Combat Leadership' book.

"What then is our perceived policy towards the proxy war in J&K? Indian policy appears to be on one hand to eliminate as many 'terrorists' as possible to force a political solution and at the same time accept security forces casualties as acceptable. What has not been factored is the intangible and intrinsic aspects of terrorist staying power of fresh recruitment, home-grown or externally sponsored, and the attitude of the local population," Lt Gen Brar writes.

The Army cannot be deployed on internal security duties in 'aid to civil power' or 'disturbed areas' without the mandated legal sanction and protection. The Armed Forces Special Power Act (AFSPA) was enacted for this purpose.

"Unremitting Pakistan sponsorship of the proxy war would and should result in moving up the escalatory ladder to the full conventional level to deter and punish. That response is precluded due to lack of capability or 'hollowness'. Handling insurgencies has followed a pattern of 'military pacification' followed by 'political purchase'. J&K is essentially and ultimately a political problem," the ex-DCIDS writes.

In the past the military shrugged off the politician and politics as not concerning them. The politician's disinterest in matters military was a consequence of total ignorance of such matters. While the ignorance remains, the new found interest of the political class is driven by political mileage and not the interest of the military or national security.

"The country has failed the Army by not providing the clarity of objectives, legal framework, capability and ethical backing. The senior military leadership has failed the rank and file by not taking the inbuilt correctives within the military justice system and discipline to deal with any actions outside the laid down parameters, if there was any transgression, and not standing by the rank and file if there was none and they were being hounded on false grounds," the general laments.

Blurb
"Politics and judicial intervention has practically left the soldier devoid of protective cover while operating in disturbed areas, with resultant prosecution and confusion." – Lt Gen N S Brar (Retd), Deputy Chief of Integrated Defence Staff

MISSION VICTORY INDIA – III
'Give responsibility of national security to Chief of Defence Staff'

The responsibility of national security must be given to the Chief of Defence Staff (CDS) not the National Security Adviser (NSA) because he is well equipped in dealing with threats to national security, while NSA must focus on strategic affairs and regional environments, senior veteran and former Infantry battalion Commanding Officer, Colonel Rajinder Kushwaha (Retd) writes in the upcoming book 'Mission Victory India – Key to Combat Leadership'.

"Security forces must have a free hand. Appeasement and softness are the biggest enemies of internal security measures. Armed forces of a nation are organised and equipped to deal with these threat to national security. Therefore, the responsibility of national security must devolve upon armed forces, whether it has a Chief of Defence Staff (CDS) or not. Defence Minister can take on this role till government decides to appoint a CDS. But with the fast spreading insurgency and militancy across the nation, the need for a CDS is becoming utmost," Col Kushwaha writes.

According to him, the NSA cannot take on this role because he must focus on strategic affairs and regional environments.

"NSA can only advise the Ministry of Defence but he cannot be the executive authority. The Ministry of Home Affairs (MHA) must focus on law and order for which it has the Central Reserve Police (CRPF) and state police forces," he writes.

There is a lot of confusion between national security and law and order problems. Not only this, national security has been further sliced into internal and external security and being assigned to different organs of the Central Government.

"NSA to MHA; MoD to State governments, have, thus, all become executive authorities to conduct national security operations. National security cannot be segmented into compartments and thus distributed as sweets to different proponents. It must have a single executive authority, whether it was internal threat or external threat," he demands.

He argues in the book that when there are so many bosses, confusion has to take place as it did during terrorist attack on Pathankot Air Force base on January 1, 2016 and more recently during terrorist attack on Sunjuwan Military Garrison on February 11, 2018.

"Lack of clear cut definition and areas of responsibilities make everyone rush into it to get their pound of flesh. National security cannot be segmented into compartments and thus distributed as sweets to different proponents. It must have a single executive authority, whether it was internal threat or external threat. Unfortunately, India has divided this role between Home Ministry and Defence Ministry. This needs to change now," the retired Colonel concludes.

Blurb
"With the fast spreading insurgency and militancy across the nation, the need for a CDS is becoming utmost." – Col Rajinder Kushwaha (Retd), ex-Infantry Bn Commanding Officer

MISSION VICTORY INDIA – IV
'Paramilitary forces need restructuring to deliver better results'

With Army performing the core tasks of country's paramilitary forces (PMF), the Central government must merge the various PMFs, which are performing the same tasks to ensure better results and save crores of exchequer's money, senior veteran Major General V K Madhok (Retd) has written in the upcoming book 'Mission Victory India – Key to Combat Leadership'

A tax payer is puzzled at the scale and range of our 10 lakh or so Para Military Forces (PMF) – the 4th largest in the world. Though an indispensable requirement, these continue to proliferate at an unrealistic and unimaginable pace.

Today, India has 15-16 types of PMFs: CRPF, BSF, NSG, ITBP, CISF, DSC, Assam Rifles, RPF, SSB, India Reserve Battalions, and some more outfits like the Command Battalions for Resolute Action (COBRA), a commando force of nearly 10,000 personnel organised on the lines of Grey Hounds in Andhra Pradesh.

"Question is do we need these forces at this scale when finally, for instance, after Dantewada incident in 2010 (75 jawans of CRPF killed by Maoists), we are still wanting the Army and are now going to recruit ex-Servicemen for the tasks. If that be so, then the PMF need a serious look and total restructuring," Maj Gen Madhok writes.

Assam Rifles, a 31 Battalion force is now raising another 31 Battalions for the Indo-Myanmar border. The raising of each Battalion costs 10-12 crore. According to him, departmental battles at Delhi, duplication of command and control channels has indeed led to unhealthy rivalries between the Army and the PMFs.

He proposes that those PMF whose purpose is to guard the international border during peace and which are currently deployed for this purpose should be merged and re-designated as 'Border Guards'. In this category fall the BSF, Coast Guard, ITBP and the state armed police. These forces would need an army orientation except for the Coast Guard, who are meant for the Navy.

"Each force should be commanded by a senior service officer. The recruitment should be based on the service pattern. The entire PMF should have a single code of conduct and one set of regulations. Above all, this force should be under the Ministry of Defence and not the Ministry of Home Affairs," asserts the veteran officer.

Blurb
"Multiplicity and resultant lack of coordination are an obstacle and a serious handicap in tackling terrorism. Therefore, we are now asking for the Army to counter it."
– Maj Gen V K Madhok (Retd), former Division Commander

MISSION VICTORY INDIA – V
'Public-Private partnership model can fill up officer shortage'

A successful 'pilot project' in military-civil existing between the Punjab government's Armed Forces Preparatory Institute (AFPI) and private school in Mohali, Punjab can enable Centre to consider it as the feeder for military's officer cadre since Sainik school system nowhere meets India's need for officer induction into the defence forces, writes Maj Gen Raj Mehta (Retd) in the upcoming book 'Mission Victory India – Key to Combat leadership'.

Country has 26 Sainik Schools (21 more have been proposed and Rs 80 crore earmarked for them, as per a PTI report of 11 August 2017 on Parliamentary proceedings). In a written reply to Parliament, Rajya Raksha Mantri S R Bhamre stated that the 26 Sainik Schools in 2016, fed 159 or 29.33 per cent cadets and the five Military Schools fed 31 cadets or 5.1 per cent cadets to the NDA in 2016.

"A total of 215 cadets came from India's official 'feeder' institutions for NDA entry, leaving the balance 140 (out of 355) to come in from outside the official system. This is where the Shemrock School-Armed Forces Preparatory Institute (AFPI), Punjab public-private partnership (PPP) comes in to the picture for imparting quality education to young military aspirants," Maj Gen Mehta writes.

This 'PPP' model has resulted in a staggering 111 cadets joining India's elite military training academies since 2012. It can help in replacing the Sainik School bridging the gap in officer cadre.

It has sent 22 cadets to the NDA in June 2018 against a vacancy of 355 which is 6.2 per cent of the NDA batch strength. Also, in the May-June 2018 passing out of commissioned officers from India's defence academies, Shemrock-AFPI had 21 officers passing out from Indian Military Academy, Naval Academy, Air Force Academy and Officers Training Academy.

"There cannot be but deep concern about why the feeder institutions, which have been set up at great initial and residual cost, aren't doing enough to send more officer candidates to the NDA even as we have a daunting shortage of around 13,100 officers in the defence forces persisting for decades which even limited women officer entry and short-term measures such as increase in Short Service Commission induction has not been able to resolve.

Blurb
"The PPP model is an initiative needing exploitation by the government as one out-of-the-box, cost-effective way of ending the logjam of crippling officer shortages in India's armed forces."

MISSION VICTORY INDIA – VI
'Urgent need to review selection process for officers'

There is an urgent need to move from existing personality based selection system in Services Selection Board (SSB) to a cognitive based process of selecting future officers, former SSB President and present Chairman of Odisha Public Service Commission, Brigadier L C Patnaik (Retd) writes in forthcoming book 'Mission Victory India-Key to Combat Leadership'.

Existing personality variables in Officer like Qualities (OLQs) focus more on social effectiveness and adjustment, based on concept of behavioral process and observable responses, neglecting the mental process, which actually meditates the stimulus and response.

"Cognitive assessment provides time course for information processing, reaction based measurements to provide baseline of assessment and subsequent monitoring. Rise of reliable cognitive function assessment tools have given more options for assessment and needs to be incorporated in our selection systems," Brig Patnaik states.

Physical Efficiency Test (PET) can also be introduced at the Services Selection Boards (SSBs), to include elements like one mile shuttle run, pushups (30), sit ups (30), chin ups (10). The above tests should be assessed on a gradation scale and marks obtained to be included in the overall assessment.

"On the day of screening Test (Day 1) the current assessment based on Picture Perception and Description Test should be replaced by Cognitive Assessment Test and the Physical Efficiency Test (PET). The Psychology Test and GTO assessment could be suitably modified on cognitive assessment tools to reduce the duration so as to complete the test in one day; thereby reducing the overall duration to four days, instead of present five days," he states.

"There is a need to develop suitable software to assess the correlation between assessment and training to be shared periodically between the assessors and trainers to review their own mechanism. The existing procedure is outdated and devoid of sincerity in purpose," Brig L C Patnaik the former SSB President and present Chairman of OPSC writes.

The Defence Institute of Psychological Research (DIPR) had proposed a De-novo approach to the selection system for the Armed Forces with redefined attributes and jugular variables in personality traits without keeping the future fluidity in the nature of warfare. The Ministry of Defence (MoD) has directed DIPR to reconsider the proposal. It is recommended that the Chief of Staff Committee and Chief of Integrated Defence IDS need to advise DIPR based on the views deliberated in the five volumes of "Victory India". (Series concluded)

Blurb
"The existing selection procedure for armed forces officer cadre is outdated and devoid of sincerity in purpose." – Brig L C Patnaik (Retd), former SSB chairman